THE GREAT PIERPONT MORGAN

Books by

FREDERICK LEWIS ALLEN

*

ONLY YESTERDAY

THE LORDS OF CREATION

SINCE YESTERDAY

THE GREAT PIERPONT MORGAN

(*with* AGNES ROGERS)

THE AMERICAN PROCESSION

METROPOLIS

I REMEMBER DISTINCTLY

*

JOHN PIERPONT MORGAN

The Steichen Camera Portrait

The Great Pierpont Morgan

By

FREDERICK LEWIS ALLEN

Harper & Brothers Publishers

NEW YORK

1949

C-Y

CONTENTS

PREFACE

I FIRST encountered Pierpont Morgan's personality some fourteen years ago, when I was working on an informal financial history called *The Lords of Creation* and read his testimony at the Pujo investigation—that testimony which is cited in the first chapter of this book, and again in the last few pages. Here, I thought, is an extraordinary man, strikingly different from the other financial and industrial princes of his day, and different, too, from the impression which he made upon the public mind. Ever since then I have played with the idea of writing about him at greater length. But not until 1947 could I find the time to begin it; and as soon as I went to work, the difficulty of the task became obvious.

This difficulty lay in the nature of the evidence about him. In the first place, it was curiously scanty. He himself had been very reticent, unwilling to be interviewed or written about. This reticence continued in his son, who both worshipped him and was reluctant to have anything written about him; and it spread like a contagion among his family and associates. Furthermore, most financial reporting tends to be impersonal and to give few dramatic glimpses of men in action; and the contemporary financial chroniclers had walked with special circumspection when they approached 23 Wall Street. There were legends and anecdotes galore, but many of them were of uncertain veracity. Finally, what evidence had accumulated about Pierpont Morgan was strikingly divided between the one-sidedly laudatory and the one-sidedly derogatory.

Pierpont Morgan's son-in-law, Herbert L. Satterlee,

had written a detailed biography of him, rich in evidence as to various personal matters; but it was grossly flattering, occasionally inaccurate on business matters, and quite lacking in any perspective upon his father-in-law's financial operations and their significance. Accounts of Morgan, written and oral, by others who had been close to him seemed to me likewise to present him in an unbelievably benign aspect; these accounts could not be brushed aside and were often revealing, but could hardly be taken at their face value. And on the other side were a number of books, such as Lewis Corey's *The House of Morgan* and Matthew Josephson's *The Robber Barons,* which while helpful on the facts of many transactions seemed to me wholly unreliable as to Morgan's motives and total impact upon the American economy; for they had apparently been written on the assumption that if a great capitalist did something which could be ascribed to any one of five motives, the duty of the historian was to ascribe it to the worst of the five, brushing aside all evidence which suggested laudable intentions and eagerly underlining any evidence which suggested base ones. Between the conscientiously flattering and the conscientiously hostile accounts of Morgan there was room enough to drive a ten-ton truck. (There were other books of a more judicial nature, notably Carl Hovey's *The Life Story of J. Pierpont Morgan* and John K. Winkler's lively *Morgan the Magnificent,* but they were confusing to work with, for it was sometimes hard to know when they were presenting verified facts and when they were embroidering gossip or legend.)

Believing as I do that it ought to be possible to write about a man of note, whether he be a master of capital or a labor leader or a politician, without being wholly swayed by prejudice for or against the type of institution which he represented, and believing especially that it is a disservice to history to depict the conflicts between men of opposing social and economic ideas as conflicts between saints and sinners, when common sense should tell us that human beings are not thus compartmented, I have tried to steer a true course between the Morgan-praisers and the Morgan-dispraisers. Pierpont Morgan was a man with whom I would have disagreed strongly on most political and economic issues if I had been his contemporary. To me he represented a trend in the direction of economic affairs which had to be altered for the good of the country. But I am also convinced that he was a man great in character and force, whose immense influence was in many respects salutary. What I have tried to do, therefore, has been to show what sort of man he really was; how his ideas developed out of his background and the traditions of the group to which he belonged, and out of his experience; how both his ideas and his actions conflicted with those of others whose background and experience differed from his; and how they influenced, and were affected by, the course of American history.

Owing to the nature of the evidence, this has not been easy. As to the facts in this book I have been scrupulously careful, rejecting unverifiable legend. As to the interpretation of Morgan's impulses and ideas and view of affairs, that is my own. I have tried to ask myself, "From all the evidence available, and from whatever intuition I may have acquired about human nature, and especially about the impulses and ideas of men whose background and circumstances and position have in one way or another been comparable to Morgan's, why do I think he acted as he did?" Obviously, some readers will feel that I have accepted too naïvely the testimony of his admirers; others, that I have followed too closely the reasoning of his detractors. All I can say is that the picture painted here represents the fairest judgment I know how to bring to bear upon an extraordinary man who has never yet been adequately depicted, in his true colors, against the background of the times upon which his influence was so prodigious.

F. L. A.

THE GREAT PIERPONT MORGAN

Chapter One

JUDGMENT DAY

A FEW days before Christmas in the year 1912, John Pierpont Morgan, the most influential banker in the world and the mightiest personal force in American business life, was called to testify before an investigating committee in Washington. This group—a subdivision of the House Committee on Banking and Currency—was popularly known as the Pujo Committee, because its chairman was Arsène Pujo of Louisiana; and its aim was to demonstrate, through evidence brought out in its protracted hearings, that there existed in America a "money trust"—that a small group of New York bankers, headed by Pierpont Morgan, held such a grip on the money and credit resources of the country, and so dominated the big industrial and railroad corporations through "interlocking directorates," that in effect the whole American economy lay under their control. Day after day the Pujo Committee had spread its evidence on the record, and now the inquiry was coming to its climax. Pierpont Morgan himself, the head and front of American banking power, was going to take the stand.

He was an old man now, well along in his seventy-sixth year. His hair, which had been dark in his youth, and then steel gray, was white and thin. Even his big straggling mustache, which had remained black until old age approached, was graying. Now as always the first thing that caught the attention of anyone who saw him for the first time was his nose, for it was bulbous and flaming red as the result of a baffling skin disease that had fastened itself upon him progressively during his later years. Only when one had accustomed oneself to the sight of this hideous and dismaying feature did one note his extraordinary eyes, whose burning intensity had so often held men in awe of him. But those eyes were tired now. The vital force in him was waning; though no one in the committee room could know it, he was within four months of his death. This was to be his last public appearance, his last accounting for his stewardship.

2

All his active life Morgan had spent a part of each year in Europe; now that he had virtually retired from business, his travels during this year 1912, while characteristically magnificent, had been exceptionally protracted.

New Year's Day of 1912 had found him already on the way from New York to Europe, dozing and playing solitaire in his private suite on a liner headed for Cherbourg. He had traveled by special train from Cherbourg to Paris, where he visited the American Ambassador; then had crossed to London to superintend the packing of part of his vast art collection for shipment to New York; and then, after a short stay at Monte Carlo, had proceeded to Egypt, where he had taken a party of friends up the Nile. They had traveled in his own river steamer, an all-steel vessel especially built to his order; and the party had included, characteristically, a bishop and several attractive ladies. One day in Cairo Morgan visited the gold bazaar, bought a liberal collection of bracelets, necklaces, and other gold ornaments, and on returning to the hotel spread them out on a table in his sitting room, crying to the ladies, "Now, help yourselves!"—which, after some hesitation, they did.

From Egypt he had moved on to Rome, where he was granted a private audience with King Victor Emmanuel;

to Aix-les-Bains, where he took the cure; to Venice, where he took part in the inauguration of the new Campanile, to whose construction he had subscribed; to London and Paris, where he purchased two fifteenth-century tapestries. Then he had boarded the *Corsair,* his private yacht, the finest in the world, to be the personal guest of the German Kaiser at the Kiel Regatta. A flying trip to Rome—where he turned the first sod for the building which he had enabled the American Academy to build—and he was ready to leave for the United States. During the rest of the year 1912 he had put in some weeks of business at his office, had taken a cruise of several weeks on the *Corsair,* had testified in Washington before a committee investigating campaign expenditures, had inspected an art gallery which he had presented to the city of Hartford, had promised to give Hartford a library too, and had attended the consecration of a new chapel for St. George's Church in New York, of which he had long been senior warden.

Not wholly a relaxing year for a man of seventy-five; and now Pierpont Morgan was in Washington again to face a new set of congressional inquisitors, with their elaborate charts designed to show how a network of influence and control reached from 23 Wall Street, the headquarters of J. P. Morgan and Co., by way of banks and trust companies and the directorates of industrial corporations, throughout the whole structure of American business.

He had been very tired during the preceding days in New York, when his partners and the firm's lawyers had tried to brief him on what he should say. They took a dark view of the impending proceedings, which they looked upon as insolent, crafty, and no doubt inspired by the lowest motives of personal ambition on the part of the congressional investigators; and Morgan himself was depressed. As his son-in-law later wrote, "His feeling about this examination in Washington was that the people down there were going to 'make a show' of him. . . . The more his counsel warned him about possible plots and pitfalls, the more annoyed and apprehensive he got. For him the trip down to Washington was not a pleasant one, and at the hotel after dinner he told the lawyers he needed a rest and devoted himself to his cards." In moments of anxiety or crisis solitaire had always been his recourse; there was something that responded to his inner constructiveness in this creation of order out of haphazard disorder.

The next morning he traveled to the Capitol in a big square-topped limousine and walked beside his daughter Louisa and his son Jack through the staring crowds to the committee room—an old-fashioned figure in a heavy velvet-collared overcoat and high silk hat, walking slowly, with a stick. The committee room was packed, and the crowd outside was kept in order by policemen. Presently the examination of the day's chief witness began, following the traditional formula.

Q. Where do you reside, Mr. Morgan?

A. New York City.

Q. Are you senior member of the partnership or firm of J. P. Morgan & Co., bankers, of New York City?

A. I am, sir. . . .

Q. Does your New York house do a general banking business?

A. We try to, sir.

Slowly the examination unfolded. It was as if—through the agency of the Pujo Committee—the American public were asking this man, at the close of his extraordinary life, "Tell us, before it is too late—have you really controlled American business? And if so, how is it done? And do you think it right that any man, in a republic which hopes to be a genuine democracy, should wield such authority?"

3

Samuel Untermyer, counsel for the Pujo Committee, a shrewd and well-prepared lawyer, conducted the examination. Morgan's son and daughter and his partners and lawyers were uneasy lest the old man break down under Untermyer's questioning. They need not have been. Morgan was a direct and co-operative if singularly determined witness. He took no refuge in the evasions or lapses of memory or vague circumlocutions which often afflict business executives when they confront congressional committees. He answered clearly and stoutly; when he could not remember a fact or figure he said he would be glad to have it looked up and produced for the committee later. And he spoke with completely satisfied assurance.

When Untermyer, having established that some seventy-eight interstate corporations carried bank accounts with J. P. Morgan & Co., and that their deposits totaled over eighty-one million dollars, asked Morgan if he thought it was a wise thing to permit publicly owned corporations to make deposits with a private banker, he answered firmly, "I do, sir." Untermyer further brought out that a great many railroad corporations had made J. P. Morgan & Co. their fiscal agent, so that the Morgan firm had become the designated channel through which these railroads must sell all their securities to the public, and thus had become also their sole source of investment funds; and Untermyer went on to ask, "Don't you think it would be better for these great interstate railroad corporations if they were entirely free to sell their securities in open competition than that they should be tied to any banking house, however just might be its methods in the issue of such securities?" Morgan answered, "I should not think so." When he was asked whether the fact that there were a few men (such as Morgan himself and his partners) who served on the boards of directors of many banks did not tend to prevent those banks from competing for deposits, his answer reflected a colossal confidence. "I should doubt it," said he. "I have been in business for a great many years in New York and I do not compete for any deposits. I do not care whether they ever come. They come."

With all the ingenuity of a trained trial lawyer, Untermyer tried to get Morgan to admit that he exercised great power. Morgan would have none of it. He said he exercised no power at all. It was as if he were asserting that all the elaborate charts prepared by Untermyer's aides were so much nonsense.

The audience in the committee room was ready for this sort of denial; of course this organizer of huge corporations, this consolidator of banks, this master of the authority of money would be expected under such circumstances to minimize his own status; but presently Untermyer's verbal rapier would find a weak spot. Morgan was denying too much. He was not only—against all reason—denying that he controlled the reorganized railroads for which he had named the voting trustees who named the directors; he was actually denying that if he himself were voting trustee for all the railroad systems of the United States, this would concentrate control of them in him. He was denying that there was any way in which one man could get a monopoly of money, or control of it.

Yet as the questioning persisted, it became apparent that these denials on the old man's part were not merely tactics in his battle of wits with Untermyer; they came from something deeper in his nature, something that commanded the audience's respect. Morgan was insisting that what ruled the financial world was not money, but character.

"Is not commercial credit based primarily upon money or property?" asked Untermyer.

"No, sir," said Morgan; "the first thing is character."

"Before money or property?"

"Before money or anything else. Money cannot buy it. . . . Because a man I do not trust could not get money from me on all the bonds in Christendom."

How could anybody hear those words—so dubiously applicable to the facts of the business world in general, yet clearly so valid to the old gentleman in the witness chair—without wondering what manner of man this was, what principles had ruled his long career, and by what conjunction of circumstances and events he had come to a place where people could honestly believe that he was the ruler of America?

Chapter Two

THE MATERIALS OF A CAREER

AMONG the men who wielded far-reaching authority in American business at the beginning of the twentieth century, Morgan was unusual in his origins. John D. Rockefeller's father had been a pitch man of uncertain repute—an itinerant salesman of patent medicines—and Rockefeller himself had begun his working life at sixteen as a $4-a-week clerk in a commission merchant's office in Cleveland. Andrew Carnegie had been born in a weaver's cottage at Dunfermline, Scotland, and after having been brought to the United States in his early childhood had gone to work at thirteen as a $1.20-a-week bobbin boy in a Pittsburgh cotton mill. Among the subsequently mighty bankers, George F. Baker, a country boy, had begun as a clerk in the New York State Banking Department at Albany; James Stillman's father had been well-to-do but had suffered reverses, and young Stillman had entered business life at sixteen in a small position in the cotton business. And even the great railroad organizer, E. H. Harriman, though he had had wealthy friends and moderately prosperous relatives, had been unable to get to college and had been introduced to business by way of a job as a broker's office boy at $5 a week. The prevailing pattern was of the sort prescribed by Horatio Alger: begin work as a boy, without benefit of higher education; work furiously, with a single eye to business; and thus rise to the top.

There were to be sure other men, like the Astors and Vanderbilts, who had inherited wealth and were forces to be reckoned with at the turn of the century by reason of that wealth; but they represented a waning and undynamic authority compared with the Rockefellers and Carnegies and Harrimans. Morgan was unique. Nobody could call him undynamic. Yet by contrast with the Horatio Alger heroes of his time he had been born to rising wealth and social position, and before he was twenty had enjoyed opportunities for travel, university education, and international acquaintance such as Rockefeller and Carnegie could hardly have dreamed of.

Morgan's grandfather, Joseph Morgan, came from a Massachusetts farm to Hartford, Connecticut, in 1817; ran a coffee house or tavern, and then sold it to become the proprietor of the City Hotel in Hartford; prospered as a hotelkeeper, and invested on a considerable scale in Hartford real estate; helped to organize a canal company and steamboat lines and the new railroad which connected Hartford with Springfield; and finally became one of the founders of the Aetna Fire Insurance Company. A solid citizen, hearty, hardworking, shrewd in a bargain, and God-fearing withal, Joseph Morgan was the perfect pattern of the up-and-coming Yankee enterpriser of the early nineteenth century.

Joseph Morgan's son, Junius Spencer Morgan, was born in 1813, before his father arrived in Hartford; and Junius, too, was put into business without benefit of a college education. He got a taste of commercial life in New York and then spent a number of years in a drygoods merchant's firm in Hartford. But in his late thirties he moved to Boston to become a partner in the booming firm of James M. Beebe & Co., which conducted and financed foreign trade transactions, particularly in cotton; and by that time, as a result of his father's expanding wealth, he was able to bring considerable capital with him to put into the Boston firm, which thereupon became J. M. Beebe, Morgan & Co. But Junius Morgan did not remain long in the work of financing those exports and imports which made the Boston of the eighteen-fifties a hustling center of clipper-ship trade with Europe and Asia. After only a few years he was invited to go to London to become a partner of George Peabody, a Yankee who had built up a respected and very profitable international banking house there. And when, during our Civil War, George Peabody retired, the Peabody firm—an important link in the system of financial communications between imperial London and industrializing America—took the name of J. S. Morgan & Co. In short, Junius Morgan, helped along on his career by his Hartford father's well-invested savings, became a man of wealth and of international influence.

Thus it happened that Junius Morgan's son, John Pierpont Morgan, grew up in an atmosphere of financial security, rising business prestige, and rising worldly consequence.

2

The house in which Pierpont Morgan was born on April 17, 1837, was an ample one, his grandfather's house at 26 Asylum Street, Hartford; nothing palatial, but a substantial urban building three stories high and six windows wide across the front. (It is gone now; in 1948 its site, in a somewhat run-down commercial district between more progressive business areas, was part of a lot occupied by a six-story branch office building of The Travelers—with a paint shop and a record shop on the ground floor, and bowling alleys next door, and a technical institute and movie theater across the way.) At the time of Pierpont Morgan's birth, his father was still a young Hartford merchant, but his grandfather was already a man of considerable means.

Young Pierpont—"Pip," as they called him in his boyhood—went first to a small private school for young children in Hartford, then to a public grammar school, then to a boarding school at Cheshire, Connecticut (while his father was moving to Boston and becoming established there); then to the English High School in Boston, a public school of exceptionally high standards; then (as the family moved abroad to London) to a private school in Vevey, Switzerland; and finally for over a year to the university of Göttingen in Germany. There was always plenty of money behind him, and of educational opportunity, and of New England belief in breadth of education.

Inevitably he early absorbed, through inheritance and through the very air of the commercial Hartford of the eighteen-forties, certain traditions and tastes characteristic of the Yankee business community. First, there was the tradition of businesslike thrift. There was nothing finer than to be a good business man, and the very mechanics of a business operation were alluring. When Pierpont was just reaching his twelfth birthday, he and his cousin Jim Goodwin, after the immemorial fashion of twelve-year-olds, got up a show for which they sold tickets to their families and indulgent friends—a *Grand Diorama of the Landing of Columbus*; not only did Pierpont keep strict account of every penny received and disbursed, but he prepared afterward an accurate balance sheet of the whole operation, headed "Morgan & Goodwin, Grand Diorama Balance Sheet, April 20, 1849." Other boys in other eras might play at being sea captains, or firemen, or airplane pilots; to this boy in pre-Civil War Hartford there was a tingle of fascination in being able to set down assets and liabilities in perfect order. After Pierpont had moved to Boston, in his mid-teens, he and Jim Goodwin carried on a steady correspondence which combined boyishly occult references to girls they both knew in Hartford, with reports of purchases they had made for one another; and Pierpont used to like to sign his letters to Jim, "Truly yours, Goodwin, Morgan & Co.—J.P.M.—To Messrs. Goodwin, Morgan & Co.'s Agent at Hartford."

He not only kept a diary, in a clear handwriting that by the time he was fifteen was graceful and well formed, but kept a series of precise personal account books; and so firmly was this habit acquired that twenty years later, when he was married and traveling abroad with his wife and children, he still committed to a blue leather account book, in his fine slanting hand, the exact record of the francs he had spent on such items as *3 bouquets, 18*; *postage 1.40*; *cab, 1.80*; *oranges, 1.70*; *mineral water, 18*; *postage, 1.50.*

Along with the thrift went godliness: church attendance twice on Sundays, family hymn-singing Sunday evenings, and the building of a robust religious faith, which was destined to stand almost unmodified throughout his life. Long afterward Morgan's friend, Dr. William S. Rainsford, the rector of St. George's Church in New York, wrote that Morgan's faith was like a "precious heirloom"—"a talent to be wrapped in its own napkin and venerated in the secret place of his soul . . . in safe disuse." But this did not mean that it was something with which he appeased God and the congregation on Sunday for ungodly conduct during the week. It meant simply that to him religion was something as solid and unquestionable as the stones of St. George's, even though most of the time it was out of sight and out of mind; and that business success, too, while quite separate and on a more mundane level, was indubitably valid. In the Hartford and Boston of the mid-nineteenth century, devotion to the competitive warfare of business—with few holds barred—and devotion to God and the church and the creed had been two mutually comfortable parts of a whole life.

The first thing Morgan ever collected in his youth, aside from stamps, was the autographs of Episcopal bishops. He went on to become not only a formidably successful banker but a tireless vestryman and church warden, a giver of parish houses and cathedral chapels, an energetic attender of triennial Episcopal Conventions. When in the skeptical year 1913 he died, and his will was made public, those who had known him only by reputation gasped at the way in which the document began; how on earth could this monarch of Wall Street, this worldly yachtsman, this lordly spender of millions, have written those tremendous introductory words?—

"I commit my soul into the hands of my Saviour, in full confidence that having redeemed it and washed it in His most precious blood He will present it faultless before my Heavenly Father; and I entreat my children to maintain and defend, at all hazard and at any cost of personal sacrifice, the blessed doctrine of the complete atonement for sin through the blood of Jesus Christ, once offered, and through that alone."

There was no mystery: this, deepened but unchanged, was the faith in which Pierpont Morgan had been raised in the Hartford of the eighteen-forties.

3

In such communities, Yankee penny-counting thrift was often mitigated by the conviction that travel was a sound investment; and as Junius Morgan moved along from Hartford to Boston and then to London, his son was able to profit increasingly by chances to see the wide world. When Pierpont was a pupil at the English High School in Boston, at the age of fifteen, he was crippled by a bad attack of inflammatory rheumatism and needed a rest and change. Thereupon his family packed him off in a sailing ship to the Azores, in company with their friend Mr. Dabney, the American consul at Horta on the island of Fayal; and there the boy spent several months—living alone at Silva's Hotel in Horta, spending only part of his time with the Dabneys, and learning otherwise to enjoy being quite on his own.

His letters home from Horta give us a revealing glimpse of him at fifteen. They were exceptionally mature for a boy of his age—long, clearly and capably written, marred by only a few youthful clichés, and packed with varied and detailed observation. They showed a zeal for factual precision, as when, in his account of the voyage from the States on the sailing ship *Io,* he noted, "We had five ladies on board and three gentlemen besides myself. Of these, three ladies and one gentleman were seasick, and as it very singularly happened those who escaped with the exception of Mr. Dabney were those who had never been to sea before." He set down for his parents careful accounts of the whitewashed stuccoed-over houses, of the gardens and what grew in them, of the currency and prices of Horta, and of the ships and shipping; the latter he studied with especially close attention, liking to go aboard the ships in port and hear about their trade. And he wrote at length about the presents he was sending home to his family—oranges, bottles of wine, baskets, silk stockings and a bonnet for his mother, and artificial flowers made of feathers, which he packed most carefully so that they would not be damaged. He was methodical, too:

noted in his diary the temperature on rising, at noon, and at bedtime.

Some signs of aesthetic appreciation appeared in his letters: of the mountain toward which his hotel window looked, across the water, he wrote: "Pico is a very beautiful mountain and it seems to me as if I should never tire of looking at it. It varies so both as to clearness and color. I often sit before a window facing it and watch the various changes which take place so often." But mainly he was a tireless factual observer with an eye for the business aspect of events. When the *Io*, on a subsequent visit to Horta, was badly damaged in a heavy storm while in port, Pierpont reported: "Later in the day I went with Captain Pillsbury to examine the rigging, etc., but it was so broken that he thought it was not good for anything. Had the *Io* gone ashore the Underwriters would have had a nice bill to pay, for she is insured for $25,000 and her cargo for $10,000 more, and none of the cargo had been landed at all. Mr. Dabney of course and everyone else here seems to be so delighted that she escaped, for she would have been a great loss to the whole island. Towards night the gale moderated. Thermometer 57.57.59."

When Pierpont arrived at Horta he had been very weak from his illness, and spent much of his time playing chess with a certain Dr. Cole who had also come to Horta for his health, and reading and writing letters; but his condition improved so rapidly that before long he was taking considerable walks and going to parties with the Dabney girls; and his gain in size was prodigious. On his arrival on November 20 (1852) his weight was 126 pounds; a month later it was 138 and he was complaining that his pantaloons were too tight; by March 21 it had reached 150. In April, his island cure successfully completed, he left the Azores by steamship for England in order to join his family for a tour of the Continent. It was on his solitary voyage to England that he formed the enduring habit of jotting down each day, in orderly figures clearly legible even when crowded into the limited space of the back of a calling card, the exact latitude and longitude reached at noon and the mileage of the day's run.

This prolonged boyhood expedition, along with his subsequent schooling among students of many nationalities at Vevey and at Göttingen, and his holiday visits to his family in London, gave Pierpont Morgan while he was still in his teens a familiarity with foreign life and ideas and an international outlook which in those days of slow ocean travel were exceptional for a young American. The farthest west he ever went in the United States as a boy was to Buffalo and Niagara Falls; in August 1854, when he was seventeen and about to enter school at Vevey, he and Jim Goodwin set out by the newly built Erie Railroad to Buffalo, returned by rail to the Hudson Valley, visited Saratoga, Lake George, and Lake Champlain, crossed Vermont and New Hampshire by stage to Crawford's Inn in the White Mountains—and then, because their cash was giving out and they would not appeal to their families for help, proceeded partly on foot and partly by stage to Portland, where they took an inexpensive boat to Boston, arriving with their money quite gone. Not a very extended American trip for a boy who was about to live for years abroad; but in those days the New England of the merchants and the bankers faced east.

4

The level-eyed, methodical boy was growing up to be a big, bulky man, a six-footer. You would hardly have called him handsome, but he was responsible looking, with round strong features, a rather large and expressive mouth, and a fine direct gaze. He was not athletic, though in those days—and until he was well on in years—he was active and liked to walk and climb mountains and had a normal enjoyment of sports. It was perhaps the result of frequent invalidism as a boy that his favorite games should have been whist and chess. Like many youths, he was cursed with a bad complexion; at least once, when he was nineteen, he stayed away from a dance at Göttingen that he had very much wanted to go to because he was ashamed of the eruption on his forehead. In school he was by no means a conspicuous student, though in his later years at English High he stood near the top of his class. But he developed a very sharp head for mathematics, and when he left Göttingen, the professor of mathematics there assured him that he was making a great mistake to go into business: he should stay on, perhaps become the professor's assistant, and even possibly—if he worked diligently and fortune favored him—succeed to the professor's own august chair.

He was a sociable fellow, with a relish both for playing chess with men of twice or thrice his years and for organizing dances at Vevey, where—as he wrote to Jim Goodwin—his participation would cost him "about $5.75 a night, but that is dog cheap when you can laugh, talk, and dance with such a beautiful girl as Miss H. as much as you choose."

In the year 1857, when Pierpont was twenty, there was a farewell party at Göttingen and his university days were over. After a short visit to England, he left his family and crossed to America to begin his business career as a junior accountant with Duncan, Sherman & Co., private bankers, in New York.

5

To the business of Duncan, Sherman & Co. at 11 Pine Street in downtown Manhattan this six-foot youth brought an energetic and enterprising spirit, mathematical acumen, great confidence, and a useful tie with the Peabody banking house in London. Within a year he demonstrated the enterprise and confidence in a way that brought acute if momentary alarm to his business seniors.

He had gone to New Orleans to make a several weeks' firsthand study of the cotton and shipping business. He spent a good deal of time exploring the waterfront, ranging from dock to dock and boarding the vessels tied up there to find out how their imports and exports were handled. One day, boarding a ship, he found it loaded with coffee in bags and learned that its captain was in a quandary: the man to whom the shipment had been consigned could not be found, and the captain, consulting his Brazilian headquarters, had been instructed to dispose of the cargo of coffee as best he could. Pierpont saw an opportunity. He went off with samples of the coffee in his pockets, made the rounds of the local merchants, collected orders, returned to the ship, and bought *the entire cargo* with a sight draft on Duncan, Sherman & Co. The next day, within a few hours of the time when his superiors in New York began spluttering with rage at his temerity, he was able to telegraph them that he had sold every bag of coffee in the cargo to various merchants at a neat profit, and was forwarding to Duncan, Sherman & Co. the checks made out in payment. What the men in New York had supposed to be a foolhardy operation had been a methodically prudent one; he had collected orders for every bag before he bought the shipload. But it had been a bold transaction for a neophyte of twenty-one, and characteristic in that he had not bargained for a quarter or a half of the cargo, but for the whole thing. No half-measures for him.

Pierpont's most obvious asset—his intimate connection with the English banking world—was imperiled very soon after he took his desk at Pine Street; for the Panic of 1857 was raging, the Peabody firm in London was in dire straits, and one day the rumor ran about New York that it had had to suspend. Finding that the new transatlantic cable lines were being monopolized at the moment by press messages, Pierpont went down "to Mr. Field's"—the office of Cyrus W. Field, who had laid the cable only a few years before—and was able to bring back the welcome news that George Peabody & Co. had been saved by a credit of a million pounds from the Bank of England. As the panic abated the connection began to regain its value, for the shortage in the Peabody till had been merely temporary; and within four years it enabled Pierpont, at twenty-four, to leave Duncan, Sherman & Co. and go into business on his own.

It was very much of a one-man show that he ran at first. He was George Peabody & Co.'s American representative, selling bills of exchange on the London firm and acting generally as its agent in New York. At first he did not even have a clerk to help him; he sold bills all morning, posted his books in the afternoon, and spent half his evenings writing letters to George Peabody & Co. or to his father—the letters to his father being long, detailed, and candid reports of his business operations, his personal news, and the general state of affairs in America. He continued writing candid letters like these until his father's death in 1890. Toward the end of his life, coming upon the entire file of them in the library at Dover House, the Morgan country place outside London, finding them full of intimately confidential data and unreserved expressions of opinion about people, and fearing that some biographer or historian might make such items public, he burned the entire collection!

Meanwhile he had settled into the agreeable life of a young gentleman-about-town. He roomed comfortably with his somewhat older friend Joe Peabody, a nephew of George Peabody of London, in what was then the fashionable uptown district of Manhattan; they lived first on West Seventeenth Street and then on East Twenty-sixth Street. (In those pre-Civil War days the solid blocks of brownstone houses reached up Fifth Avenue only to about Thirty-seventh Street; northward of that point only a few scattered urban buildings had invaded the market-gardens of the Manhattan countryside. And although William B. Astor, the city's wealthiest man, had built a house for himself as far north as Thirty-fourth Street—on the corner where the Empire State Building now stands—the chief center of polite society was still the neighborhood of Washington Square; and the center of entertainment was at Broadway and Fulton Street, far downtown, where stood Barnum's celebrated American Museum. There was no such thing as a tall building in the whole town; the city skyline was broken, not by skyscrapers, but by church spires.) Pierpont's account books for his earliest months in New York throw a glimmer or two of light upon his life as well as upon the prices of 1857-58: they contain such items as *Lunch .30, Dinner 1.00, Omnibus .06, Paper .02; To Hartford 2.65, Supper .37, Collection .25, Tolls .20, Feed .35, Horse and buggy to Middletown 3., To New York 3.25; Cap 2., Gloves 1., Barber .12, London News .15, Lunch .28, Dinner at Everett House 1.; Tickets to Philharmonic Concert 3., Church collections 1.25, Charity Five Points Mission 10.,*

Seidlitz powders and sugar .37, Opera tickets 8., Adele 1., Sleighride 13.62.

Gradually, young Morgan made a considerable acquaintance among the substantial families of the city; and he threw himself with as much gusto into Sunday-evening hymn singing at the Babcocks', or country walks at the Osborns' in the Highlands of the Hudson, as into evening gatherings of young people at the Sturgeses', who owned what was said to have been the first grand piano in New York. He had a sizeable income from his family, good prospects, high spirits, and the sort of gusto that made every party of young people revolve about him.

6

One might have foreseen for him a wholly reasonable and orthodox marriage. A few years before, when he was at Göttingen, he had written to Jim Goodwin, who had expressed a tender interest in a Hartford girl who was studying to be an opera singer, a letter that was positively elderly in its counsels of prudence: "Your career in life like mine," he had written, "depends on our own individual exertions, our courses though widely apart will both be in the mercantile sphere, and from this cause it becomes our duty to select for our wives those who, when we go home from our occupations, will ever be ready to make us happy and contented with our homes." Pierpont might have seemed to be following his own sage advice when he soon fell in love with Amelia Sturges, a girl of impeccable Manhattan antecedents. Yet what happened next took him clean out of the pattern of frugal and ambitious calculation which he seemed to have been setting for himself up to this time.

We must bear in mind, however, that in his inheritance, along with the blood of the shrewd Morgans, there was a more romantic and headlong strain: his maternal grandfather had been the Reverend John Pierpont, clergyman, poet, and man of reckless principle, who as pastor of the Hollis Street Church in Boston had been threatened with the loss of his pulpit if he would not stop preaching abolitionism and other indiscreet measures of social reform, and had defied the pillars of the parish, preached a last undaunted sermon, and then resigned.

In the spring of 1861, just as the Civil War was beginning, Amelia Sturges—or Mimi, as she was generally called—came down with tuberculosis. By autumn she was gravely ill. Pierpont decided that she must be taken to a warmer climate—and that he would marry her and take her there. His business? That could go hang; and anyhow his loyal cousin Jim Goodwin could be persuaded to come down from Hartford and look after the office for an indefinite time. Nothing—nothing in the world—mattered but Mimi.

So on October 7, 1861, he and Mimi were married, though by that time she was so weak that she could not stand alone. A few close friends gathered in the front parlor of the Sturges house on East Fourteenth Street in New York; in the back parlor, behind folding doors, the minister took his place; then Pierpont carried Mimi downstairs in his arms to the back parlor, the folding doors were opened, and he held her upright during the brief wedding ceremony. Then he carried her to a carriage outside, drove with her to the pier, and took her abroad with him—first, by way of England, to Algiers, and then, in desperation when her strength continued to fail, across the Mediterranean to Nice.

It was all to no avail. Mimi died only a little over four months after the wedding.

A widower at the age of twenty-four, Pierpont Morgan

returned to New York. Slowly he began to pick up the pieces of his life and put them together again. On the first of September of that year 1862 there appeared in the *New York Times* a modest advertisement to the effect that he was now ready to engage in business under the style of J. Pierpont Morgan & Co.

Chapter Three

GROPING FOR DIRECTION

THE New York to which young Morgan returned after his brief and tragic adventure in marriage was seething with Civil War business.

For us of today, who instinctively think in terms of total war, it is hard to realize how very untotal was the conflict of 1861-65, at least in the industrial North. Morgan did not enlist because for some time his health had been a source of concern to him: he had been subject to dizzy spells, even fainting spells (these seemed to have some obscure relation to the state of his complexion, for when his skin was clear the dizzy spells were more severe). But even for many of the healthiest young business men of that time the question of enlisting hardly rose to the level of consciousness; of those who rose to the top in American business in later years, very few had ever put on a uniform. When the draft was instituted in 1863, Morgan took advantage of the curious regulation which permitted one to hire a substitute to take one's place in the Army; but this too was a fully accepted practice. It is a striking fact that in the draft of July 1863—immediately after the critical Battle of Gettysburg—only a little over three per cent of those whose names were drawn actually became "draftees held to personal service"; the rest failed to report, or were exempted for physical disability or other reasons, or were exempted by paying a $300 "commutation," or furnished substitutes!

Meanwhile the industrial boom which led Charles A. Beard to call the Civil War the Second American Revolution was beginning its reckless course. The shifting fortunes of battle, the sharp expansion of manufacturing under the impact of war orders, and the westward push of trade toward the Pacific kept the speculative markets in turmoil. And under these circumstances the marts of the Wall Street district of New York seethed with energetic speculative activity. There was plenty of excitement for anybody in the gyrations of Erie stock, the gold dealings in Mr. Gilpin's Exchange and Reading Rooms, and the wild attempts of the aldermen of New York City to make a killing in Harlem Railroad shares—so much excitement, in fact, that to many men in the street the news from the bloody battlefronts of the South was interesting chiefly for its possible effect upon the course of prices.

During these wild years young Morgan, just starting in business for himself, got mixed up in two dubious enterprises which in recent years have been made much of by hostile writers. One was the Hall Carbine Affair. In the summer of 1861—just before he married Mimi—Morgan lent $20,000 to one Simon Stevens, who was engaged in selling to General Frémont, for $22 apiece, carbines of an outmoded style which had been bought by one Arthur M. Eastman *from the War Department itself* for only $3.50 apiece. The deal was a scandalous one, reflecting both gross incompetence on the part of the War Department and profiteering greed on the part of Stevens. More than forty years later the record of the episode was combed over by Gustavus Myers in his *History of the Great American Fortunes* and Morgan's part in it was represented as that of a fellow-conspirator with Stevens; and this version of the story thereupon appeared in book after book and article after article. But a later and even more diligent piece of research by R. Gordon

Wasson of J. P. Morgan & Co. has unearthed a wealth of detailed information from primary sources which puts a somewhat different light upon the matter.

That Morgan lent Stevens the $20,000 is beyond doubt. How much he knew at that moment about what Stevens was up to we shall probably never know; but there is no evidence that he had previously known the man, though Stevens' sister had once been a schoolteacher of his at Hartford and Stevens' brother was known to Junius Morgan in London. At the earliest moment when Morgan could detach himself from the operation, he did so. Within a month he was refusing to lend Stevens more money (Stevens got it elsewhere), and within six weeks he had been paid and was out of the business entirely. He did not share in Stevens' profit; his commission for his services (aside from $156.04 interest on the loan) was $5,400—a rather small sum to have been subsequently described by Myers as "the real beginning of J. Pierpont Morgan's business career." The only reason why Morgan's name figured in the scandal later was that—as a War Department Commission stated—"Morgan having loaned Stevens money, the carbines passed into the possession of Morgan as a security for the advance thus made, and were by him delivered to General Frémont, under the sale made by Stevens to him; and the bills against the government were made out in favor of Morgan." Although the Hall Carbine scandal was promptly aired, being investigated by two congressional committees and by a special War Department commission, Morgan himself was never called before any of them nor personally censured by any of them; apparently they were convinced that his connection with the business was not only brief but incidental. Nevertheless it was an ugly thing to have been involved in, however inadvertently; Morgan, at the age of twenty-four, had at least been headstrong, injudicious, and a bad judge of the character of a well-connected but disreputable customer.

The other episode—which has likewise been vigorously aired in recent years—took place after Mimi's death, and involved a speculation in gold. During 1863 Morgan and a young man named Edward Ketchum bought gold quietly and in small amounts; then all at once they conspicuously shipped abroad half of what they had acquired, in order to lift the price and sell the remainder of their hoard at a handsome profit. The scheme worked, and according to some reports they divided a profit of $160,000. From one point of view this was a legitimate, if crafty, speculative coup. It was probably regarded in 1863 somewhat as, let us say, a successful short sale of securities was regarded in 1931, or as a gamble in wheat prices was regarded in 1947: it seemed reprehensible to people distant from the exchanges but quite acceptable to people engaged in the constant push-and-pull of speculative trade. Yet from another and larger point of view this gold deal was a shabby operation, since it was in effect an attempt to depreciate, at least temporarily, the national currency in time of acute emergency. It is quite possible that Junius Spencer Morgan, hearing of it, may have breathed more easily in the knowledge that his son would henceforward have an older and wiser head in the office with him. (At about this time Charles H. Dabney joined Pierpont as senior partner and the firm became Dabney, Morgan & Co.) For once again the young man had been a bad judge of character: his crony in this deal, Edward Ketchum, came of a highly respectable family but subsequently got into other speculations which turned out disastrously, and in the collapse of the Ketchum firm forged a large number of gold checks and thereupon went to prison.

2

Quite aside from these adventures, the war years were busy ones. Young Morgan had his hands full at times putting through sales of American securities on behalf of the Peabody firm's anxious English clients, who doubted if the Union would survive and wanted to unload their American holdings. And what with a variety of other sorts of transactions, he prospered strikingly; his personal income for the year 1864 was no less than $53,286.

A photograph of him taken in 1862, shortly after Mimi's death, suggests how that tragedy had marked him: there is an intensity in his gaze such as no earlier picture had revealed, and it shows a much older-looking young man. His hair, parted on the left side, is longish and grows thickly above his ears after the fashion of the time; he has a small mustache now, and wears a high stiff collar.

Gradually, as time went by, his spirits were restored. As early as the summer of 1863, when he organized a party of friends to tour the White Mountains by four-horse stage, stopping at the Profile House at Franconia for a week, he made all the arrangements for them and bossed the whole expedition as was his wont, and seemed to his companions to be enjoying himself fully. And just as the Civil War came to an end he married again.

His bride in this second and more tranquil marriage was Frances Louisa Tracy, a pretty and sweet-natured girl whose family were people of substance in New York. Her father had come to New York from Utica and had become one of the leading lawyers of the city; and as he had several charming daughters, the Tracy house on

Seventeenth Street had long been a favorite haunt of Pierpont's. He and Fanny—as Frances Louisa was called—were married at St. George's Church on May 31, 1865.

With the gentle Fanny he now settled down to years of brownstone domesticity, first at 227 Madison Avenue and then at 243, in what were then the northernmost reaches of residential habitation in the city proper. The Murray Hill district was just being built up; Madison Avenue reached only to Forty-second Street, a few short blocks north of where the Morgans lived, and beyond that lay fields and farms; from the new brownstone houses rising along the Avenue one could look to the east, across vacant lots, to the masts of the shipping moving up and down the East River. Within the next decade Pierpont's wife bore him four children: Louisa (who later became Mrs. Herbert L. Satterlee); John Pierpont (who succeeded him in 1913 as head of the family firm); Juliet Pierpont (who became Mrs. William P. Hamilton); and Annie Tracy (who, as Anne Morgan, was to become well known for her work in French war relief and other charities).

A hulking, solid-shouldered young man with a strong, large-featured face and an emphatic mustache and striking hazel eyes, Morgan settled down into playing the orthodox role of active young business man, citizen, and churchman. Apparently he had now learned to select his customers and companions with ample circumspection. He was elected to the highly respectable Union Club. He became a member of the board of managers of St. Luke's Hospital, was busy in the affairs of the Y.M.C.A., helped to organize both the Metropolitan Museum of Art and the Museum of Natural History, and became a vestryman of St. George's Church in Stuyvesant Square. If you had a good cause to promote and wanted on your committee a young fellow with good connections, a wide acquaintance, unlimited energy, and a sort of innate force which made people tend to go his way, people would suggest that you consider young Morgan, the promising son of that Hartford man in London who had succeeded George Peabody and whose international banking firm was now called J. S. Morgan & Co. Yet as Pierpont turned thirty there was still little sign of the direction in which his character and peculiar talents would lead him.

In the late summer of 1869, however, when he was thirty-two, something happened which one can see now, in retrospect, as a sort of preface to his subsequent career.

3

The Northern victory in the Civil War had opened up to the industries of the expanding country, and to the railroads, an exciting prospect of growth—the industrial exploitation of a continent. Factories were booming, new inventions burgeoning, railroads pushing to the Pacific; and in the rush to take advantage of the new opportunities, ethical scruples were being tossed aside more heedlessly than at any other time in our history.

It was during the decade following the Civil War that Daniel Drew, while treasurer of the Erie Railroad, secretly printed new shares of Erie stock by the thousands and threw them on the market whenever it suited his speculative purposes; that Jay Gould and Jim Fisk conspired to corner the gold supply of the country, that the Grant Administration was honeycombed with graft, that Boss Tweed's corrupt regime ruled New York City, that the Crédit Mobilier scandals sullied the record of Western railroad financing, and that Gould and Fisk and Drew bribed legislators and judges with a cynicism and casualness unmatched before or since in the annals of American fraud.

In the summer of 1869 Jay Gould, who was both a railroad executive and a stock-market gambler, and seldom hesitated to wreck a company which he controlled if this suited his speculative purposes, was the undisputed master of the Erie Railroad. Gould cast covetous eyes on a newly completed line between Albany and Binghamton, New York, that was called the Albany & Susquehanna; he wanted the line as a profitable adjunct to the Erie, offering it a useful connection with New England. So he sent agents with bags of money to buy up shares which had been subscribed to by towns along its right of way, and he further tried to displace the existing management and directors of the road by getting complaisant judges to issue a flock of injunctions against them. Gould was vigorously countered by President Ramsey of the Albany & Susquehanna, who with his friends induced other judges to issue counterinjunctions against Gould. So complete was the resulting judicial confusion that at one time in August the conflict between the two factions became a minor civil war, with officers of the law at the Binghamton end of the line making arrests in accordance with the dictates of Manhattan judges who took orders from Gould, and officers of the law at the Albany end carrying out the decrees of upstate judges who sided with Ramsey; and there was actually a time when hired thugs battled for the control of a tunnel along the way and two locomotives manned by the hirelings of the respective groups collided with a fine smash. Day after day the New York papers carried news stories about the progress of this feud, which they called "The Susquehanna War." As the date of the annual stockholders' meeting at Albany —September 7—approached, it was manifest that the

Gould forces would try, by force or wile, to unseat the directors favorable to President Ramsey, and that the Ramsey forces must be ready for the fray.

The day of the meeting offered a spectacle probably unmatched in the history of that ordinarily sedate institution, the stockholders' meeting. The bearded Gould was not in Albany; but his right-hand man, the dandified Jim Fisk, with his waxed mustache, was on hand to further Gould's designs, wearing a speckled straw hat with a blue ribbon; and in profitable roguery Fisk was as adept as any rascal in the land. He was accompanied by an exceedingly untidy gang of forty or more ruffians whom he had brought up by train from New York and had fed that morning at the Union depot restaurant in Albany; subsequently these men were referred to delicately by the Supreme Court of New York as "such as in common parlance would doubtless be classed among the roughs and fighting men of the city." Each carrying a proxy—for they were now to play the part of Albany & Susquehanna stockholders—these ragged but muscular characters were lined up by Fisk in a meeting room already crowded with railroad officials, lawyers, and stockholders.

Word came that two of Ramsey's tellers had been stopped on their way to the meeting by an officer of the law armed with one of those injunctions which certain Manhattan judges, who enjoyed good living more than good reputations, would issue on behalf of Gould and Fisk at the drop of a hat. And just before the scheduled time for the meeting, President Ramsey himself was likewise arrested on a charge engineered by Gould. Apparently the Gould-Fisk tactics were to disorganize the Ramsey forces by such arrests, and then to hold an election which their strong-armed gang of "stockholders" would control. But Ramsey managed to get bail in the nick of time to participate in the proceedings. What then happened was that *two* stockholders' meetings took place, with the tellers at one table counting votes for the Ramsey candidates and the tellers at the other table counting votes for the Gould-Fisk candidates, and each party claiming victory for its side. Surveying the tangled results of these rival elections, and of assorted injunctions, counter-injunctions, arrests, counterarrests, lawsuits, and counterlawsuits, the Governor of New York in disgust then called upon the Supreme Court to settle the whole issue; and weeks later it delivered judgment—in favor of the Ramsey board and all its works.

As one of Ramsey's chief aides, Pierpont Morgan took part in this incredible episode, but just how much part is not clear. His devoted son-in-law and biographer, Herbert L. Satterlee, represents him as standing guard at the head of the steps leading to the meeting room and, with the aid of Ramsey, physically throwing Fisk and the leading toughs downstairs. But it is quite clear from detailed contemporary accounts that Fisk entered the meeting unopposed; it was not on September 7 that he was thrown downstairs, but a month earlier, when he made another foray on the Albany & Susquehanna offices with the idea of capturing the company's stock transfer books; and since Satterlee himself places Morgan in California at that previous date, it seems doubtful whether the young banker had to make any physical show of prowess. Some other recent writers, including Matthew Josephson in *The Robber Barons,* perhaps succumbing to the tendency of narrators long-after-the-fact to place undue emphasis on the participation in any event of a man subsequently famous, have referred to the Ramsey party in the dispute as the "Morgan-Ramsey party." No contemporary account that I have seen pays Morgan any such compliment. But it is certainly true that Morgan was called upon, as a reliable and active young financier with a quick head for strategy, to help Ramsey, and that his name headed the list of directors chosen by the Ramsey faction and subsequently confirmed by the upstate court.

It is doubtless true, too, that the victory of his side added to the solidity of Morgan's reputation in downtown New York; for the Mephistophelean Gould and the hard-shelled playboy Fisk were formidable adversaries. And one may perhaps hazard a further conclusion. Earlier that summer Pierpont Morgan, accompanied by his wife and two friends, had taken a trip to the Pacific Coast over the newly completed transcontinental railroad line. It had been his first Far Western visit. On the way out they had spent twelve days in Chicago; then they had boarded one of the earliest Pullman cars for a journey on which, as they crossed the Plains, they could see from the car windows a Pawnee war party, squads of scouting United States Cavalry, herds of antelopes, and immigrant trains winding slowly westward. They had visited Salt Lake City (where they talked with Brigham Young), and San Francisco, and the Yosemite, and then had returned East, again by Pullman. Is it not unreasonable to guess that this expedition gave Morgan a fresh and lively sense of what new frontiers there were for the railroad industry to conquer, and that it must have been a shock to him, immediately on his return home, to see a part of that industry demoralized by a lawless battle for control? And is it not also likely that to him, who had a deep instinct for order, the Battle of Susquehanna may have seemed an object lesson in the disorderliness of competition gone hog-wild?

By instinct, if not by reason, most business men hate competition, at least when they are selling rather than buying. A man's competitor is the fellow who holds down his prices, cuts away his profits, tries to seize his markets, threatens him with bankruptcy, and jeopardizes the future of his family. It is only when the business man mentally sets competition alongside some order of things even less attractive to him that he becomes its devotee. To a young man in 1869, monopoly, as an alternative, had no such connotations as it carries today; government control was something that only a few wild theorists talked about; and even government regulation of competition seemed a pretty remote possibility—and might very well appear to involve, furthermore, an unpalatable complication of the anarchy of competition such as had been brought about by Gould's cheerful prostitution of the New York judiciary. It is hardly an accident that most of the Americans who at the beginning of the twentieth century were charged with being monopolists had got a good look in their youth at competition at its savage and unbridled worst, and had decided to try to do something about it. At the age of thirty-two Pierpont Morgan saw at close range what the Battle of the Susquehanna did to a small fragment of the railroad industry. It brought corruption, confusion, waste, and loss; and his systematic soul detested it. Surely, he may well have thought, it would be better if instead of fighting thus like cats and dogs, people could be brought together to combine forces for the peaceful and orderly and profitable development of railroad properties.

4

During the next year or two Morgan became deeply depressed about his health. He felt perpetually tired, slept badly, had severe headaches, had recurrences of his old fainting-spell trouble; and he began to think that, having already made a good deal of money—enough to live on thereafter—he might as well retire. The term for which the partnership of Dabney, Morgan & Co. had been organized was coming to an end; the elderly Mr. Dabney wanted to retire; the faithful Jim Goodwin talked of returning to Hartford. Why not just wind the whole thing up, get out of business, and take as many years as might be necessary to recover his physical well-being? So he reasoned in a letter to his father in London.

What, one wonders, would have been his future, and how would the course of American business have been affected, if he had succumbed to this despondent idea? But it happened that at about this time his father was engaged in putting through one of the boldest operations ever known in international finance. The French had just been soundly defeated in the Franco-Prussian War of 1870; Paris was surrounded by German forces. To the city of Tours went Junius Spencer Morgan, head of the London firm that had once been George Peabody & Co., and agreed with the French ministers there to support them in their hour of trial by floating a loan to the French Government of 250,000,000 francs—fifty million dollars—in the form of six per cent bonds which he would take at the price of 80. It was a stiff price, but it was also a dangerous gamble. To sell the bonds he organized a group of bankers to which was applied the French term "syndicate"—a term which was then new. At first the sale of bonds went badly, and Morgan had to buy back a considerable number of them at a discount. But after the war the French credit rallied; the value of the bonds quickly rose to par; and Morgan's judgment was justified. His firm not only made a resounding profit on the French bonds—probably five million dollars or more—but won for itself in the world of international finance a place second only to that of the Rothschilds.

With a deal like this in hand, Junius Morgan would appreciate more than ever the future value to him of having his son in a strongly entrenched position to sell European securities for him in the United States and to negotiate for American securities which J. S. Morgan & Co. might distribute in Europe. And here was that son flirting with the idea of retirement—and at the age of thirty-three!

Somewhere about this time he wrote to the young man in New York, "I have had a visit from Mr. A. J. Drexel, of Drexel & Co., Philadelphia. It is possible he may want to see you about a certain matter, and if he does I hope you will go to see him."

Drexel & Co.—established by old Joseph Drexel, an immigrant portrait painter turned financier—had become an important private banking house, second only in Philadelphia to the great house of Jay Cooke. It had set up a London branch, Drexel, McCulloch & Co., and it also had a Paris house, Drexel, Harjes & Co. But its New York connections were unsatisfactory. What could be more promising for it than an alliance with young Pierpont Morgan, who not only was building up a sturdy reputation of his own, but also—what was presumably more impressive—was the son and American representative of the great J. S. Morgan of London? One day in May 1871, Anthony J. Drexel (old Joseph's son, and now the leading spirit of the Drexel firm) wired young Morgan asking him to come on to Philadelphia for dinner.

Somewhat mystified, Morgan took a train to Philadelphia, went to Drexel's house, and dined with the Drexel family. After dinner Drexel and he adjourned to the library.

"Morgan, I want you to come into my firm as a partner," said Drexel; and then proposed, more specifically, that they join forces to set up in New York the firm of Drexel, Morgan & Co., the Drexels and Morgan each contributing capital to it and sharing the profits half-and-half.

Morgan protested that he was in wretched health and that he had been thinking seriously of leaving business altogether. He said that anyhow he could not enter such an alliance, inviting though it might be, unless he took a year off at the outset. Drexel saw no objection to such a prolonged holiday; and so that evening they reached an agreement, written down by hand on a small sheet of paper. And on the first of July, 1871, the new firm of Drexel, Morgan & Co. began business—whereupon Pierpont Morgan promptly sailed with his wife and young children to spend over a year abroad.

5

The new association proved highly profitable. By 1873 Drexel, Morgan & Co. began to break into the field of distributing United States Government bond issues, a field which for some time had been monopolized by Jay Cooke's banking house in Philadelphia. Teaming up with Levi Morton's firm in New York, which was allied with the Rothschilds abroad, Morgan was given a chance to sell an issue of bonds along with Cooke. The sales went badly, the times being inauspicious, but it was something to be placed by the Treasury on a par with the notable financier of the Civil War; and when, a few months later, Cooke plunged into bankruptcy in the panic of 1873, Morgan found himself without an equal rival. For in those days there were far more wealthy investors in England and on the Continent than in the United States, and there was nothing more important to a distributor of government bonds than to have the means of selling them abroad. So a man who not only was already the dominant figure in the Drexel-Morgan firm, with the Drexel capital to aid him, but also had at his disposal the machinery of J. S. Morgan & Co. in London and Drexel, Harjes & Co. in Paris, and in alliance with Levi Morton could put into action also the international salesmanship of the great Rothschild firm, found himself one of the key figures of American finance in the eyes of the United States Treasury, despite the fact that not yet did one American citizen in a thousand know his name.

On a little sheet of paper which he carried about with him in his wallet, Pierpont Morgan wrote down the "reserves" contributed by each partner to the business of Drexel, Morgan & Co. in the years 1871, 1873, 1874, and 1875—that is to say, the part of each member's share of the annual profits which he did not take out as personal income but put back into the business to add to its financial backlog. Usually each member took out half of his share and put back half; perhaps in 1871, since the firm was newly formed, he put back a larger proportion than half. At any rate, here are Pierpont Morgan's contributions to reserves in those years: for 1871—$727,-649.21; for 1873—$202,253.03; for 1874—$324,572.60; for 1875—$200,820.58. If Pierpont in those three latter years kept as personal income (not subject to any income tax) an amount equal to what he was contributing to reserves, clearly he was making out very handsomely indeed—especially as they were dismal years for business in general.

6

He had his offices, now, in a sumptuous and strategically located building just erected by the Drexels at the corner of Broad and Wall streets—a six-story white marble building with a corner entrance and, high above it on the roof, a sort of hexagonal cupola. The splendor of these new quarters offered majestic evidence of his rise in the world; and they were to serve him throughout the rest of his active business life, for it was not until within two or three years of his death that the Drexel Building was removed to make way for the present much lower and solider building at 23 Wall Street.

Uptown, he and Fanny and the children occupied a brownstone house at 6 East Fortieth Street, just a few steps from Fifth Avenue, across which rose the embankment of the Croton Reservoir (on the site of the present Public Library). It was a unit in one of those rows of high-stooped brownstone houses which gave the residential districts of New York their prevailing air of somber monotony; but it was a very proper house by the standards of the Rutherford B. Hayes period, with a plethora of Victorian furniture. In its elongated, high-ceilinged, heavily curtained drawing room there were amply upholstered chairs, a sofa with a fringe hanging down in front, and sundry small tables of maximum inutility and instability; there were fine rugs superimposed upon a flowered carpet; every horizontal surface—mantels, tables, shelves—carried its freight of ornaments and knickknacks; and if Pierpont had not yet become a notable collector of art, at least there was hardly a foot of wall space not covered with pictures elaborately framed in gold, hanging one above the other.

And up in the Highlands of the Hudson—at Highland Falls, just south of West Point—the Morgans now had a country place, Cragston, which Pierpont had purchased by cable when he was abroad in 1871. It was one of the most comfortable estates in what was then a fashionable summer district. Some two miles south of the village of Highland Falls the entrance driveway of Cragston turned in from the main road that ran along the bluff high above the west shore of the Hudson; turned downhill toward the river, swung through woods, skirted a green meadow through which ran a little brook, and then twisted up the slope of a knoll just above the river bank. Here stood the house, a very ample, broad-eaved, gabled structure, a hundred feet long or thereabouts, three stories high, built of white clapboard; its front windows looked southward across a fine lawn toward the hills opposite Bear Mountain. (In 1948 the house had become a terrible blackened wreck; for after Morgan's death the place had been sold, had gone through various vicissitudes, and finally had been visited by fire. Three great brick chimneys still stood and the walls were partly intact, but the roof had mostly fallen in, charred wainscoting hung at crazy angles, and the stairs and floors were gone. Outside, the long grass of the one-time lawn—half overgrown now—was matted and unkempt. Even so, one's mind's eye could reconstruct the Cragston of old: a very commodious though unpretentious country house, surrounded by rolling acres of field and grove, with the river glittering below it; a place that would commend itself to a man who enjoyed exercising a substantial hospitality and appreciated the English county tradition.) Here the growing Morgan family now spent a good part of the year.

Still Pierpont's health troubled him. He had frequent colds and headaches, and to his humiliation the recurring inflammation of the skin of his face began to settle in his nose; this was the beginning of the unending affliction of *acne rosacea* which was destined to disfigure him increasingly as time went on. But there were compensations. He was a rich man now, and life was beginning to expand.

The Morgans went on frequent trips abroad, and now when they were in England they would find themselves either in Junius Morgan's fine city house at Prince's Gate, facing Hyde Park, or at his agreeable country estate, Dover House, at Roehampton in the western outskirts of London. In 1877 they spent almost a year abroad; in Egypt they chartered a steamer to go up the Nile and had their pictures taken in front of the ruins of Karnak in a group of eighteen—family, friends, doctor, maid, dragoman, waiter, and consular agent—Pierpont standing very straight and solid looking, with pith helmet, knickerbocker suit, wing collar, and a long walking stick.

When they were at Cragston, Pierpont liked to entertain guests a dozen at a time, sending them up the river to Highland Falls on the punctual steamer, *Mary Powell*, while he, who was usually too rushed for such a leisurely jaunt, would go up the Hudson by train and be met on the eastern shore by his tidy steam launch, the *Louisa*, which would ferry him across the river. At Cragston he would go for long walks with his mastiff Hero, when his recurring headaches were not too troublesome; sometimes he would go riding, or driving in the surrey; or he would take his guests to inspect the cattle that he was beginning to breed. On Sunday mornings he piled everybody into a big wagon like an omnibus, climbed up on the high front seat in his frock coat and straw hat, and drove them all to church, where he handed over the reins to the coachman; and of course hymn singing was obligatory every Sunday evening that he was there. He loved parties and expeditions, and ran them to the last detail; when you were with Pierpont Morgan, you found yourself doing just about what he had planned for you to do. On the evening of the Fourth of July, when he put on a majestic show of fireworks, the guests and neighbors would sit quietly on the porch and gasp with satisfaction at the flares of brilliance against the night sky which arched above the black shapes of the hills across the river —but it was Pierpont who managed the whole exhibit.

He was beginning to think of breeding collies in addition to cattle, and wondering whether he might not acquire, in addition to the pair of smart horses which drew Fanny's carriage, a pair of really fast trotters. And might not the launch *Louisa* soon be superseded by a real steam yacht? The depression which followed the financial and industrial follies of the post-Civil War years was slow to depart, and it was a hungry time for a great number of Americans; but he was a coming man with an ample income, and it would be fun to use it amply.

7

Still, however, he was essentially his father's son. Still his success was due primarily to his foreign connections. In a day when American railroads and American industry depended largely upon Europeans to provide them with capital, he was—in financial terms—a sort of colonial administrator: a representative in America of the financial might of Britain. But now this very fact was about to bring a new turn in his career.

In 1879 William H. Vanderbilt—son and heir of the terrific old Commodore—came to Pierpont for aid. The Vanderbilts, father and son, had brought together a number of small railroads to form the impressive New York Central system, which reached from New York all the way to Chicago, and of its shares the younger Vanderbilt now owned no less than eighty-seven per cent. He had begun to realize that this virtual one-man ownership, lucrative though it might be, had its embarrassing aspect. Vanderbilt was unpopular with the general public, and knew it. As he told a reporter later, "A public sentiment has been growing up opposed to the control of such a great property by a single man or a single family. It says we rule by might. We certainly have control of this property by right. But no matter, this public feeling exists." Vanderbilt's unpopularity was very convenient for rival financiers who wanted to put over deals at his expense; to the public these men could represent themselves as St. Georges battling a dragon. And it was handy too for legislators looking for things which could be taxed without arousing public outcry; they could slap a tax on the New York Central properties and argue that the money would come right out of the bottomless pockets of multimillionaire Vanderbilt, the almost sole owner.

A stolid man devoid of sensibility, William H. Vanderbilt had no gift for wooing the public. Indeed it was he who, three years later, when a reporter asked him whether a certain unprofitable train should not be run for the sake of the public whether it earned its way or not, replied irritably, with perfect logic but disastrous choice of language, "The public be damned! I am working for my stockholders. If the public want the train, why don't they support it?" Now, in 1879, he wanted to unload the onus of sole ownership.

The uneasy Vanderbilt went to consult Morgan because of Morgan's English connections. He told Morgan that he wanted to sell a considerable part of his interest in the road. But he wanted the sale to be conducted very privately, lest the word go round that Vanderbilt was unloading and that therefore either he or the Central must be in trouble. Could Morgan manage a private and unpublicized sale to English investors?

Morgan leaped at the chance; and working quietly, disposed of 150,000 shares of New York Central stock directly to overseas purchasers, at $120 per share, with an option to dispose of another 100,000 shares within the following year at the same price. (The total number of shares disposed of represented less than half of Vanderbilt's interest in the road, but reduced that interest so sharply that after the sale he was able to remark to a reporter, "It can no longer be said that I am the owner of New York Central.")

Not until the operation was completed, in November 1879, did any announcement have to be made, so secretly had the negotiations been conducted. When the news broke, the financial community was amazed. In the words of the *Commercial & Financial Chronicle* for November 29, 1879, "There has been one topic in Wall Street this week—the great New York Central & Hudson stock sale."

It brought about a striking change in the status of Pierpont Morgan. Now, as holder of proxies for the English purchasers, he sat on the New York Central's board as a wielder of great potential influence. For years past, on his visits to London, he had had to confront perplexed or angry Englishmen who had wanted to know why so many things went wrong with their investments in American securities. Why was America having such hard times? Why was the United States currency so unsound? Why were so many American railroads scandalously mismanaged? Why were men like Gould permitted to plunder right and left the properties in which honest Englishmen had invested? These had not been easy questions to answer, especially when put with that wounded superciliousness with which some gentlemen of London were wont to reprove a spokesman for the barbaric land across the seas. Morgan had tried to assure them that there was a prosperous future for American business, that the hard times in the United States were merely temporary, that the national currency would soon be put on a solid basis by the resumption of specie payments, and that the vendettas between railroad chieftains, and particularly their senseless habit of building parallel railroad lines in order to bring one another to terms, were passing phenomena of the youth of a great country. Now he had become the representative of these skeptical Englishmen on the New York Central board. They had been persuaded by his assurances. To himself he must admit that lawless feuds like the one in which he had found himself embroiled at Albany, ten years earlier, continued to sully the record of American railroading. Now, however, he was in a position to do something about this economic anarchy. Now he could be something more than a banker and international dealer in securities; he could help to produce some sort of order in the railroad business.

At the age of forty-two Pierpont Morgan moved out from his father's shadow and took his place, solidly on his own feet, as a regularizing and disciplining force in American industry.

Chapter Four

MORGAN THE PEACEMAKER

ON A warm morning in July 1885, two gentlemen from Philadelphia boarded a sleek black steam yacht at a dock in Jersey City for a day's cooling excursion in the waters about New York. The two Philadelphians were George B. Roberts, president of the Pennsylvania Railroad, and Frank Thomson, vice-president of the road and nephew of the great Edgar Thomson who had established its reputation as an efficient transportation system. They had come at the invitation of Pierpont Morgan to talk comfortably with him and Chauncey Depew, the diplomatic president of the New York Central Railroad.

The yacht was Morgan's own *Corsair*, a superb 165-foot vessel which he had bought three years earlier to supersede, grandly, the little steam launch *Louisa*. And the purpose of the excursion—ostensibly to offer the two Philadelphians a few hours of pleasant respite from the baking summer heat of their city—was really to try to negotiate a treaty of peace to end the most menacing railroad war of the day. Pierpont Morgan, at the age of forty-eight, was at last moving into his appointed role as conciliator among the American railroads.

The years that had intervened since he had taken a seat on the New York Central's board of directors in 1879 had been years of furious and undisciplined industrial development in the United States, and of even more furious railroad building. All over the country new lines of rails were being projected, big railroads were buying up little ones to form connected systems, and new settlers were moving into regions opened up to commerce by these avenues of steel. Railroad corporations were the biggest and most powerful units of big business. Their expanding services were stimulating immeasurably the roaring industrial growth of the country. They were attracting inventive and ambitious men, whose brains were constantly thinking up new improvements in railroad equipment and operation, and whose imaginations leaped ahead to foresee how a well-run railroad could transform a wilderness into a chain of thriving communities. But they also attracted ruthless adventurers and knaves, and their financing, construction, and operation offered extraordinary spectacles of ruthlessness and buccaneering.

To begin with, freight rates were wildly anarchic. The general practice was to keep the rates low where you faced competition, and to make up your losses by charging high where you had a monopoly of the traffic. At one time it cost only half as much to ship steel all the way from Chicago to the Atlantic seaboard as to ship it the much shorter distance from Pittsburgh to the seaboard, simply because there were several lines competing for the Chicago traffic and there was only one line available for the Pittsburgh traffic. Passenger fares, too, fluctuated wildly as the roads sought to grab one another's business: at one time the New York Central charged only seven dollars for the long ride from New York to Chicago, and the "immigrant" rate between these two cities fell all the way to one dollar. Worse even than the custom of charging less for the long (competitive) haul than for the short (monopoly) haul was the practice of discriminating between individual shippers of freight—charging reduced rates to big companies whose business was especially valuable, or who had friends, or maybe even owners, in the railroad's management, while the small and friendless paid through the nose. A legislative investigation in 1879 revealed that in a single year the New York Central had made as many as six thousand special contracts offering reduced rates (or rebates, as they were called). Throughout the country, but especially among the small business men and farmers of the West, there was naturally a continual uproar of protest at these discriminations; and needless to say, the anarchy in rates made business hazardous and unpredictable not only for those who shipped their goods over the roads but for the railroad corporations themselves. For although a road could make big money by ruthless juggling of its rates, this was a game that two or more could play at, and for the industry as a whole it was a wasteful and dangerous game.

There was also widespread buccaneering in railroad ownership—getting control of a company only to play its stock up and down in the market for one's personal profit; or getting control of two railroads and using one of them to enrich the other, again for one's personal speculative profit; or organizing a construction company to build a road at such padded "cost" that the construction company made millions and the railroad company (whose stock one could always sell) became saddled with overwhelming fixed debts.

Finally, there was an epidemic of building—or starting to build—needlessly competitive roads, which in some cases might aptly be called blackmail roads. If, for example, there was already a prosperous line running between two cities, there was nothing to prevent you from building—or starting to build—another, parallel line between them, in the hope that the management of the existing road, alarmed lest your new line ruin its business, would buy you out at a blackmail price.

This was more or less what had happened to occasion the conference on the *Corsair* in 1885. Some years previously a little group of men including the egregious Jay Gould, George M. Pullman, and General Horace Porter, had conceived the bright idea of building a railroad from New York to Buffalo right alongside William H. Vanderbilt's New York Central. It would start on the Jersey side of the Hudson, follow the west shore of the Hudson northward—just across the river from Vanderbilt's tracks—and then cut westward, avoiding the Central's heavy grades west of Albany but otherwise following it closely all the way to Buffalo.

This West Shore Road, however dazzlingly conceived, was a losing venture from the first. Vanderbilt did *not* buy it out, preferring to let it stew in its own juice, and before 1885 it was already bankrupt.

That should have been agreeable to people interested in the fortunes of the New York Central; however, there was a disquieting factor in the West Shore's predicament. A group of men interested in the Pennsylvania Railroad had been quietly buying up the West Shore's depreciated bonds. Suppose these Pennsylvania men got control of the ailing company after it had gone through the wringer of bankruptcy, and then put the mighty resources of the Pennsylvania into an effort to steal from the New York Central much of the valuable New-York-to-the-Great-Lakes traffic?

Meanwhile the Central, in its turn, had been making a foray into Pennsylvania territory. Knowing that men like Andrew Carnegie, who had big steel mills and other plants in the Pittsburgh region, were angry at the high freight rates exacted by the Pennsylvania for carrying their products to the Atlantic seaboard, William H. Vanderbilt had proposed to them in 1883 that a parallel line be built across the Allegheny Mountains from the Philadelphia region to Pittsburgh. "What do you think of it, Carnegie?" asked Vanderbilt. "I think so well of it," said the little Scotsman, "that I and my friends will raise five million dollars as our subscription." Whereupon Vanderbilt himself agreed to put in five million, and presently work began on the construction of the South Pennsylvania Railroad, which was to run westward from Reading via Harrisburg toward the Pittsburgh region.

Now in terms of ton-miles of freight carried, the Pennsylvania and the New York Central were the two mightiest railroads in the United States. The Pennsylvania stood first, the Central second. Could anything be more senseless than for these two giants of the railroad world to engage in a cutthroat war, the Pennsylvania using the West Shore to ruin the New York Central's going business, and the Central in turn using the South Pennsylvania to ruin the Pennsylvania's going business? Wasn't there plenty of room for both, without their invading each other's territory?

Morgan had watched the building of the West Shore with acute distaste—a distaste accentuated by the fact that its new tracks ran along the Hudson River shore just below his beloved Cragston; during two or three summers its construction gangs had made an infernal noise blasting at the ledges along the route and shaking the windows of his house, and there had been so many rough characters in the formerly placid precincts of Highland Falls that the Morgan children had had to be told not to go out on the highways unaccompanied. What he thought about the South Pennsylvania project is unrecorded; but certainly he felt uneasy over the fact that Vanderbilt, having declared war upon the Pennsylvania, had so lost interest in the situation as to resign the presidency of the New

York Central to Chauncey Depew and go off to Europe. Morgan felt responsible for the Central's future prosperity; were not those English investors counting on him to see that dividends were steady? And because the Drexel firm had done financing for the Pennsylvania in the past and would like to do more of the same in the future, he had every reason to want to remain in the Pennsylvania's good graces too. Surely under the circumstances this war was folly. Here, perhaps, was a chance to do something for the cause of order.

Morgan too went to Europe, took pains to return on the same liner with Vanderbilt, and talked him into permitting peace negotiations.

Whereupon, after several futile preliminary conferences with the heads of the Pennsylvania, Morgan finally succeeded in inducing Roberts and Thomson to come on from hot Philadelphia for a little run on the *Corsair*.

The agreement he proposed when his guests were settled on the yacht's deck was simple. The Pennsylvania would drop all interest in the West Shore line, permitting the Central to buy it out of bankruptcy and take a long lease on it; and in return the Central would turn over the control of the South Pennsylvania project to the Pennsylvania, to do with as it pleased.

The four men—Roberts, Thomson, Depew, and Morgan—sat under an ample awning aft of the *Corsair*'s single slanting funnel while the sharp-prowed vessel steamed slowly up the cool Hudson to the region of the beetling Highlands, and then turned about at West Point and steamed down river and out of New York Harbor as far as Sandy Hook. Depew talked, argued, reasoned. Roberts argued back. Morgan sat mostly silent, smoking a big, black cigar and occasionally putting in a massive word. Thomson appeared to have been won over, but Roberts remained unmoved. This stubborn Pennsylvania executive had begun his career as a rodman, had been a railroad builder and operator throughout, and didn't like to succumb to the will of an investment banker. The afternoon drew to a close and the *Corsair* steamed back through the harbor to the Jersey City docks; yet still there seemed to be no meeting of minds. Not until Roberts was leaving the boat did he capitulate to Morgan's inexorable logic and inexorable will. But at that moment, as he shook hands with Morgan and stepped upon the gangplank, he said, "I will agree to your plan and do my part." The war was over.

Immediately Drexel, Morgan & Co. issued a plan for the reorganization of the West Shore road, by which it was to be taken under the wing of the New York Central. And in mid-September of 1885 all work ceased on the construction of the South Pennsylvania.

Presently grass and weeds and bushes began to grow over the unfinished South Pennsylvania embankments; moss began to grow over the tunnel walls. And in due course the abandoned project for a new railroad across the Alleghenies was almost forgotten. Not for over half a century was work resumed—resumed for the completion, not of a railroad, but of a great automobile highway, the Pennsylvania Turnpike. If you should chance one of these days to drive over that magnificent turnpike, it may entertain you to know that it uses the embankments and tunnels built during the railroad war of the early eighties, and that you would not be following that particular route through the Pennsylvania hills if Pierpont Morgan, intent upon bringing order to the railroad industry, had not in the summer of 1885 taken two Philadelphians for a little spin on the *Corsair*.

2

The *Corsair* compact was hailed by the *Commercial & Financial Chronicle* as removing not only every source of discord between the trunk lines—meaning the major lines which connected the East with the Midwest—"but also the chief source of discord to the whole railroad system of the country."

It did not, to be sure, quite bring the West Shore-South Pennsylvania difficulties to an end. All sorts of legal obstacles had to be surmounted. It was during the legal planning for the reorganization of the West Shore company, by the way, that Morgan made a remark which has often been quoted (and misquoted, for that matter). Morgan had prepared a reorganization scheme and had asked his lawyer, Judge Ashbel Green, to tell him how it could be worked out legally. In a day or two Green came back and said it couldn't be done legally. Morgan, quite sure of the merits of his plan, replied severely, "That is not what I asked you to do. I asked you to tell me how this could be done legally. Come back tomorrow or the next day and tell me how it can be done." Finally it *was* done, and successfully, Morgan having himself purchased the West Shore and sold it immediately to the New York Central; and the troubles were over.

With this new, bold success to his credit, Morgan's prestige became immense, and it rose higher when, only a few days after the West Shore purchase, William H. Vanderbilt died suddenly. For it was now apparent that although Morgan was not a railroad man and hardly knew a driving rod from a coupler, there was nobody else in the councils of the New York Central who carried the weight that he did. In a day when the financial problems of the railroads underlay all their other concerns, and when most of the leading systems of the country were near the edge of bankruptcy because of the plundering and waste to which they had been subjected, a man like Morgan, who had learned all about railroad finance, whose judgment on a difficult reorganization plan had been proved sound, who stood for mutual co-operation among the railroads rather than mutual destruction, and whose word could be relied upon, stood out like a rock of safety.

One by one the managements of sick railroads came to him, as to a reliable doctor, for the financial surgery they needed. Presently he was deep in the reorganization plans of the Reading; and in the next few years he reorganized the Baltimore & Ohio, the Chesapeake & Ohio, and other lines. What matter that he was ignorant of the technical knowledge of railroading which it took railroad executives long years to master? In matters of life and death for the corporations which stood behind these executives, it was his word which counted most.

3

From Morgan's successful peacemaking flowed other striking results. Within only a few weeks of the *Corsair* conference it became clear that the principle of co-operation was being eagerly embraced, not only by the Pennsylvania and the Central, but by the other trunk lines. The officers of these lines had often tried to agree among themselves not to cut rates, but their compacts had broken down. Now, however, there was a new feeling in the air that the owners and heads of the companies meant business, and freight rates and passenger fares began to rise from the low points to which harsh competition had driven them. By the following spring the *Commercial & Financial Chronicle* could cheerfully report that passenger fares between New York and Chicago, which as we have seen had got all the way down to seven dollars, had advanced to twenty dollars for first class and seventeen dollars for second class, "the final step in that restoration of rates which had its origin in the trunk line settlement of last summer." And in the same conservative journal there was another announcement which reads somewhat oddly today:

> *Anthracite Coal Combination*—Representatives of the various coal companies met at the house of Mr. J. Pierpont Morgan this week, and informally decided to limit coal production and maintain prices. The new coal combination agrees to mine 33,500,000 tons of coal this year. Last year's output was 31,600,000 tons. An advance of 25 cents a ton was made by the companies on the following day. . . .

What had happened was that Morgan, having succeeded with one peace conference, had decided to try another one. The anthracite coal business was then almost wholly in the control of several railroad companies which served eastern Pennsylvania—the Reading, the Pennsylvania, the Lehigh Valley, the Delaware & Hudson, and others. Morgan wanted to do something to help the Reading, whose officers had been angry when he had stopped the project for the building of the South Pennsylvania line, which would have been a very handy adjunct to it. He was now reorganizing the Reading; what better way of showing his interest in its future than by a little peace conference on prices and production between the heads of all these coal-producing railroads—the meeting to be held, not on the *Corsair*, for it was March and the weather was unseasonable for yachting, but at his house? There was then no Sherman Anti-trust Law (a fact which explains the frankness of the news report); the agreement was perfectly legal. But it was, of course, a competition-throttling, monopolistic move, and there was a loud public outcry. Said the *New York Times*, indignantly: "In plain language, this means . . . a tax upon an important commodity at the will of the combination. . . ."

It is doubtful if Morgan saw much difference between ending railroad wars and ending competition in the coal industry. This, too, in his eyes, was co-operation in order that all might prosper.

4

Such agreements as Morgan's peacemaking had encouraged were brittle at best. As Arthur Twining Hadley wrote years afterward, "Each [railroad] company is at the mercy of its agents. They will try to steal business from rival concerns by cutting rates. If they are allowed a commission on sales, they will divide it with the buyer; if they are not allowed such a commission they will find a hundred different ways, less obvious but hardly less effective, of rendering a rate agreement nugatory." Sometimes even the men who gathered round a table to decide on the price they would all charge had their tongues in their cheeks; as a leading industrialist remarked, a price compact usually lasted about as long as it took the quickest man to get to a telegraph office or a telephone and put in a selling order at a lower price. Among the trunk lines there remained a semblance of co-operation, largely as a result of Morgan's influence; but over the country as a whole the granting of rebates and the sale of blocks of tickets by railroad passenger agents to scalpers went right on, as did the building of rival and blackmail lines, especially in the West. In short, the industry was still in an anarchic condition. By the end of 1888 so few American railroads were earning enough money to pay dividends on their swollen capital that the English investors to whom Morgan felt responsible were protesting vehemently, and he decided that it was time to turn on the heat.

So now he called a new and much larger and more ambitious conference; and this time he allied with him, in issuing the call, several other investment banking houses. It was as much as to say, "We represent the owners of your companies. These owners are sick and tired of the way you are behaving. They want earnings. And to that end they want you people to co-operate."

By this time there was a new element in the picture. Public fury at the behavior of the railroads had led a number of state legislatures, as early as the eighteen-seventies, to try to regulate the lines within their state borders; and when, in 1886, the Supreme Court of the United States had decided that only the federal government could regulate interstate commerce, it had been manifest that some sort of federal law would have to be passed. So in January 1887 the Interstate Commerce Act was adopted at Washington. It sternly forbade rebates and any sort of discrimination in rates, and it set up an Interstate Commerce Commission to see that freight and passenger rates were reasonable and just, and to require public disclosure of all rates charged. This, to be sure, was little more than a gesture to placate indignant farmers and business men, especially in the West and South; for after its frequent fashion, Congress had given the law enforcers so little authority that there were dozens of ways of circumventing them, and if these failed, one could always go to court and get a decision against them. The almost incredible fact is that between 1887 and 1905, of the cases appealed from the Interstate Commerce Commission which got all the way up to the Supreme Court *fifteen out of sixteen* were won by the railroads against the shippers or other complainants who had brought them!

Naturally, Morgan had been opposed to the passage of the Interstate Commerce Act. He had thought that the abuses in the railroad industry could best be cured by the sort of reform measures upon which he was engaged—substituting co-operation for competition, and honest financing for buccaneering. He had a deep contempt for politicians, and thought that people like himself could handle things much better. He wanted to see the railroads of the country respectably run, at profits steady enough and large enough to maintain the value of their securities; and if reliable men ran these enterprises, who but a demagogue could object? The trouble with these ignoramuses in Washington, he felt, was that they seemed to make no distinction between the crying abuses of the industry and the perfectly sound action it must take to maintain values.

Nevertheless, the law was on the books; and so, when a great company of railroad presidents from all over the country gathered at Morgan's brownstone house in December 1888 and January 1889, one of their first moves was to set up a committee to confer with the Interstate Commerce Commission. But that was a polite gesture toward the nominal authority over the regulation of railroad abuses. The nearest thing to a real authority was the big, solid man with the red nose and fierce eyes who sat at the head of the table at the library in his own house and spoke for the investors who owned the roads.

One can measure the height to which Morgan's prestige and influence had risen by the fact that when the conference of railroad presidents met for its adjourned sessions on January 8 and 10, 1889, every major railroad west of Chicago and St. Louis was represented except the

Chicago & Alton and the Southern Pacific—and the absence of Huntington of the Southern Pacific was said not to signify any opposition to Morgan's purpose. Even Jay Gould, who at the time was head of the Missouri Pacific, had accepted Morgan's invitation. The presidents of the trunk lines were there too—Roberts of the Pennsylvania, Depew of the New York Central, King of the Erie, Mayer of the Baltimore & Ohio, Sloan of the Lackawanna, Wilbur of the Lehigh Valley. And representatives of several leading investment banking houses on both sides of the water were likewise on hand—not only Drexel, Morgan & Co., but also Kidder, Peabody & Co., Brown Brothers & Co., J. S. Morgan & Co., and Baring Brothers.

It was too much of a gathering of lions to be an altogether calm occasion. At one point Roberts of the Pennsylvania pointed out sharply that there wouldn't be much trouble about the building of ruinously competing lines if investment bankers didn't provide the money to finance them; to which Morgan a little later replied:

"In regard to the remarks made informally by Mr. Roberts, about building parallel lines and the position of the bankers thereto, I am quite prepared to say in behalf of the houses represented here that if an organization can be formed practically on the basis submitted by the committee, with an Executive Committee able to enforce its provisions, upon which the bankers shall be represented, they are prepared to say that they will not negotiate, and will do all in their power to prevent the negotiation of, any securities for the construction of parallel lines, or the extension of lines not unanimously approved by such an Executive Committee."

That cumbersome sentence bears all the earmarks of a statement dictated to a secretary during a hurried recess in a big meeting, and then submitted to other men for suggested revisions, until in the end it bulges obesely with qualifying and amplifying phrases. Yet in effect it was clear enough. What Morgan wanted the railroad presidents to do was to make among themselves a definite agreement not to cut rates, not to build unnecessary competing lines, and so forth. He wanted them to put teeth into this agreement, so that any man who broke it would suffer penalties. And to show his own good faith in making so drastic a proposal he was producing a firm pledge that the investment bankers, for their part, were quite ready to play ball.

The meeting appeared to end successfully. The men who sat crowded in Morgan's library agreed to set up an association of presidents, pledged to live up to the Interstate Commerce Act and also to maintain rates, with a board of managers to arbitrate disagreements between them. Just how strong the teeth actually were was a matter of conjecture from the outset, however. After the presidents had filed out of the library and dispersed on Madison Avenue, a group of the Westerners adjourned to hold a rump session of their own at the Hotel Windsor, and one of them was quoted as saying, "We did not swallow whole the arrangement evidently prepared for us." And the *New York Times* reporter, writing his front-page story for the following morning's paper, led off with an obviously ironical paragraph:

> The New York bankers triumph. The Western railway presidents surrender. Hereafter they will be good. There will be no more rate-cutting and no more railroad wars of any sort whatever—nothing but peace and plenty.

The reporter's cynicism was at least partly justified. Rate wars and competitive gouging did not come to an end. The following year Morgan held another conference at his house, and that one, too, failed to end the chaos in the industry. He began to realize that wherever he really *must* have order, he would have to impose it himself.

Chapter Five

NO. 219

ON THE east side of Madison Avenue between Thirty-sixth and Thirty-seventh streets, on the gentle slope of Murray Hill, there had stood since the early eighteen-fifties three massive brownstone houses with ample gardens behind them. All three belonged to members of the Phelps family of Phelps-Dodge copper fame. They embodied the undemonstrative grandeur of respectable prosperity, and Pierpont Morgan had long been impressed with them. And so, when in 1880 it had become clear to him that the high-stooped house at 6 East Fortieth Street was no longer adequate for the needs of his family's expanding life, he bought the southernmost of the three houses—the one at the corner of Thirty-sixth Street, which had originally belonged to Isaac N. Phelps. (It stood where the white marble annex of the Morgan Library now stands, and roughly resembled the remaining brownstone house at the corner of Madison and Thirty-seventh, which at this writing—1948—is the sole survivor of that group of three Phelps houses.) And he employed Christian Herter to remodel the building, moving the street entrance to the Thirty-sixth Street side, utilizing the whole Madison Avenue front for a bay-windowed drawing room, and adding a conservatory on the opposite or eastern side, where it would catch the morning sunlight. In the autumn of 1882 the Morgans moved in; and this house, No. 219 Madison Avenue, remained their town residence throughout the rest of Pierpont's life.

It was quite satisfactory to him, and remained so. Already when he took possession of it the tide of fashion was moving northward. The Vanderbilt family was engaged in an orgy of simultaneous mansion building along the west side of Fifth Avenue between Fifty-first and Fifty-eighth streets, thus establishing a pattern which was destined to last for decades: the proper place for a prince of industry or finance to build himself a palace was on Fifth Avenue, preferably somewhere between St. Patrick's Cathedral and the corner of Central Park, or else a little farther north, on the east side of the avenue fronting the park. William H. Vanderbilt's new house at the corner of Fifty-first Street was a huge brownstone structure; next to it on the north was another, also of brownstone, built for his daughters. Farther uptown, at the northwest corner of Fifty-seventh Street, his son Cornelius was putting up an even more immense palace of brick and stone. But it was another son of his, William K. Vanderbilt, who was really leading the fashion in residences; for his house at Fifth and Fifty-second, designed by William Morris Hunt, was built of limestone and was a translation to Fifth Avenue of certain features of the design of the fifteenth-century house of Jacques Coeur at Bourges. From now on New York's native brownstone would begin to seem a little old-fashioned; the apt material for a millionaire's house would be limestone, or even marble; and American architects trained at the Beaux Arts, and faithful to the notion that beauty and grandeur were both European by nature and both susceptible of happy transplantation to our crude American shores, would vie with one another in adapting the designs of famous châteaux, castles, and palaces to the residential uses of stock-market speculators and holding-company promoters. It became fashionable not only to imitate the general effect of, say, the Doges' Palace or one of the châteaux along the Loire, but also to import bodily various architectural details and accessories, much as if Western Europe were one great builders' supply store.

Already the trend toward helter-skelter importation had set in boldly. For though the William H. Vanderbilt mansion had been made of sedate brownstone, by the time it was ready for occupancy, early in 1882, visitors to it found themselves passing, in the vestibule, a huge malachite vase, eight feet four inches high, which came from the Demidoff family palace of San Donato, outside Florence; entering the house through gold-overlaid portals which were replicas of Ghiberti's "Gates of Paradise" doorway; moving into a large central hall which the architect liked to call the "atrium," and which contained columns of red African marble, an especially designed British-woven oriental carpet, a Gobelin tapestry, a chimney piece with bronze figures by a sixteenth-century French sculptor, a French bust of Semiramis, a Japanese statue of Neptune, and a German bronze of a female falconer. After having submitted to the impact of these imposing objects from all over, it must have been something of a relief to the Vanderbilts and their friends to be able, in the library, to sink into plain American fringed rocking chairs. In later years when the lust for outfitting houses with imported objects had reached its apogee, the thing was done on an even grander scale; thus, for example, the traction magnate, William C. Whitney, equipped his Fifth Avenue house with a plate-glass and iron grille gate from the Doria Palace at Rome, and a ballroom brought over in sections from a castle in Bordeaux.

With such nonsense Pierpont Morgan would have no truck. He shared the rising veneration for the art of the Old World and subsequently became a collector and importer of it on a tremendous scale, but he didn't want to subdue his domestic life to it. His brownstone house was large, dignified, comfortable, and in every way suitable to his position. In due course he consented to have his drawing room done over from more-or-less-Pompeian into more-or-less-French; and still later, when his collection of books had long since overflowed not only the bookshelves of the house but also the cellar room which he used for storage, he built a marble Renaissance library on Thirty-sixth Street next door to his house, and incorporated into its interior design many of the architectural trophies of his chase for art; but even then he wouldn't change the original library at No. 219. It was just about right for him, and that was that.

This room was the center of his life at home. It was here that he held his important conferences, whether of railroad presidents or of churchmen. It was a large room with a very high ceiling. The walls were paneled higher than a man could reach with Santo Domingo mahogany; the general effect was so imposingly dark that in later years the household staff referred to the room as the "black library." In an arched alcove there was a tiled fireplace flanked by settees, and near the middle of the carpeted floor there was a big, ornate knee-hole walnut desk. The room reflected the late-Victorian unwillingness to leave any foot of wall space unoccupied; there were even paintings hung in the narrow and lofty interval between the wainscoting and the ceiling. But above all it conveyed a sense of somber and dignified comfort. It was a haven of masculinity within a home; and though in later years Morgan traveled like a prince and spent millions on masterpieces, he never quite relinquished the idea that home was a hearth, cluttered perhaps with mementos of one's expeditions, but not a show place.

2

Here at No. 219 the Morgan family spent the winter months. During the rest of the year—from April to October or thereabouts—they made their headquarters at Cragston; and just as they stood fast on Murray Hill despite the northward drift of wealth and fashion, so they remained loyal to the Highlands of the Hudson all the rest of their lives, despite the waning popularity of a region that the rising generation of affluent New Yorkers would soon condemn as much too hot in summer compared with, say, Newport or the north shore of Long Island. To such decrees of fashion the Morgans were indifferent. In the complex of social groups in the well-to-do Manhattan of the eighteen-eighties, they belonged neither to the aristocracy of the old Dutch families, who would probably have classed them as "new rich," nor to that (overlapping) Society with a capital S which was dominated by Mrs. Astor, shepherded by Ward McAllister, and aspired to by upcoming millionaires and their wives. For membership in this circle of the fashionable they were certainly not too newly arrived; they just had little taste for it. Pierpont Morgan, for one, didn't care for balls, cotillions, gilt chairs, chatter, lackeys in livery, or social emulation. He preferred solid comfort, solid dinners, solid people; butlers in discreet black coats; and if there was occasion for splendor, his own sort, on his own terms.

He belonged to what in Europe would be called the *haute bourgeoisie,* and in New York might—to borrow a word applied recently by Cleveland Amory to Bostonians—be called the Proper New Yorkers: a vaguely defined group of men who had plenty of money, were engaged in large corporate business or finance, voted the Republican ticket, believed in the sanctity of property, subscribed to sedate and conservative newspapers, held a low view of most politicians and practically all Democratic politicians, and an even lower view of "labor agitators"; who belonged to the right sort of church (preferably the Episcopal Church, which as Clarence Day put it was "a sect with the minimum of nonsense about it—no total immersion, no exhorters, no holy confession"); served on the boards of well-established charities, hospitals, and museums; joined reputable clubs such as the Union or perhaps the Union League, where they would be unlikely to be troubled by hearing any queer ideas; had a proper taste for good cigars and good wines; had decent manners, at least toward one another; and expected their wives to be charming and angelic, but not to know anything about their business affairs or for that matter about any affairs of moment. Morgan himself had little social traffic with artists, musicians, writers, scholars, or with professional men generally, except corporation lawyers and such architects or lawyers or physicians as he or his firm might have occasion to engage professionally. His social world was a world of business gentlemen of English descent and Protestant affiliations.

His life at No. 219 was a fabric woven upon a pattern of strict routine. Church at St. George's on Sunday morning, with perhaps a walk home afterward—this mile and a half or so on foot being his nearest approach to exercise after he gave up riding when he was in his forties. (The sedentary life was the rule rather than the exception among the business men of New York in the eighteen-eighties, when there was no golf, little tennis, no squash or racquets, and no country-club life.) Friends or relatives in to supper Sunday evening. Hymn singing after Sunday supper. Dr. Rainsford of St. George's Church to breakfast Monday morning. For some years, the Mendelssohn Club, a choral society, on Wednesday evening—presumably to please Fanny, for Pierpont's inability to hold a tune was marked, despite his undaunted appetite for what Satterlee called "strenuous, tuneful hymns."

He dressed for a business day in a frock coat, a hard winged collar, and an Ascot tie; this was the costume of his kind in Wall Street, and only on the hottest days was it considered proper to remove the coat for certain office chores, such as the signing of papers. He ate a solid breakfast, and delighted in having his children—in later years, his grandchildren—on hand then. In the pre-telephone days there was a private wire between his house and his office, on which reports and quotations were printed on a tape, news-ticker fashion; he would send a child into the next room to bring him the tape, so that he could scan it at the breakfast table and write messages or orders for the child to type off on the machine; he especially liked to get the quotations on foreign exchange and perhaps to do a little arbitraging—the simultaneous purchase and sale of dollars, pounds, and other currencies so as to net a profit on the fluctuations of the moment. Long experience and a lightning mathematical mind enabled him to see at a glance what the winning operation would be, and he enjoyed these little gambles. Then he would proceed to his office—preferably, as the years went by, not by the elevated railroad but by horse-drawn cab. At the end of the day's work he might stop off at the Whist Club or the Union Club for some cards, or might call briefly on a friend; but as often as not he would go straight home, lie down on the sofa in his study, pull an afghan over him, and sleep until it was time to dress for dinner—which he did with great rapidity: he prided himself on being able to hurry upstairs just as the first guests arrived, and come down again only six minutes later in tails and white tie. The Morgans gave a good many dinner parties and dined out often, and in addition Pierpont took in many stag dinners. The last item of his daily routine was a few games of solitaire, his constant solace.

There was a pattern of routine during the Cragston months too. He always spent Thursday there as a midweek holiday—a custom which dated back to his earliest business days, when there had been long letters to write to London on Friday night, and he had had to spend most of Saturday at his desk. (He still wrote those voluminous letters to his father, until the latter's death in 1890.) Now the *Corsair* took him to Cragston for the Thursday respite and again—usually with a house party of guests—for a short week end. Cragston was expanding; now he could show his guests his new cow barn and his prize cattle, as well as the Cragston Kennels, where he was breeding blue-ribbon-winning collies. Yet for all the amplitude of the place, with its stables of driving horses, saddle horses, and ponies, its farm buildings, its grass tennis courts, its subordinate buildings to house the servants, and its numerous guests, it remained essentially a place of unostentatious domestic comfort, typified by the sight of the Morgan children playing what they called polo on the two donkeys Beelzebub and Apollyon up and down the field by the brook.

3

Upon this pattern of domestic routine, however, was superimposed another pattern more individual and more splendid. First of all, there was the magnificent *Corsair.* Before he bought her in 1882 he had had rooms at the Fifth Avenue Hotel which he occupied on weekday nights when the family were at Cragston; now he spent most of his leisure time aboard the great yacht. She would lie at anchor in the North River and he would pile guests into a little naphtha launch to go out and dine aboard her; usually he slept there. She not only did ferry duty to Cragston, but frequently took him off on cruises, sometimes with his family, sometimes with a party of friends. An especial group of cronies, which originally included George Bowdoin (a partner), Charles Lanier, Frank K. Sturgis, David Egleston, and William Turnbull, made privileged use of her, and while she was laid up for the winter used to continue the association by dining at one another's homes in turn, calling themselves the "Corsair Club." She was a big yacht, but not big enough to suit him as his fortunes waxed, and so in 1890 he engaged J. Frederick Tams to superintend the building of *Corsair II*, which was 39 feet longer and also roomier belowdecks; she measured 204 feet on the water line, 241½ feet overall. On such a superb pleasure boat one could live and entertain like a prince.

Each year, furthermore, he had been accustomed to go to London, usually in the spring, to maintain touch with his father's old office at 22 Old Broad Street and to take a short holiday on the Continent; now these annual expeditions tended to become longer and more elaborate. As time went on, no more did Fanny accompany him; she remained enveloped in domesticity at 219 and at Cragston. Usually he took along one of his growing daughters. A busy stay at Prince's Gate or Dover House, and he would be off for Paris, where the Hotel Bristol (which was run by his father's ex-butler) always let him have the same corner suite on the *premier*; he might go on to the Riviera, or visit Rome (for which he had a special veneration), or take the cure at one of the great watering places. Several months might elapse between the day when he boarded an eastbound liner in New York and the day when, approaching the city on his return voyage, he would spy the *Corsair*, decked with pennants, coming down the harbor to welcome him home. These were months when he moved out from under the shadow of the strict conventions of Murray Hill and enjoyed the more varied company of men and women of the world.

Somewhat as royalty must reinforce the current code of respectability by careful visible observance of all the forms held dear by commoners, yet is implicitly granted a license to range more widely when the eyes of the people are turned the other way, so this prince of finance could live by a more relaxed code aboard the *Corsair* and on his continental journeyings. Like many an American man of that era of sheltered and shackled womankind, Pierpont Morgan believed that it was necessary for the safety of the republic that his wife and daughters, and the wives and daughters of all right-thinking men, should be kept unsullied from contact with anything so gross as profanity, outspoken talk, or for that matter politics and business affairs; and also he enjoyed with unashamed gusto not only the freer talk and freer conduct of gentlemen apart from their ladies, but also the company of those women—widows, perhaps, or actresses, or simply defiers of convention—whose wit and beauty had escaped the confines of a dulling respectability. Despite his swollen nose and his often brusque manner, Pierpont Morgan was immensely attractive to many women of all ages; his force and directness and his inner and sometimes abashed kindness won for him an astonishing allegiance. He liked to shower gifts upon them; at least one or two he presented with houses or set up financially for life. Exactly what his relations were with them, this particular biographer does not care to inquire; he would prefer to respect the privacy of private life. Yet it might be reasonable to observe that in an era when an unmarried woman was considered already lost to decency if she so much as dined alone with a man, and when even a widow would be considered to have removed herself beyond the pale if she dined with him on his yacht, gossip portrayed in flaming colors many companionships that today would attract no attention whatever; and also that in an era when most men sought their own ways, often shabby, of escaping from the constrictions of the Victorian proprieties, Morgan's ways were simply grander. He had his own standard of personal conduct: to try to behave like a gentleman. Part of the time he lived by the rules of nineteenth-century gentility, and part of the time he was free to make his own rules; but there is no reason to believe that his own standards did not govern him throughout.

4

Not only in business but in other affairs too, Morgan's personality put him naturally in command in any group of men who had a problem to deal with. No railroad executive ever adequately described him in action at a business conference, but the Reverend W. S. Rainsford, rector of St. George's Church, could sketch him in words as he took charge of a vestry meeting of the church, and Rainsford's account of a session at No. 219 in the early eighteen-eighties is illuminating.

It was in 1882, three years before the *Corsair* conference, that Rainsford, a man of fiery religious and social convictions who had been occupying a pulpit in Canada, was invited to become the rector of St. George's. At that time the church was in bad shape. The congregation was dwindling, there was a floating debt of $35,000, and the institution's influence seemed to be waning. The senior warden was Charles Tracy, Morgan's father-in-law; Morgan himself, then forty-five years old, was only a vestryman; but it was significant that when Rainsford arrived in New York to meet with the wardens and vestry, it was to the house into which Morgan had just moved that he was directed.

Mr. Tracy presided at the meeting, which was presumably held in the "black library." He explained the state of affairs in the church and asked Rainsford whether he would consent to become its rector. Rainsford demurred; he didn't know whether he could cope with such a situation; and he sketched out the sort of work he would like to do. As often happens in sessions of this sort, the conversation began to ramble inconclusively; they seemed to be getting nowhere. Then Morgan spoke up (I quote directly from Rainsford's autobiography):

> "Mr. Rainsford, will you be our rector? If you consent I will do what I can to help you carry out this plan." Turning to the others, "Gentlemen, do you agree with me?" Then, again turning to me, "Will you accept our unanimous call?"
>
> At once I replied, "I will, on three conditions."
>
> "Name them."
>
> "First, you must make the church absolutely free. Buy out those who will not donate their pews. Second, abolish all committees in the church except the vestry, and only reappoint such as I shall name. Third, I must have an annual fund of $10,000 for three years, independent of my salary, to spend as I see fit on church work. My salary I leave to you."

Dead silence followed. I saw Mr. Morgan look around the circle of tense faces. Then he looked full at me and said one word: "Done."

5

What is a conservative? The word, like its antonyms "liberal" and "radical," carries such a freight of special political and economic connotations that it often bears little relation to the actual human impulses to which it is applied. In the strict sense of the word meaning "disposed to maintain existing institutions," there was a strong conservative strain in Pierpont Morgan's temperament. He cherished old family rites. There must always be a gathering of the Morgan clan for Thanksgiving dinner, with an invariable menu. He loved the traditional Christmas ceremonies: the dressing of the tree on Christmas Eve, a carriage trip with one of the children to distribute presents; church on Christmas morning, and then a family dinner. (For several years, when his children were young, he used to dress up as Santa Claus.) In his religion, unchanged since his Hartford days, he especially warmed to what was venerably traditional. When he liked anything—the furnishings of his library or of his yacht, a certain suite at a hotel, a house or scene hallowed by association—he wanted to keep it as nearly as possible unchanged. In his later years, as a collector, on a gigantic scale, it was always old things that he collected, books and manuscripts and works of art loaded with venerable tradition: he was associating himself with the beauty of bygone times, which nothing new could possibly match.

In politics and economics too, he was what most of us would call deeply conservative. He voted the Republican ticket steadily except in 1884, when he disapproved of

Blaine and cast his ballot for the fearlessly honest Cleveland, who was certainly no apostle of quick change. He objected to any sort of government intervention in business. In his son-in-law's biography of him there is a passage describing the prosperity of 1881 which reflects the conservative nineteenth-century attitude: "There were not many problems in the national life of the day. Immigration was practically unrestricted. Work was plentiful. Food and clothing were cheap. Everybody was busy. Labor was not yet unionized. The organized attempts to stir up discontent and raise class feeling had not been begun. Pierpont was making money, as was almost everybody else who was engaged in sound business. . . ." That passage would probably have struck Morgan himself as reasonably stated. If you had reminded him that the Reading Railroad's anthracite workers in the valleys of Pennsylvania, for example, were sharing only microscopically in the benefits of national prosperity, being virtually peons of the company, overworked and underpaid, the glare he would have given you would have signified that this was wholly irrelevant: that new inventions and new industrial processes, sensibly applied by well-financed and expanding companies, were one of the answers to general poverty; that churches and charities were another; and that—in the words of William Graham Sumner—"the yearning after equality is the offspring of envy and covetousness, and there is no possible plan for satisfying that yearning which can do aught else than rob A to give to B; consequently all such plans nourish some of the meanest vices of human nature, waste capital, and overthrow civilization." As for politicians being of any value in combatting poverty, Morgan had seen enough of them in the Albany & Susquehanna business and in subsequent litigations to be convinced that they were low fellows who bleated about the poor and were always ready to sell their services for a handout from the rich. People like himself, who helped business secure capital and tried to keep it on an orderly and solvent basis, were doing more for the general well-being than all these yawpers put together.

Most of us would call such sentiments—which were pretty representative of downtown business sentiment at that time—extremely conservative. Yet the label is misleading to the extent that it suggests that Morgan wanted to see things stand still. On the contrary, he was constantly intervening in businesses to reform and strengthen them in his own way, merging little railroads to make big systems, clearing the way for new construction, and (in later years) utilizing new legislation such as the New Jersey holding-company law to speed these new developments. In a real sense it was he and the other fabricators of giant industries, and the lawyers and legislative draftsmen inventing new corporate devices, who were the radicals of the day, changing the face of America; it was those who objected to the results who were conservatives seeking to preserve the individual opportunities and the folkways of an earlier time. You might question the direction in which Morgan was moving; but that he was moving fast, and with a purpose which seemed to him to be to the country's benefit, is certain. In this the major sphere of his life, he was not a brake, he was an engine.

Nor did his love for old customs and old traditions prevent him from hastening technological change. He was one of Thomas A. Edison's earliest backers. He put money into the Edison Electric Light Co. as early as 1878, when the coming of electric lighting systems was only a hope. When, in September 1882, Edison's first power station for lower Manhattan was completed, the

Drexel Building was one of the first ones to be equipped (with 106 bulbs). Edison came to that building to turn on the lights for a brief experimental test; and when, at about five o'clock on the afternoon of Monday, September 4, 1882, the switch was finally thrown at Pearl Street, it was to Morgan's office that Edison returned, along with five of his associates, to turn on the lights again in his backer's presence, while "throughout a third of the downtown district little lamps began to glow." (One of those five other men, incidentally, was Samuel Insull.)

At that time Morgan was completing the alterations to 219 Madison Avenue, and he seized the opportunity to install the new lights there, thus making his house the first residence in the world to be thus lit throughout. Then began a chapter of troubles. There was no central power station in that part of the city, an engine had to be installed in a cellar under his stable, and an engineer had to visit this plant daily to get up steam so that the generator would operate. The gas lamps which had been installed in the house were used for the new electric-light bulbs, and this caused all sorts of troubles with the wiring. There were frequent short circuits or failures of power; once the lights died out at 11 P.M. while the house was full of guests, because the Morgans had forgotten that the engineer went off duty then. Neighbors complained of the noise of the motor; one even alleged that it gave off smoke and fumes which tarnished her silver. And when the lamp on the big desk in the middle of Pierpont Morgan's library was wired—a new problem to Edison's assistant, Everitt H. Johnson, who had previously wired only wall lamps—the inevitable happened: there was a short circuit and then a fire which ruined the rug and the desk and filled the house with the odor of charred wood.

The next morning, according to Satterlee, Johnson arrived at the house when Morgan was at breakfast. He went into the library and surveyed the wreckage, apprehensive lest the banker lose all future interest in financing Edison's enterprise. "Suddenly he heard footsteps, and Pierpont appeared in the doorway with a newspaper in his hand and looked at him over the tops of his eyeglasses. 'Well?' he said. Johnson had been formulating an explanation ever since he had heard of the fire and was preparing to make elaborate excuses. Just as he opened his mouth to speak, he saw Mrs. Morgan behind Pierpont. Catching Johnson's eye she put her finger on her lips. Johnson took the hint, and looked dejectedly at the heap of debris. After a long minute's silence, Pierpont said, 'Well, what are you going to do about it?'

"Johnson answered, 'Mr. Morgan, the trouble is not inherent in the thing itself. It is my own fault, and I will put it in good working order so that it will be perfectly safe.'

"Pierpont asked, 'How long will it take to fix it?'

"Johnson answered, 'I will do it right away.'

" 'All right,' said Pierpont, 'see that you do.' And he turned and went down the hall and so on out.

"The result of the new installation was so satisfactory that Pierpont gave a reception, and about four hundred guests came to the house and marveled at the convenience and simplicity of the lighting system."

The morning after the reception, when the financier Darius Ogden Mills visited the Drexel Building to buy a thousand shares of Edison stock, Morgan waylaid him and told him that he would permit his partners to make such a sale only on one condition, "that for every share of Edison stock that they buy for you, they buy one for me." And still later, when a million dollars was needed to build an uptown power station, he subscribed half of the amount himself.

That would not seem to be evidence of wholehearted resistance to change. It is evidence, rather, that this was the sort of change which kindled Morgan's imagination: a wonderful invention, a wonderful investment, a wonderful chance for corporate promotion, and withal the germ of a great new industry which would shed its light over the whole country.

Chapter Six

RAILROAD REORGANIZER—AND EMPEROR?

LIKE a general whose supreme tactical opportunity comes when the battle is going badly, Morgan had to wait for a time of financial and business disaster to come into his own as a really decisive power in the railroad industry. During the eighteen-eighties, as we have seen, he had ended one railroad war, had had some practice in reorganizing bankrupt or hard-pressed railroad companies, and had tried, with only indifferent success, to persuade the railroad chiefs of the country to end voluntarily the sort of corporate knifing and gouging that seemed to him to be imperiling the investment standing of the nation's most important industry. Now he was to step into a position of unprecedented authority in that industry. The opportunity came during the financial hurricanes of the mid-nineties.

For more than four years—1893, 1894, 1895, 1896, and part of 1897—the United States was tormented by what we would now call a major depression. (In those days they spoke of the Panic of 1893 and of the "hard times" which followed.) Business which formerly had been prosperous went into the red; factories shut down; bankruptcies multiplied; wages were cut; workers by the millions lost their jobs, and year after year faced the recurring nightmare of unemployment; and there was industrial strife, bitterness, and unrest—from the Homestead Strike of 1892 to the Pullman Strike of 1894, the pathetic march upon Washington of "Coxey's Army," and many another dramatization of the anger and bewilderment of the time.

One of the most dismaying things about that depression was the epidemic of financial bankruptcy among the railroads. In some cases one would have had to go back many years to find the chief cause of financial trouble: it lay in the speculative looting and blackmail competition and gross overcapitalization to which company after company had been subjected during the preceding two or even three decades. In other cases there had been more recent waste, mismanagement, or folly. But in each case, as passenger and freight traffic declined and red ink replaced black ink on the company's books, the moment came when the managers of the line no longer had money in the till to pay their debts and joined the melancholy procession to the courts of bankruptcy. According to Alexander Dana Noyes, the financial historian, within the short space of two years nearly one-fourth of the total railway capitalization of the country passed through these courts, and by the middle of 1895 no less than 169 railroads with 37,855 miles of track—amounting to more than one-fifth of the total mileage of the country—were being operated by receivers. Nor were little shoestring lines the only ones to suffer; many of the largest and proudest failed—including the Baltimore & Ohio, the Erie, the Northern Pacific, the Union Pacific, and the Santa Fe, to say nothing of the Reading, the Norfolk & Western, and the hodgepodge of lines grouped under the loose direction of the Richmond Terminal (which later became the Southern Railway System).

In every such case the railroad corporation had to be reorganized; for even the sorriest backwoods line was too vital to the life of the community—in a day when there were no automobiles, no trucks, no busses—to be permitted to go out of business. This meant that somebody had to invent a plan by which the company's debts could be whittled down to a point where it could safely meet all its interest payments out of current revenue. If the plan was to succeed, it must look fair and workable not only to the courts but also the various groups of clamoring creditors; and it must also assure new investors that the reorganized company would be a safe and profitable thing to put their money into.

The job of planning and putting through such a reorganization had almost nothing to do with railroading as you or I would have thought of railroading—with locomotives, timetables, ticket agents, passenger stations, freight trains, or lines of shining steel rail—with the night express roaring down the quiet valley and hooting for the grade crossing, or with the daily accommodation train pulling alongside the plank platform of the country station and unloading passengers and mail bags and crates of farm produce. No expert in engine design or freight delivery or train scheduling could meet its requirements. It called rather for a mastery of money and the paper instruments which provide money. It was a job for an investment banker, with an expert in corporation accounting at one elbow and a corporation lawyer at the other. Here was Morgan's opportunity.

In almost every case the task was incredibly complex. To take a single example, the transfer of a whole series of companies and properties from the bankrupt Richmond Terminal and its offshoots to the new Southern Railway System involved executing two trustees' sales, one receivers' sale, ten foreclosure sales, six conveyances without foreclosure, and all manner of other contracts and agreements. Every one of these operations must be technically and legally correct—which required that somebody on the reorganizer's staff must have an absolute grasp of the complicated terms of innumerable bond issues, leases, and contracts. But the principal thing required of a reorganizer was that he should command confidence in the financial world—confidence that he would prepare a fair plan, that everybody who mattered would get behind it, that there was no use fighting it, that he had ample means to meet all emergencies, and that when he had completed his work the company's new bonds and shares would be widely approved as investments by bankers and brokers and men of means generally.

For such an assignment Morgan was uniquely fitted. He had his partner Charles H. Coster and his associate Samuel Spencer as his experts—Coster with his incredible mastery of detail and his uncanny ability to weigh the value of a given lease or contract; Spencer with years of railroad experience as vice-president and later president of the Baltimore & Ohio. He had Francis Lynde Stetson's legal ingenuity at his command. It had long been a favorite trick of crafty men to bring legal suit against reorganization plans in the hope of being bought off at blackmail prices. Morgan had been through this sort of experience when his reorganization of the West Shore Railroad had been imperiled by a suit brought by a minor stockholder named Belden, and he had learned that if a reorganizer is to succeed, such potential interferers must know that every avenue to the success of their maneuvers has been barricaded.

Furthermore, there was nobody in the country who could match Morgan's own experience as a negotiator among railroad executives and financiers, or his reputation for financial impregnability, reliability, and personal authority. His plans had a way of working. Bankers and brokers and executives who allied themselves with him found the alliance usually very profitable to them, and those who opposed him must be prepared for a battle against odds. Thus it came about that during the middle nineties Morgan's firm acquired the lion's share of the business of reorganizing the larger railroads. Within the space of four years he reorganized the Richmond Terminal, the Erie, the Reading, and the Norfolk & Western; in alliance with James J. Hill, the great railroader of the Northwest, he reorganized the Northern Pacific; and he played a part also in the reorganization of the Baltimore & Ohio.

2

The Morgan method, as it developed during those years, might be summed up as follows:

First, his experts estimated the minimum earning capacity of the road. Then the fixed debt of the company was ruthlessly pared down until even with minimum earnings it could readily meet its interest payments on that debt—holders of bonds being forced to accept bonds of lower yield, or stock, or both.

Second, the present holders of stock were assessed to provide the reorganized road with working funds.

Third, new stock was issued as lavishly as was necessary to keep everybody happy. In some cases the issues of preferred stock were so large that only a determined optimist could foresee the day when the common stock would be able to pay dividends; and in many cases so much stock was issued altogether that thereafter, if the company should need new capital, it could not raise it by selling more stock but would have to sell bonds instead—thus increasing once more its burden of fixed debt. In this respect the Morgan pattern of financing was shortsighted. As Professor William Z. Ripley remarked before the

Industrial Commission, although it was intended to cut down capitalization, in the long run it had "exactly the reverse effect." But for the time being it worked. And that, for the moment, was the overwhelming necessity.

Fourth, the reorganizers charged very heavily for their services. Of the Erie Railroad reorganization plan, for example, the London *Economist* said wryly, ". . . Messrs. Morgan state, with a candor which, as far as we know, has no precedent in such cases, that they are to get $500,000 cash for their trouble; and as, in addition, the syndicate which guarantees the success of the scheme is likely to get a good commission on the $15,000,000 bonds it purchases, the doctor's bill is sure to reach a million, and perhaps even two million dollars." One might qualify this statement to explain that only a small fraction of the syndicate's commission would go to Morgan's own firm. (When a new issue of securities was put on the market, a long list of banks, investment houses, and individual investors joined the syndicate, i.e., undertook to subscribe to whatever shares were not disposed of in public sale; and when the sale was over, these syndicate members shared in whatever profit—or loss—there might be. Usually the Morgan firm, as one of many members of the syndicate, received only a small part of the syndicate's total profit.) One should add anyhow that the *Economist* found the Morgan plan fair and reasonable otherwise. Nevertheless, the bill was big indeed.

If you had remarked on its size to Morgan or one of his partners, you would have been reminded that every one of these operations involved great risk. For if the new securities could not for any reason be sold at a good price (and sometimes they could not) his firm would at the least have tied up a lot of capital in an investment of dubious vendibility, and at the worst would incur a whopping loss; furthermore, the other members of the syndicate would suffer likewise, and Morgan's prestige among them would fall like lead. As he carried through reorganization after reorganization successfully, banks and big investors began to regard the Morgan name as carrying almost a guarantee of investment reliability. Nobody else in the land had such a reputation. Surely, therefore, the money value of the Morgan label was very great. Where the risk was great and the money value was great, he saw no reason why the charge should not likewise be great. In reply you might point out that it was heartless to charge heavily for an operation which involved writing off millions of dollars of investments which had been innocently and hopefully made by small investors; and from that point of view surely the size of the fees charged by bankers and their lawyers for resuscitating bankrupt corporations has long been one of the cruelest anomalies of American business. But Morgan would have scoffed at such a judgment. He would have pointed out that it was not he who had destroyed the value of a widow's second-mortgage railroad bond, but the inefficient or predatory men who had let the railroad go to ruin; that all he did was to slice off the infected growth. At any rate, the profits from such surgical operations were often immense.

Every day Drexel, Morgan & Co. were engaged in a multiplicity of lesser financial operations, on each individual one of which the profit was usually very small—dealing in foreign exchange, the sale of letters of credit, the buying and selling of securities, and so forth. It was the sale of new issues of securities, and especially it was the reorganizations, that brought in the big money, a half-million or a million dollars or more at a time, in fees or in blocks of stock that could be sold profitably if the reorganized corporation seemed likely to return to health. And these profits, while they came irregularly, tended to grow from year to year as Morgan's position in the financial world became more and more central. They were the largest source of the growing income that paid the expenses of the *Corsair* and was translated into Madonnas and medallions.

Fifth, the future control of the railroad was tied up so tightly—either through a board of directors in which Morgan partners and their friends and other men whom they trusted would be dominant, or, more likely, through a voting trust to the members of which the stockholders would surrender their voting rights—that prudent management in the future could be enforced. For Morgan had learned a lesson from what had happened to the Baltimore & Ohio and to the Reading, and was resolved that it should not happen again.

3

He himself had reorganized the Baltimore & Ohio in 1887. For a while everything had seemed to go well. Samuel Spencer, who had been vice-president of the company, was installed as president. But presently the Garrett family and their friends, under whose leadership the road had previously run into difficulties, decided to take over again; and since they still owned a majority of the company's stock, they were able to do it. They made things so difficult for Spencer that he had to resign (to become a Morgan railroad expert). They resumed their improvident course, and by 1896 the Baltimore & Ohio was once more in trouble. Not only that, but investigators looking over the books of the company found that it had been scandalously overstating its income and understating its liabilities. Again the London *Economist* expressed the dismay of English investors: "And when people here find that such malpractices as these have been carried on for a series of years, on what was believed to have been one of the best-managed of American railroads . . . it cannot be wondered at if the small degree of confidence that has been left them is still further impaired."

That sort of comment made unpleasant reading for Pierpont Morgan, who less than ten years earlier had given his endorsement to the securities of the road, and who was always conscious of the weight of English investment opinion. In the second reorganization of the Baltimore & Ohio he played only a passive part; but while this was still proceeding, a group of James J. Hill's friends bought a controlling interest in the stock of the road and Hill sought Morgan's aid; and the result was indicative of Morgan's resolution that no one again should have a chance to run away with the property and ruin it. For the voting control of the reorganized road was placed for five years in the hands of a voting trust of five men, including Coster (a Morgan partner), Louis Fitzgerald (a firm ally), and three other men whom he and Hill regarded as trustworthy.

The adventures of the Philadelphia & Reading were somewhat similar—if more spectacular. This company, too, had been reorganized by Morgan during the eighteen-eighties. For a brief time it had been held in the grip of a voting trust. But after it was freed of this grip, a headstrong president, A. Archibald McLeod, embarked upon a course of management more ambitious than prudent. He leased or bought other railroad lines with the notion of getting a monopoly of the anthracite coal business; and then, not content with that, he launched a scheme for giving the Reading road a lion's share of the business of carrying anthracite coal to New England. To this end he purchased not only a minor interest in the Boston & Maine Railroad but also a controlling interest in the New York & New England Railroad, a smaller line which crisscrossed southern New England.

Morgan was furious. In the first place, McLeod was acting with outrageous improvidence. The Reading Railroad's treasury could ill afford such large and diverse expenditures and commitments. (As a matter of fact, McLeod had been doing a very rash thing: he had been buying those New York & New England shares in his own name, on margin, and taking securities out of the Reading's treasury to put up with the brokers as collateral—a fact which hastened the road's ruin.) In short, McLeod was guilty of jeopardizing the safety of an investment which Morgan had sponsored.

In the second place, what McLeod was doing offended Morgan's conviction that each railroad should develop its own territory and not invade other roads' spheres of influence. Had he not worked long and hard, as a peacemaker, to try to enforce this principle? The Reading had no business going into New England.

In the third place, this invasion touched Morgan personally. He had recently become a director of the New York, New Haven and Hartford Railroad, to which he had long been emotionally attached because of his Hartford beginnings. This road was a meager thing indeed when he took his seat on its board in 1892. It owned outright only 141 miles of road (reaching from the outskirts of New York City to Springfield, Massachusetts, with a few short branch lines). It leased or partly owned 503 miles more, but its trains had to go over lines owned by other people even to reach Boston. To Morgan this seemed ridiculous. He had a vision of a single unified railroad system covering most of New England, and obviously the New

Haven must be its nucleus. The first thing he did for it when he became a director was to buy for it the Housatonic Road, to extend its reach northward. He was planning also to annex the Old Colony, in order to give it satisfactory access to Boston. And here, suddenly, was this wild man McLeod barging right into the southern New England territory that rightly, he thought, belonged to the New Haven!

Finally, McLeod, when Morgan remonstrated with him, had been openly defiant. Had he not been heard to say that he would rather run a peanut stand than be dictated to by J. P. Morgan?

Very well, then; if McLeod wanted war, he should have it. Morgan was no peacemaker when he felt that he himself or his interests had been attacked. Now he made it clear to those to whom he talked that he was through with McLeod's management of the Reading, and that he would have no use in the future for anyone who came to McLeod's aid. Then, on February 17, 1893, there was a sudden onslaught on the stock of the Reading Railroad—and also the New York & New England Railroad—on the Stock Exchange: a cascade of selling orders which was widely, and probably with good reason, attributed to Morgan's hostility to McLeod.

The result came swiftly. Only a few days later the officials of the Reading Railroad had to go into court and ask for the appointment of a receiver. As McLeod later said, "The raid drove our securities down until we had no recourse but to entrench ourselves behind a receivership. The attack was on both sides, for it not only shut off our source of supplies and impaired our credit, but brought upon us demands from creditors which we could not comply with."

Thereupon the job of reorganizing the road went to

Morgan. McLeod departed under pressure. And—lest anybody try such nonsense again—the reorganization provided for a voting trust to run the road for at least five years, and a board of directors which included Coster, Stetson, and several Philadelphians who saw eye to eye with them.

4

Morgan not only meant to make it impossible for any road for which he had assumed responsibility to squander its funds or to invade his friends' territory; he also meant to make it impossible for any speculator to upset his orderly plans. During this same period the officers of the Richmond Terminal came to him and suggested that he reorganize the property. Now the Richmond Terminal (or, more formally, the Richmond & West Point Terminal Railway & Warehouse Co.) was the nucleus of a group of loosely connected Southern railroads. Its stock had long been a football of speculation; to large numbers of men in the Wall Street area the job it did in carrying freight and passengers was of trivial interest compared with the gyrations of the price of its shares on the stock market. Morgan investigated the situation, found that most of the common stock was then held by a few men, and decided that he would not touch the reorganization job unless these men would deliver their shares into his keeping while the intricate negotiations were going on. He didn't want to run any risk of these men playing any speculative game while he was at work. The principal owners were Calvin Brice, Samuel Thomas, and W. P. Clyde. They came into the office of Drexel, Morgan & Co. to talk the thing over. According to the subsequent memory of a man who was present at that session, Clyde, the last to come in, settled himself on the long sofa in the partners' room, listened to Morgan's proposed terms, and then drawled, in a voice which suggested a smacking of the lips:

"Well, Mr. Morgan, I've bought Richmond Terminal at 7 or 8 and sold it at 15 twice in the last few years. I see no reason why I shouldn't do it again. So I fear I cannot join with the others in asking you to deal with the property."

Under the circumstances, Morgan was quite content to have somebody else try to reorganize the Richmond Terminal. The Central Trust Company undertook the job; and only when the Central Trust's scheme had failed, and Morgan was approached again, and the owners dutifully agreed to deposit their shares with him for safekeeping, did he proceed. And this time, in order that the future of what became the Southern Railway might not be jeopardized by speculators less intent upon seeing that it was soundly managed than in riding its shares up and down hill, he tied up its control tightly. Samuel Spencer went in as president, and the last word in the direction of the system lay with a voting trust of three men: Morgan himself; his frequent ally and trusted collaborator, George F. Baker, head of the First National Bank of New York; and his old and intimate friend and fellow-member of the Corsair Club, Charles Lanier.

5

In each of these specific cases which I have been describing, the company in question came—as many other concerns, railroad, industrial, and banking, were in the future to come—under what was known as Morgan control. This involved immense power. But the nature and limitations of that power have often been misunderstood, and therefore a word or two of explanation and interpretation may be in order.

The word "control" brings to mind a picture of a sort of omnipotent being sitting at a central switchboard from which he manipulates every policy and every transaction of a concern. Yet any large business concern is a loose aggregation of departments which run to a very large extent on their own, facing problems many of which are puzzling even to the head of the concern; and if this is true of a single company, it is all the more true of a varied collection of companies and of the men who sit in a banking office and supposedly "control" them. Usually the representatives of the House of Morgan on the board of directors of a company were content to sit and listen to what went on, merely assuring themselves that the company's funds were not being wasted, that its executives were not going berserk in their competitive battles with other concerns, and that stock-market plungers were not playing hob with it. Even when—as in the three cases of the Baltimore & Ohio, the Reading, and the Richmond Terminal—voting trusts were set up to prevent such abuses, the grasp of Morgan and his friends upon the company's affairs, while strong as iron, was sometimes so loose as to be almost impalpable. The members of the voting trust might know only two or three of the company's executives by sight, let alone know about the decisions which these men faced from day to day, or what sort of enterprises the various departments of the business were engaged in. Neither Morgan nor Baker nor Lanier, for example, could probably have told you what were the chief operating problems of the Southern Railway. (Indeed it can be argued that the very fact that the supreme authority over a railroad so often lay in the hands of men inattentive to engineering advances tended to prevent that rapid renovation of equipment for the lack of which the industry later suffered.) These bankers saw a railroad company as a group of men and a set of books; if the figures were satisfactory, and were vouched for by reliable men, everything was all right and no further attention need be paid to its affairs.

Yet that is not quite all. For beyond this extremely limited control reached the Morgan influence, a thing impossible to measure because it was based upon imponderables. These included the desire, on the part of company executives and bankers and the men of the business community in general, to remain on good terms with a man whose backing had a solid dollars-and-cents value; the knowledge that business deals in which he took part had a way of becoming extremely profitable, and that if you played ball with him you might have a chance to reap some of these profits; the feeling that his judgment was so weighty among bankers that if you went counter to it, some banker whose favor you might need in the future might look upon you with a bilious eye; and the final fact that there emanated from Morgan himself a personal force which men felt it was rash to challenge. A question asked by him at a directors' meeting, a remark attributed to him in the gossip of the Street, carried inordinate weight. This sort of authority could not be diagrammed as the Pujo Committee tried to diagram it, but it was very real.

There is one more thing to be noted. Pierpont Morgan felt that the corporations for whose securities he had assumed responsibility must be in "safe hands." That meant, primarily, the hands of men who were not dreamers, or irresponsible, or crooked. He wanted no Jay Goulds within reach of any corporate pocket which he had helped to fill. He wanted no reorganization plan of his to be subject to upset by a holdup action like Belden's, or by what he thought of as trickery of any sort. He took an active dislike for Edward H. Harriman because Harriman, opposing his plans for the Dubuque & Sioux City Railroad in 1887, managed to have the votes of a majority of the stockholders—votes which had carefully been assembled by the Morgan forces—thrown out on the ground that proxy voting was illegal in the State of Iowa. It *was* illegal; Morgan's lawyers had slipped; but Harriman's tactics seemed to him shifty, and so he included Harriman, too, among the owners of unsafe hands.

What, then, were truly safe hands? Well, those of honest and capable men who lived by a code of conduct which permitted one to rely upon oral agreements with them. There were a good many businesses in which, if one were dealing with the head executives, one knew one would have to watch one's step. Some of these men one couldn't avoid dealing with, for they had indispensable knowledge and authority. When, for example, Morgan subsequently organized the Steel Corporation, he had to rely heavily for the time being upon many steel executives who were plungers by nature, and possessed what one of his partners subsequently referred to, very delicately, as "an undeveloped sense of trusteeship." But he preferred to deal with men of his own sort, who followed the code of the gentleman. When he asked railway presidents to meet him on his yacht, or in his library at home, this was partly to be out of the reach of prying eyes, but it was also, I think, because he had a sense that an agreement reached in a personal setting such as these would have the same sort of validity as one reached over the coffee cups at a private dinner party; if the men who made it were fit to associate with, they would feel constrained to live up to it, even if no contract had been written down on paper.

Morgan was attempting to enforce the code of the gentleman.

It was easier, of course, to deal with men who were recognizably gentlemen in the first place. And if one happened to be—by nature and by long association with the men of the English banking world—patrician in one's tastes, this often meant men who belonged to the same club, as it were, whose intellectual and social background was similar. With them one knew just where one stood and the understanding could be complete. And it was better yet to deal with tried and trusted friends; their hands were the safest of all.

Now as it happened, Morgan was a man of increasingly formidable will, whose friends tended to agree with him, or be swayed by him, because of the sheer weight of his personality. Thus it was likely to happen that these friends dealt with things very much as he would, or even consulted him and did as he advised. And so, in the end, it not infrequently turned out that the "safe hands" were hardly distinguishable from his own.

6

After his series of reorganizations, in the mid-nineties, Morgan occupied a position unprecedented in American railroading. He had long been influential in the councils of the New York Central; now he was at least influential, if not dominant, in those of the Erie, the New Haven, the Reading, the Norfolk & Western, the Southern Railway System, and the Lehigh Valley (in which his friends now had gained voting control). In alliance with James J. Hill, he was influential in the Northern Pacific, the Baltimore & Ohio, and Hill's own Great Northern. The Jersey Central was dominated by his close ally, George F. Baker of the First National Bank. And the Pennsylvania,

Lackawanna, and Delaware & Hudson were all in hands generally friendly to him and his notions of community of interest. In short, the managements of most of the leading railroads of the East were at least deferential to his wishes, and through the Great Northern and the Northern Pacific his sphere of influence reached all the way to the West Coast.

The authority that Pierpont Morgan exercised over this great network of lines was very limited indeed, as I have already tried to suggest. At the most, it amounted to a veto power over anything that he and his colleagues regarded as hurtfully competitive or financially reckless; at the least, it amounted to little more than an opportunity to keep informed as to what was going on. In any case, it was sufficient to assure that no new Jay Goulds or Daniel Drews could run amuck, and that the management of American railroads would be more respectably and responsibly conducted than in earlier years. From the evidence available, I do not believe that it was Morgan's primary and conscious intent to build a "railroad empire." Rather, he believed in order, believed in reducing competition to a minimum, believed in protecting the solvency of properties which he had backed; and the logical way of producing this state of affairs seemed to him to be to provide the railroad managements with supervisors who would see things as he did, and to make war on all disturbers of the peace. But his confidence in his own rightness was so colossal that it was not always clear whether the primary offense of a man like McLeod was that he had been reckless or that he had got in Morgan's way. And so the pattern of domination and influence and friendly consultation that had emerged by 1897 looked to observers very much indeed like a railroad empire, with Pierpont Morgan as the emperor.

Chapter Seven

GOLD FOR THE GOVERNMENT

PRESIDENT GROVER CLEVELAND was desperately worried. Ever since the beginning of his second term, misfortunes had rained upon him. He had been established in the White House only a few weeks when the Panic of 1893 had convulsed the business world. In the wake of the panic had followed other troubles—widespread and acute unemployment, the Pullman Strike, a tragic destruction of the corn crop by drought, and a fall in the price of wheat to less than fifty cents a bushel. Worst of all, in the eyes of this stubborn, conscientious, conservative President, the credit of the United States Government had been a recurring source of deep anxiety. For the Treasury's reserve of gold—the buttress of its stability—had been dwindling.

This reserve had been alarmingly depleted when Cleveland had taken office. Again and again it had been shored up by emergency measures—and then had crumbled away again. And now, as the month of January 1895 drew to a close, it seemed all too likely to vanish utterly within a few weeks—or even a few days. The President faced the grim prospect of a new panic.

The trouble was multifold. In the first place, legislation of long standing not only permitted men who held the kind of paper dollars called legal tender (or, more colloquially, greenbacks) to turn in these notes at the Treasury and receive gold for them, but also—absurdly—provided that when the notes were exchanged for the gold they were not extinguished but must be reissued, and could thus be used again and again as a means of drawing out gold. In a time of general confidence such a law was not necessarily embarrassing; but in a time of business depression, when men became uneasy about paper promises to pay and wanted to wrap their hands around things of unquestionable value, it invited what Grover Cleveland called an "endless chain" of withdrawals of gold from the Treasury. Nor was this the only reason for the gold shortage. For because of the depressed state of business and the ineptitudes of the framers of the new Wilson Tariff Act, the government's revenues were not keeping pace with its expenditures; it was running at a loss, and at times actually had to dip into its gold reserves to pay its day-to-day expenses. And meanwhile a succession of business bankruptcies in the United States had so disturbed European investors that they were unloading their American securities, thus hastening the flow of gold away from America to Europe. For all these reasons the gold reserve kept melting away.

Several times Cleveland's Secretary of the Treasury, John G. Carlisle, had either gone to the New York bankers and persuaded them, as a patriotic measure, to exchange some of the gold in their vaults for government notes, or else had issued bonds and with the proceeds of their sale had bought gold for the Treasury; thus disaster had been deferred. But now, on the morning of Monday, January 28, 1895, the gold remaining in the reserve had fallen far below the amount considered the necessary minimum for safety, which was one hundred million dollars. It had been reduced to only a little over fifty-six millions, and the amount was shrinking daily.

On that Monday, January 28, three millions and three-quarters were withdrawn. On Tuesday, three millions were taken out. On Wednesday, nearly three millions and three-quarters. At that rate, the reserve would last scarcely three weeks—and who could tell when the trickle of gold might not become a torrent? The emergency was immediate and acute.

What could be done? Float another bond issue to raise money with which the government could buy more gold? But the last one had been floated less than three months before, in November 1894. Surely such a measure would advertise all too well the desperateness of the situation. And besides, it took time to prepare and advertise an issue of bonds for public bidding—and now there was no time to spare.

Could Cleveland turn to Congress for emergency help? On Monday the 28th he did so, in a brief emergency message. But the chances of relief from Congress were small indeed. For during these years of depression and unrest a strange thing had been taking place.

In the early nineties the long-gathering resentment of Western and Southern farmers, and of small business men and workmen generally, against the business abuses of the time had boiled over, and they had angrily formed the Populist party. This party's 1892 platform had been radical not only in the accepted sense of the word but also in its stricter sense; for it had contained many drastic proposals which went to the roots of the abuses of the day. (One might almost describe the Populists as vociferous left-wing New Dealers born long before their time.) They had gathered such a large following that in 1892 they carried four states, won a million votes for their candidate for the Presidency, and swept into office five senators and ten representatives. But as time went on and conservative opinion solidified against them and discouragements multiplied, more and more of the indignation which Populism had crystallized began to concentrate itself upon a single cause—the cause of "free silver." The perennial susceptibility of desperate men to panaceas which involve formulae too complex for the average man to understand—a susceptibility which in later years was to win converts for Technocracy and Social Credit—led millions of people to believe that it was gold which was at the root of their troubles; that the wider circulation of silver would enable Kansas farmers to make a profit on their wheat, and would restore the reduced wages of Pennsylvania steel workers; and that any plan designed to protect the government's gold supply was a plan to enslave the plain people of America.

During those years, as Mark Sullivan has written, "The average American in great numbers had the feeling that he was being 'put upon' by something he couldn't quite see or get his fingers on; that somebody was 'riding' him; that some force or other was 'crowding' him. Vaguely he felt that . . . his economic freedom . . . was being circumscribed in a tightening ring, the drawing-strings of which, he felt sure, were being pulled by the hands of some invisible power which he ardently desired to see and get at, but could not. This unseen enemy he tried to personify. He called it the Invisible Government, the Money Interests, the Gold Bugs, Wall Street, the Trusts. During the first Bryan campaign, the spokesmen of the West spoke of the business men of the East, collectively, as 'the enemy.' " Now, at the beginning of 1895, the Senate was largely dominated by men to whom President Cleveland's insistence upon the protection of the government's gold was the surest sign of his alliance with this enemy. And when in his emergency message of January 28 he spoke of "the preservation of our national honor and credit," they turned deaf ears.

Well then, what else could Cleveland do to avert panic?

Could the government borrow money through private bankers, who could presumably raise it more rapidly than could the government itself through a publicly advertised bond issue? Most of the gold which was currently being withdrawn from the Treasury reserve was being shipped abroad; could private bankers with European connections possibly help to bring some of it back again? On Wednesday, January 30, Secretary of the Treasury Carlisle sent Assistant Secretary Curtis to New York to consult with August Belmont, a banker whose firm was allied with the Rothschilds in England, France, and Germany. To the silver senators such a consultation would surely seem like a supplication to Beelzebub, but at least Belmont was a Democrat, and therefore not totally suspect. Curtis talked with Belmont at his home that evening, and Belmont said there was one man without whose aid no plan for restoring the government's gold reserve could succeed: Pierpont Morgan.

2

Morgan was now moving into a position of rising consequence in American finance. To begin with, he was now emphatically master in his own house. Junius Spencer Morgan, his father, was gone; the old gentleman had been driving on the Riviera on an April day in 1890 when the horses had bolted and he had been thrown heavily from the open victoria; he had lived only four days after the accident. Thereupon Pierpont had succeeded him as senior partner of the London house of J. S. Morgan & Co. Three years later, on June 30, 1893, Anthony J. Drexel had died, and after a long delay caused by the troubled financial conditions of the time, Pierpont Morgan had invited all the partners in Drexel, Morgan & Co. to dine with him at the Metropolitan Club in New

York to consider a new basis for the American firm. (This meeting, held in October 1894, was the first occasion on which all the New York and Philadelphia partners had ever been in one room at the same time.)

After dinner was over and the waiters had left the room, Morgan, the most unoratorical of men, had stood up and made one of the few speeches of his life. He proposed that the Philadelphia and New York firms should become one; that the name should become J. P. Morgan & Co. in New York, and Drexel & Co. in Philadelphia, if the Drexel heirs consented; and that the capital should be all in New York. This arrangement was later somewhat modified at the request of Edward T. Stotesbury of the Philadelphia group; the partners there were allowed to retain the earnings of Drexel & Co. in Philadelphia until these reached ten million dollars. Otherwise it went into effect at the end of 1894, so that by the end of January 1895, when Curtis went to New York to consult August Belmont about the gold crisis, Pierpont Morgan's firm in New York had for almost a month been known by his name alone. Once again it had become J. P. Morgan & Co.—a designation unused since those bitter days at the outset of the Civil War when the young Pierpont had been mourning his lost Mimi.

He had several partners in New York. Foremost among them was the brilliant Charles H. Coster, of whom Pierpont Morgan's son said long later that "his mastery of detail was complete, his grasp of a problem immediate and comprehensive, and his power of work astonishing." It was Coster who was working out the exacting details of the railroad reorganizations of the mid-nineties. "Men saw him day by day," wrote John Moody, "a white-faced, nervous figure, hurrying from directors' meeting to directors' meeting; at evening carrying home his portfolio of corporation problems for the night." Another New York partner was George S. Bowdoin, an old and dear friend of his chief's and one of the original members of the Corsair Club. Still another was J. P. Morgan, Jr., who had graduated from Harvard in 1889, had worked for a time in the London office, had come into the New York office at the beginning of 1891, had been admitted to partnership on January 1, 1892, and now, at the age of twenty-seven, had been a partner for over three years. Finally —to fill the gap left by the veteran J. Hood Wright, who had dropped dead one day late in 1894—there was the newly admitted young Bostonian, Robert Bacon. If Coster's endless labor and his untimely death in 1900 did much to give currency to the Wall Street saying that Morgan partners were likely to die young of overwork, Bacon's spectacular good looks bore out another generalization about the firm: that Pierpont Morgan liked handsome men. Perhaps there was in this preference an element of compensation: a man who, suffering from *acne rosacea,* knew that his own physical appearance sometimes struck beholders with dismay was glad to be accompanied by a partner as superb looking as this young man from Boston, who had been captain of the Harvard football team, had rowed No. 7 on the university crew, had excelled at sparring, the hundred-yard dash, and the quarter-mile, had been president of the Glee Club, and had graduated as chief marshal of his class. Hence the Wall Street saying, "When the angels of God took unto themselves wives among the daughters of men, the result was the Morgan partners."

All these men—the diligent and harried Coster, the friendly Bowdoin, the earnest young Jack Morgan, the handsome Bacon—stood in awe of Pierpont Morgan. In the words of James Brown Scott, "They were lieutenants, not commanders." Everything hung on his almighty word.

His prestige among financiers and business men generally had risen too within the past few years; for the railroad reorganizations which have been described in the preceding chapter of this book were well under way, and already his success with them was impressive. It was recognized, too, that as a master of international finance he stood alone.

3

On the morning of Thursday, January 31—the morning after Curtis' conference with Belmont at the latter's house—a cable from J. S. Morgan & Co. in London reached Pierpont Morgan in New York:

> N. M. Rothschild & Sons have sent for us, asked us if we would act with them Europe *re* U. S. Government securities. A. Belmont & Co., New York, have cabled them Assistant Secretary of Treasury coming see him [sic] today to offer 4% Bond. We replied we will be most happy act in concert with them provided you A. Belmont & Co. acted together U. S.
>
> N. M. Rothschild & Sons cable A. Belmont & Co., New York, see you, also that our opinion is jointly that public will not take any loan not specifically gold bonds at any price satisfactory to U. S. Government.

That was interesting to Pierpont Morgan—but also discouraging. He had received three days earlier a somewhat similar cable message, though in less immediate terms, from his brother-in-law Walter Burns, the acting chief of the London firm. The earlier message had likewise made the point that there was no hope of selling in Europe a United States bond not specifically payable in gold; now this new message reaffirmed it. Well, there seemed to be little hope that Congress, in its present temper, would authorize a bond issue specifically payable in gold. So the impasse continued: it looked unlikely that the government could borrow money quickly on terms satisfactory to European investors. But the earlier message had been "strictly confidential, for your own use only," and Morgan had done nothing about it. This one he could do something about.

Presently, August Belmont appeared to consult him, and the two of them thereupon walked across the street from the Drexel Building and conferred with Assistant Secretary Curtis at the United States Subtreasury. Curtis was seeing the heads of most of the chief international banking houses that day, getting their views of possible ways of meeting the emergency, but it was Morgan and Belmont alone with whom his negotiations at once took definite and positive form. Morgan had been giving the problem long and intense thought, and as a result he was able to cable London that very day as follows:

> Have had consultations with A. Belmont & Co., also Assistant Secretary Curtis. Without further authority Congress, any loan specifically gold impossible, although feeling necessity such action growing.
>
> The situation, however, is critical and we are disposed to do everything our power avert calamity and assist Government under the power it actually possesses; besides which, should dislike see business largely hands Speyer & Co. and similar houses, who more sanguine European loans than your cables indicate.
>
> We have requested Secretary Curtis to obtain from Government answer to following questions:
>
> "Would the Government make a private contract with a syndicate for the sale of 50,000,000 with option of 50,000,000 additional, such a contract to be considered a state paper and confidential and not to be divulged until syndicate issue completed? Bonds to be 4's or 5's at discretion of syndicate and delivered wherever sold." [Then followed further financial details.]

If can obtain such exclusive contract should feel inclined form syndicate on 3⅝ to 3¾% basis provided at least 25 million could be sold or underwritten in Europe. It is essential restoration confidence and stoppage gold withdrawals that it be known such negotiations made, and £5,000,000 in Banks of England, Germany, France available shipment here if necessary.

We think if this negotiation can be made will be most creditable all parties and pay good profit.

We can secure co-operation best parties this side including leading National Banks.

We all have large interests dependent upon maintenance sound currency United States. Important use every exertion success negotiation. Great factor is European absorption even temporarily of bonds. Public here keenly alive that feature. We appreciate importance gold instead coin bonds, but no authority such at present. . . .

Curtis went back to Washington. Rumors began to circulate that a syndicate of bankers headed by Pierpont Morgan was coming to the rescue of the gold reserve by an immediate loan of money to the government. There was suddenly a new feeling of hope in the air; the stock market closed strong; and although on that day nearly two and a half million dollars in gold had been withdrawn from the Treasury reserve—all for export by Saturday's steamer—by evening it was said that some of it might not be exported at all. Had the tide already turned?

4

The tension in Washington was terrific. Night after night the Cabinet was meeting at the White House, and some of the men most directly concerned with the problem of the gold reserve—the President, Secretary of the Treasury Carlisle, Attorney General Olney, and the President's one-time private secretary and present Secretary of War, Daniel Lamont—would on occasion stay in session till dawn, debating endlessly over alternative plans for meeting the crisis. They considered the proposal brought by Curtis, and the next day, Friday, February 1, Morgan was able to cable to London, "Curtis telephones from Washington indications favorable. He will reach here eleven tonight." That Friday morning, while the *New York Times* was thundering editorially for congressional action in response to Cleveland's plea, saying, "The situation that confronts the Senate involves the honor of the United States throughout the world," it was the front-page news report headed BOND ISSUE COMING SOON that caught excited attention in the Street. Again the stock market leaped. Better yet, only $1,257,000 was withdrawn from the gold reserve—and $1,800,000 was returned to it! As Morgan cabled to London, "Improvement public feeling today, with nothing known and nothing done, indicative what will follow successful conclusion business."

That night Morgan conferred with Curtis on the latter's arrival back in New York, and the next morning, Saturday, February 2, they had a long session with August Belmont at 219 Madison Avenue, considering a multitude of details. There seemed to be only one likely hitch in the negotiations. The press and public had acquired the idea that the four per cent bonds would be issued to the syndicate at a price to yield 3½ per cent. The Treasury insisted on 3½ per cent. Morgan was asking for 3¾ per cent, expecting privately to be able to compromise on 3⅝ per cent. But surely that gap could be closed. Curtis took the detailed proposal back to Washington, promising to telephone the answer at three o'clock Sunday afternoon.

5

On Sunday the telephone message came, but it was merely to the effect that the matter was still under consideration and that a messenger would soon start for New York bearing a letter from Secretary Carlisle. This was a little disquieting. Morgan cabled to London, "The situation here tonight Sunday is this. The public and press believe the negotiation practically completed without knowing any details whatever but only price assumed to be 3½ per cent. We feel bound use every exertion complete negotiation. Effect of abandonment upon all interests would now be worse than if never begun."

The messenger, who was Curtis' private secretary, Lawrence O. Murray, arrived in New York Monday morning with his letter. It was a bombshell. The negotiations were off.

The Administration had had a change of heart, induced presumably by three things: the fact that the price was high, the fact that the drain of gold from the Treasury reserve had for the moment ceased (because of this very negotiation), and the grave political hazard of the undertaking. Already Democratic newspapers were shouting with dismay at the notion of a private deal between the government and a Republican Wall Street capitalist. Joseph Pulitzer's New York *World* was warning Cleveland and Carlisle that they were delivering themselves to the money interests, and was advising the President to hold out for a three per cent loan, saying in bold type, "If the banks won't take it, the people will." And so the decision had been made to make a public call for bids for the purchase of government bonds.

Morgan was appalled. He did not believe that a public sale of bonds could possibly succeed at this critical juncture. He consulted with Belmont. To abandon now the negotiations for a private sale would be disastrous for the government, they agreed. Belmont started for Washington on the ten o'clock train Monday morning. Morgan waited in New York to communicate with Secretary Carlisle, and finally reached Assistant Secretary Curtis by long-distance telephone and told him in the strongest terms that it would be fatal to announce a public issue of bonds. Curtis presently reported that Secretary Carlisle reluctantly agreed to delay the announcement for a day; Morgan said that Belmont was on his way to Washington, and he himself would start for Washington that afternoon, and that he thought he had a right to be listened to. And he sent two cables to London. The first said:

> Monday morning. Do nothing further about negotiations until you hear further from us. We have received letter this morning by messenger from Secretary of Treasury which apparently withdraws all attempts European negotiations. We are completely loss to understand. Will cable you later. Strictly confidential and for your use only.

The second cable said:

> Consider situation critical. Politicians seem to have absolute control. Shall make strongest fight possible for sound currency. If fail and European negotiations abandoned it is impossible overestimate what will be result United States. . . .

Then he took the *Congressional Limited* for Washington, taking with him his counsel, Francis Lynde Stetson (who would be an especially useful ally because he had been President Cleveland's law partner), and handsome young Robert Bacon. Only one thing, he thought, could prevent the utter failure of his cherished plan—and a panic of incalculable severity: he himself must talk to Grover Cleveland.

6

It was cold and windy when he arrived in Washington that Monday evening, and his reception was cold. When he alighted from the train he was met on the station platform by Daniel Lamont, the Secretary of War. Lamont told him that President Cleveland would not see him. As to what happened during the rest of the evening, the accounts of various chroniclers differ; I shall follow mainly Satterlee's version, which seems to me at this point to have the ring of truth. According to this account, Morgan said shortly to Lamont, "I have come down to Washington to see the President, and I am going to stay here until I see him." Then he strode off to the cabstand.

Stetson left him to drive to the White House, where he made a futile attempt to see Cleveland to arrange an appointment. Morgan, with Bacon, took another cab, and started off as if for the Hotel Arlington; but then—because at the Arlington, which was known to be his usual Washington headquarters, he would be under close observation by reporters and others—told the driver to take him to the house of his friend Mrs. J. Kearney Warren on K Street, while Bacon went on to the Arlington without him.

Mrs. Warren, an old friend of his parents and of his own, was a little bewildered by his surprise visit. He told her that he could not explain it to her, but he was in hiding, awaiting a telephone call; nobody must be admitted to the house while he was there; she must tell her servant that she was not at home to callers. Then—to quote Satterlee—he "sat and smoked before the fire, apparently listening to Mrs. Warren's talk, but did not speak." At the end of an hour or so the telephone rang. It was Bob Bacon, who had persuaded that dour New

Englander, Attorney General Richard Olney, to talk to Morgan. The banker thereupon took a cab to Olney's house, explained to him vehemently the importance of a conference with Cleveland, and then went on to the Arlington Hotel, where, according to the *New York Times,* "as Mr. Morgan stood for a moment at the desk he was asked by a newspaperman if his visit had anything to do with the bond issue. He returned a diplomatic reply and hastened to the elevator."

Belmont, arriving in Washington before Morgan, had seen Secretary Carlisle at his house toward the end of the day and had exercised his best powers of persuasion to the effect that the President must talk with the bankers. Now there was nothing more to be done. Morgan, in his suite at the Hotel Arlington, settled down to play "Miss Milliken," his favorite game of solitaire, while he thought the situation out. The hours went by and he was still playing. It was well after three before the last lights went out in the Morgan rooms.

7

Sometime that night or early in the morning of Tuesday, February 5—the evidence is conflicting—came a welcome message from the White House: the President would see Mr. Morgan. The banker gathered with him Belmont, Stetson, and Bacon, and together they walked to the White House through the bitter cold and biting winds of that midwinter morning.

At the White House they were shown upstairs and ushered into the presence of the burly President. Secretary Carlisle was with him. Cleveland said that a public issue of bonds had been decided upon. There was a delay while the two officials went over early reports from the Subtreasury in New York which indicated the probability of further withdrawals of gold that day—possibly disastrous withdrawals. There were more interruptions —telephone calls, messages—and at one time the President left the room and was gone for the better part of an hour. Then, at last, came the moment when Cleveland turned to Morgan and asked him what he had to say.

With that tremendous certainty which gave his words impressive weight, Morgan made his argument. Withdrawals of gold had begun again. There was not time enough for a public issue. The only possible solution lay in a private and immediate arrangement such as the one the mere prospect of which had stopped withdrawals cold the week before. And he introduced a new idea: that in a certain old law dating from Civil War days—Section 3700 of the Revised Statutes, he thought it was—the government was authorized *to buy coin and pay for it in bonds.* Why should the government not buy gold coin from the syndicate—coin gathered partly in the United States, partly in Europe—and pay for it with this new private bond issue?

According to Satterlee, this new idea was Morgan's own; he had recalled during the night, as he played solitaire, that in his gold-trading days during the Civil War he had heard of such a provision. According to Allan Nevins' life of Cleveland, it was Curtis' idea. It does not matter. What matters is that the law books were sent for, that Section 3700 was found to be the perfect answer to the situation, and that the continuing arguments of Morgan and Belmont carried the day.

Cleveland had been wary of Morgan at first; as he said many years later, "I had a feeling, not of suspicion, but of watchfulness. . . . I had not gone far, however, before my doubts disappeared. I found I was in negotiation with a man of large business comprehension and of remarkable knowledge and prescience . . . of clear-sighted, far-seeing patriotism."

"Mr. Morgan," said the President, "what guarantee have we that if we adopt this plan, gold will not continue to be shipped abroad and while we are getting it in, it will go out, so that we will not reach our goal? Will you guarantee that this will not happen?"

"Yes, sir," answered Mr. Morgan instantly. "I will guarantee it during the life of the syndicate, and that means until the contract has been concluded and the goal has been reached."

That was an immense commitment. He was pledging himself to control what for years past had been uncontrollable—the course of international exchange and international gold shipments. Not to do his best, but to succeed. And he was a man who did not make pledges lightly.

No final agreement was arrived at during this White House session. It was decided to wait until Thursday, when an Administration bill to meet the crisis was to come before the House of Representatives, before acting, lest it be said that the Administration had gone ahead without exhausting every possibility of congressional help. But the essential victory had been won. Cleveland had been persuaded. As Pierpont Morgan got up to leave that upstairs room in the White House, someone noticed what looked like a lot of brown dust on his knees and on the carpet by his feet. Without realizing it, he had been crushing into fragments the cigar which, long hours before, he had brought into the room unlighted.

8

Later that day he cabled London, "Received your cable of yesterday. Impossible convey any just idea of what have been through today, but we have carried our point and are more than satisfied."

The message went on to outline the basis of the forthcoming deal. The syndicate would deliver to the government gold equivalent in ounces to 60 million dollars, payment for them to be made in bonds at a rate "equivalent to a purchase of the bonds on a 3¾% basis, one half gold to come from Europe. . . ." And the syndicate, as far as lay in their power, would "make all legitimate efforts to protect the Treasury of the United States against the withdrawal of gold pending the complete performance of this contract."

Pierpont Morgan went home to New York, waited anxiously until Thursday, and then, as the Administration's Springer Bill went down to its expected defeat in the House, returned to Washington, saw Cleveland and Carlisle again briefly, and on Friday morning went to the Treasury Department with Stetson, where the final details of the contract were worked out and the document was signed.

The cold wave of the early part of the week had now turned into a blizzard, accompanied by temperatures close to zero in the northeastern states and by blinding winds; traffic was crippled, ferries tied up, trains stalled; and as a result August Belmont, who had started from New York to Washington by Thursday night's train, did not arrive until the early afternoon. But he got there in time to sign the contract. As a matter of fact, it would have mattered little if he had been further delayed, for Morgan had been informed by cable from J. S. Morgan & Co. in London that the Rothschilds authorized him to sign on Belmont's behalf if necessary; and anyhow, Cleveland had already, even before the signatures were affixed, notified Congress of the arrangement and thus given authoritative public notice that relief for the government's gold reserve was at hand.

9

An uproar of protest at the news arose from the silverites and those other Americans who regarded Wall Street as the enemy. What seems astonishing to us today, as we contrast the relative powers of the government and of private financial groups at the present time with their relative powers in the mid-nineties—the fact that the United States Treasury was forced by circumstances to deal with two private bankers almost as if they had been plenipotentiaries of an independent state of more ample resources—seemed to these observers not so much astonishing as outright scandalous.

The price of the private bankers' aid looked high. In the final contract they had secured the bonds on the basis of a 3¾ per cent yield; not the 3⅝ per cent that they had been ready to compromise on, nor the 3½ per cent that the public had expected; and since the public announcement of the deal at once relieved the pressure on the Treasury, there was a sharp rise in the market value of the new bonds which were about to be issued. The 3¾ per cent yield was equivalent to a price of 104½; presently the temporary "allotment certificates" which represented these bonds while the actual instruments were being engraved were being bid for on the market at the much higher price of 120—a fact which of course suggested that the original figure had been much too low. On February 14, young William Jennings Bryan of Nebraska, not yet renowned as a Presidential candidate, said in a speech in Congress, "I only ask that the Treasury shall be administered on behalf of the American people and not on behalf of the Rothschilds and other foreign bankers." The New York *World*, speaking scornfully of "bank-parlor negotiations," called the agreement "an excellent arrangement for the bankers. It puts at least $16,000,000 into their pockets. . . . For the nation it means a scandalous surrender of credit and a shameful waste of substance."

Nor was this all, for it was widely—and of course baselessly—whispered that Cleveland had profited personally by the deal. As Allan Nevins has put it in his life of Cleveland, "By hundreds of thousands, hard-headed Americans believed that Cleveland and Carlisle had sold the credit of the republic to the Morgans and Rothschilds and had pocketed a share of the price."

But certainly the syndicate operation proved a thumping success. On February 20 the new United States Government bonds were put on sale simultaneously in New York and London, and presently the transatlantic cables were ticking off messages of triumph. From London, J. S. Morgan & Co. sent word, "Subscription enormous. Subscription books closed noon; open only two hours." And from New York came the return message from J. P. Morgan & Co., "We have closed our books. Subscriptions something enormous. We offer you all our sincere congratulations." And a little later: "We are quite overwhelmed by success of transaction. We send you our deepest heartfelt congratulations. You cannot appreciate the relief to everybody's mind, for the dangers were so great scarcely anyone dared whisper them. . . ."

10

And after that? The success continued. Within a few weeks the New York banks associated with the syndicate had turned in to the Treasury, in payment for the new bonds, large amounts of gold collected in the United

States; and, in payment for bonds issued abroad, a steady stream of gold was crossing the Atlantic westward. "You can ship any gold you choose," a cable from Morgan in New York had explained; "bar gold, sovereigns, U. S. gold coin, Napoleons. Assay Office will receive and give coin value." To protect the Treasury against simultaneous withdrawals of gold which would have nullified these gains was a more difficult undertaking; but so well did the members of the syndicate keep their pledged word to do this that before the end of June the Treasury's reserve of gold had grown until it had crossed the safety line of 100 million dollars.

Years later, Grover Cleveland told George F. Parker that when the negotiations were over he asked the head of the syndicate, "Mr. Morgan, how did you know that you could command the co-operation of the great financial interests of Europe?" And Morgan replied, "I simply told them that this was necessary for the maintenance of the public credit and the promotion of industrial peace, and they did it."

After June 1895 the situation became more difficult, and the syndicate was put to considerable expense to prevent the outflow of gold from America by complicated and hazardous dealings in drafts on London, conducted at a loss. And after the syndicate agreement came to an end and the books were closed in the autumn of 1895, a reaction set in; for a complex of economic reasons, gold began at once to move out of the United States again. So that once more, at the beginning of 1895, the Treasury was forced for the last time to sell bonds to fortify its reserve—this time through the more orthodox method of a public sale.

The Morgan-Belmont bond issue had not brought permanent relief to the Treasury. But it had brought instant temporary relief. To say that it had prevented a panic is to indulge in guesswork. History never tells us, after we have taken Road A at the fork in the ways, what would have happened had we taken Road B. But certain it is that the financial community felt positive that the government's exchange of bonds for gold had averted dire calamity. Morgan's cable to London which spoke of "dangers so great scarcely anyone dared whisper them" was written not to impress the public—it was a private message—but out of well-informed conviction.

11

Naturally, in view of the public outcry and the whispers of graft, there was a congressional investigation of the Treasury's dealings; and on June 19, 1896, Pierpont Morgan took the stand at a hearing in the Hoffman House in New York. His forthright answers to questions reflected his complete satisfaction in the course he had taken and his overwhelming assurance. Let us listen to him for a moment, as first a friendly interrogator, Senator Platt of Connecticut, and then a hostile one, Senator Vest of Missouri, throw questions at him:

SENATOR PLATT. Why did you not want to have an issue of bonds after you had commenced your negotiations? You asked the President not to issue a call. What was your reason for doing that?

MORGAN. Because I knew that if the call was made the public would understand that the foreign negotiation had been abandoned.

PLATT. It was a well-known fact that you had commenced a negotiation.

MORGAN. I did not care about anything except to get the gold for the government. I had but one aim in the whole matter—to secure the gold that the government needed and to save the panic and widespread disaster that was sure to follow if the gold was not got.

PLATT. Then it was understood that when you were negotiating, shipments ceased?

MORGAN. Absolutely; and they did not commence again until a month afterwards.

PLATT. And so your real purpose, as I understand you, in this transaction was not the idea that you could take this bond issue and make money out of it, but that you could prevent a panic and distress in the country?

MORGAN. I will answer the question, though I do not think it is necessary in view of all that I have done. I will say that I had no object except, as I have stated, to save the disaster that would result in case that foreign gold had not been obtained.

SENATOR VEST (*moving to the attack*). If that was your sole object, why did you specify in your telegraphic communication to Mr. Carlisle that your house, or you and Mr. Belmont, were to have exclusive control of the matter?

MORGAN. Because it was absolutely impossible for more than one party to negotiate—to make the same negotiation for the same lot of gold. It would only have made competition.

VEST. If the gold was abroad, I take for granted that anybody could get hold of it who had the means to do so. If you were actuated by the desire to prevent a panic, why were you not willing that other people should do it, if they wanted to?

MORGAN. *They could not do it.*

VEST. How did you know?

MORGAN. That was my opinion. . . .

VEST. Do you believe that the government could have

made any better terms with anybody else than it made with yourself and Mr. Belmont at that juncture?

MORGAN. I do not, sir.

VEST. Do you believe that gold could have been obtained from abroad on any better terms?

MORGAN. I do not. It was difficult enough to obtain it, as it was.

VEST. Was your house engaged in shipping gold abroad up to this time, or at about this time?

MORGAN. We never have shipped one dollar of gold abroad for the last three years.

12

When Senator Vest, a little earlier, asked the direct question, "What profit did your house make upon this transaction?" Morgan replied flatly: "That I decline to answer. I wish to state that I am perfectly ready to state to the committee every detail of the negotiation up to the time that the bonds became my property and were paid for. What I did with my own property subsequent to that purchase I decline to state, except this, that no member of the government in any department was interested directly or indirectly in connection therewith."

Vest pursued the matter. "You decline to answer my question as to the amount of profits made by your firm?"

"I do, sir," said Morgan.

"Upon what terms did you dispose of these bonds that you received from the government, and to whom?"

Morgan still stood fast. "That was subsequent to the purchase," he said, "and I decline to answer for the reason stated."

J. P. Morgan, Jr., used to say that his father told him that he himself was quite willing to disclose his profit, but that for some reason August Belmont asked him not to. Be that as it may, Belmont too refused to inform the senators. Nobody seriously questioned the bankers' right to keep silence if they chose—a fact which seems somewhat remarkable to us today, since, in view of the surrounding circumstances, the transactions of the syndicate were emphatically vested with a public interest—and therefore the amount of the actual profit long remained a matter of conjecture.

As we have noted, the New York *World* charged in 1895 that "the bankers" (unspecified) made at least sixteen million dollars. In his book *The House of Morgan,* published in 1930, Lewis Corey said that "the syndicate profits ranged from seven to twelve million dollars." Other estimates, taking into account possible losses in maintaining foreign exchange in equilibrium and other expenses of the operation, and also taking into account the probability that the syndicate could not have disposed of all its bonds at the top price and raked in the whole difference as a profit, made much lower estimates, nevertheless arguing, as did the conservative Alexander Dana Noyes in his *Forty Years of American Finance,* that "the terms were extremely harsh . . . they measured with little mercy the emergency of the Treasury," or as did Nevins in his sympathetic life of Cleveland, that "after all allowances are made, the profits must be pronounced exorbitant." On the other hand, Francis Lynde Stetson said in an address that the American syndicate realized "only five per cent and interest"; and Herbert L. Satterlee went so far as to declare that "from my talks with Mr. Morgan I can confidently state that there was no profit for him at all."

Among these wildly divergent statements it was Stetson's which was the most accurate. Here are the actual figures—which so far as I know have never previously been disclosed—from the original Syndicate Book of the American Syndicate. (It must be recalled that there were two syndicates, one American, one European, with the business divided about evenly between them. These are the American figures only, from the still-existing records at 23 Wall Street.)

The American Syndicate took bonds totaling $31,157,-000, and allotted them among no less than sixty-one syndicate members—banks and private banking and investment houses. The House of Morgan took less than a tenth of the total. The largest holdings of bonds were $2,753,875 by August Belmont & Co.; $2,678,825 by J. P. Morgan & Co.; $2,600,000 by the First National Bank; $2,600,000 by Harvey Fisk & Sons; $1,800,000 by the United States Trust Co.; $1,500,000 by the National City Bank; and $1,000,000 each by the Fourth National Bank and the Chase and Hanover banks. All the other fifty-two holdings were for less than a million dollars apiece.

When the transaction was over and the books were closed, the total profit of the American Syndicate was $1,534,516.72, which was about a tenth of the figure set down by the *World*, less than a quarter of the minimum figure set down by Corey, and a shade less than the five per cent figure given by Mr. Stetson. (If interest is included—properly it should not be—the amount is increased from $1,534,516.72 to $2,079,776.47.)

Of the American Syndicate's profit, J. P. Morgan & Co.'s share was $131,932.13. In addition the Morgan firm received half of the American Syndicate Managers' commission of three-quarters of one per cent; that brought in $116,841.37 more. These two sums total $248,773.50 —a little less than a quarter of a million dollars. And this, by the way, was gross profit, against which could reasonably be charged some of the general costs of doing business. (If one adds to this sum the interest drawn by the firm on its holding, the total rises by $46,879.43 to $295,652.93.)

As for Pierpont Morgan himself, presumably at the year's end he was credited with a goodly share of this profit—and also a share in the London profit, whatever that may have been.

To people outside the banking world, a profit (for the Morgan firm in New York) of a quarter of a million dollars on a single transaction looks large. But considering that it amounted to less than one per cent of the value of the bonds which were being distributed, it was not large at all—especially when one took into account the duration and complexity of the operation and the risks involved in such an unprecedented undertaking. And to Morgan himself, who was accustomed to thinking in large sums, it undoubtedly seemed a modest recompense indeed for saving the credit of the United States.

Chapter Eight

TRIANGULATION

TO FIX precisely the size and shape and position of a natural object, such as a mountain peak, the surveyor triangulates, which is to say that he looks at the object from various points of view and compares the different observations which result. Sometimes triangulation is useful in biography as well. A biographer may try to reveal his subject's terrific personal force, the awe in which he was held by those about him, the weight of the few words he spoke; his curtness toward those upon whom he had not focused his sympathies, and especially toward those whom he regarded as interrupters or interferers; his tenderness toward those who engaged his friendship; the patrician limitations of his view of other men—yet all the time this biographer is conscious that the picture he is drawing is two-dimensional and flat, and that each of the qualities which he has recorded will leap into bolder relief when observed from another direction. So I propose now to show you Pierpont Morgan through the eyes of a few contemporaries, each of whom saw him from, as it were, a different point of the compass.

Let us begin with Lincoln Steffens, writing in his remarkable *Autobiography* about the days when he himself had not yet become a redoubtable chronicler of municipal corruption but was simply an energetic and observant young financial reporter for the New York *Evening Post.* He depicts Morgan at about the time when the banker was reorganizing railroads right and left and saving the gold reserve of the United States—and also, as his prestige grew, was becoming recognizably the man revealed in Steichen's great portrait photograph.

"In those days of the eighteen-nineties," writes Steffens, "I had to do with the private bankers who are the constructive engineering financiers.

"Of these last, J. P. Morgan, Senior, was the greatest. I did not see much of him, of course; nobody did. He was in sight all the time. He sat alone in a back room with glass sides in his banking house with his door open, and it looked as if anyone could walk in upon him and ask any question. One heard stories of the payment of large sums for an introduction to him. I could not see why all the tippers with business did not come right in off the street and talk to him. They did not. My business was with his partners or associates, principally Samuel Spencer,* but I noticed that these, his partners, did not go near him unless he sent for them; and then they looked alarmed and darted in like officeboys. 'Nobody can answer that question except Mr. Morgan,' they would tell me. Well, Mr. Morgan was there; why not go in and ask him? The answer I got was a smile or a shocked look of surprise. And once when I pressed the president of one of the Morgan banks to put to him a question we agreed deserved an answer, the banker said, 'Not on your life,' and when I said, 'But why not?' he said, 'You try it yourself and see.' And I did.

"I went over to J. P. Morgan & Company, walked into his office, and stood before him at his flat, clean, clear desk. I stood while he examined a sheet of figures; I stood for two or three long minutes, while the whole bank

* Samuel Spencer was never a partner, nor, apparently, on the salary list of the firm. But as a railroad expert he was in the office a great deal, and he had a procuration for the signing of checks. At 23 Wall Street they insist today that Morgan would not have "rapped for" Spencer as he is later represented as doing. If not, this is a minor flaw in the accuracy of a revealing anecdote.

seemed to stop work to watch me, and he did not look up; he was absorbed, he was sunk, in those figures. He was so alone with himself and his mind that when he did glance up he did not see me; his eyes were looking inward. . . . I thought . . . that he was doing a sum in mental arithmetic, and when he solved it he dropped his eyes back upon his sheet of figures and I slunk out. . . ."

But one afternoon Steffens' paper received a typewritten statement from J. P. Morgan & Company about some bonds, a statement that did not make sense as written. So, says Steffens, "ready for the explosion, I walked into Morgan's office and right up to his desk. He saw me this time; he threw himself back in his chair so hard that I thought he would tip over.

" 'Mr. Morgan,' I said as brave as I was afraid, 'what does this statement mean?' and I threw the paper down before him.

" 'Mean!' he exclaimed. His eyes glared, his great red nose seemed to me to flash and darken, flash and darken. Then he roared. 'Mean! It means what it says. I wrote it myself, and it says what I mean.'

" 'It doesn't say anything—straight,' I blazed.

"He sat back there, flashing and rumbling; then he clutched the arms of his chair, and I thought he was going to leap at me. I was so scared that I defied him.

" 'Oh, come now, Mr. Morgan,' I said, 'you may know a lot about figures and finance, but I'm a reporter, and I know as much as you do about English. And that statement isn't English.'

"That was the way to treat him, I was told afterward. And it was in that case. He glared at me a moment more, the fire went out of his face, and he leaned forward over the bit of paper and said very meekly, 'What's the matter with it?'

"I said I thought it would be clearer in two sentences instead of one and I read it aloud so, with a few other verbal changes.

" 'Yes,' he agreed, 'that is better. You fix it.'

"I fixed it under his eyes, he nodded and I, whisking it away, hurried back to the office. They told me in the bank afterward that J. P. sat watching me go out of the office, then rapped for Spencer and asked what my name was, where I came from, and said, 'Knows what he wants, and—gets it.' "

2

So much for Steffens, the reporter. Let us now move our theodolite to another angle of observation and look at Pierpont Morgan through the eyes of the Reverend William Stephen Rainsford, rector of St. George's Church, the bold preacher and pioneer in church social work who, you may recall, had accepted the pulpit of St. George's in 1882 at a vestry meeting held in Morgan's house.

From that time on, Morgan had been Rainsford's devoted friend and backer. He had become senior warden of the church on his father-in-law's death; had passed the plate every Sunday when he was in New York; and had had Rainsford to breakfast every Monday morning at No. 219 to discuss the affairs of the church over an after-breakfast cigar. When in 1889 Rainsford suffered a nervous breakdown from overwork, Morgan saw to it that he was well cared for, and during Rainsford's absence made a point of reaching St. George's each Sunday morning a half hour before the service began and standing at the church door, "welcoming those he knew and did not know," and thus helping them to feel "that St. George's was a going concern." Let Rainsford say in his own words what Morgan meant to him in the dark hour of that illness:

"Then it was I proved fortunate in my friends. I had no care. Others planned my life and saved me all expense and all trouble. Of course the strongest arm under me was that of my senior warden. He was ever a man to lean on in time of trouble. You differed with him, and he with you, but when a helper was needed you turned to him, you leaned on him, and you leaned hard. He had a great heart. . . ."

After Rainsford returned to the pulpit he found that something had gone out of him; he had lost vitality and was often tired. "Mr. Morgan saw most things he wanted to see," writes Rainsford, "and he noticed the change in me. Soon after my return, in his quiet way, he drew me aside one day and, slipping a paper into my hand, said, 'Don't work too hard; you ought not to have to worry about money. Don't thank me, and don't speak of it to anyone but your wife.' He had created a modest trust fund for me and mine. So he lifted from my shoulders a burden that has crushed the life out of many a good soldier. . . ."

Again, when Mrs. Rainsford was gravely ill for a long time at the Roosevelt Hospital, Morgan, "who at that time was carrying a load of responsibility heavier, perhaps, than any other man in the United States carried, except its President, found time again and again to bring roses to her sick room, and would wait outside her door till the nurse permitted him to lay them by her bed."

The close association between these two men was a strange one. For Rainsford was by nature a radical reformer, a passionate democrat. He believed in the "social gospel"—the pre-eminent importance, in Christ's teaching, of the duty of active neighborliness to all men. He wanted to make the church itself a friendly place to which men and women of every sort would come for companionship, enjoyment, solace, and practical help. To Morgan, the conservative and traditionalist, all this was strange. Morgan's religious faith, unquestioned and unchanged since his Hartford boyhood, was something set sacredly apart from daily conduct. As Rainsford interpreted him, "His mental qualities drew him strongly to the ecclesiastical side of the Episcopal Church's life. Its very archaic element, its atmosphere of withdrawal from the common everyday affairs of men, answered to some need of his soul." Morgan regularly attended the triennial national Episcopal conventions, and according to Rainsford, "The floor of the convention, the association with men who were, by virtue of their office, guardians and exponents of a religious tradition, beautiful and venerable, had for him an attraction stronger than any other gathering afforded. He would cast all other duties aside and sit for hours, attentively following the details of the driest of debates, on subjects that could interest only an ecclesiastic." How explain such a man's loyal partnership with a clergyman to whom the church was first of all an organization to energize and inspire a humble-hearted friendship among men?

Perhaps Morgan recalled how desperately his grandfather, the crusading John Pierpont of Boston, had missed the support of the congregation of the Hollis Street Church; perhaps he had resolved that he himself would never be so blindly obstructive as those Bostonians had been. More likely the chief reason was that when Morgan believed in a man he believed in backing him with full faith and with few questions; and Rainsford, a big, handsome, straightforward fellow who knew how to meet loyalty with loyalty, attracted his belief. At any rate, despite his misgivings over Rainsford's program of social work, he gave the clergyman his sustained support, and even went so far as to build for St. George's a parish house —Memorial House, given in memory of his wife's parents —which was the first building of its kind in New York. But the story of Morgan and Rainsford would not be complete if it omitted a rift between them which opened up in the middle eighteen-nineties, not very far in time, probably, from Steffens' confrontation of Morgan at 23 Wall Street.

I draw my account of this episode directly from the one in Rainsford's autobiography, *The Story of a Varied Life,* abbreviating it somewhat but quoting from it lavishly and presenting the whole episode as Rainsford himself saw it.

3

The meetings of the vestry of St. George's Church were held at eight-thirty in the evening in the Corporation Room at the Parish House, with the rector as presiding officer. One night, out of a clear sky, Pierpont Morgan rose and read a motion that the vestry be reduced from two wardens and eight members to two wardens and six members, adding, "I think the vestry will agree with me that when I get a seconder it had better be passed without debate."

Rainsford was stunned. He said that Morgan had given him no warning whatever of any intention to propose such a change. "Since I stood in your study that night when you called me to the church," he went on, "I think you will bear witness that I have never advocated any important matter in this, our church's council, without first discussing it with you. Here now you spring this revolutionary proposition on me, and on the vestry, without any warning whatever; and you ask that we should proceed to pass it without any discussion. This I cannot agree to, and I must ask you, before you get a seconder, to explain to me and to this vestry your reasons for proposing so important a change. We have done good work together, constituted as we are. If a small vestry is for St. George's a better vestry, there must be some reasons for it. What are your reasons for it?"

Thereupon Morgan "very unwillingly" got on his feet and explained that the vestry's role in the church was different from that of the rector. The rector's part was to teach and inspire; the vestry's part was fiduciary and its obligations were financial. "I am its senior warden and responsible officer," said Morgan. "I am aging. I want at times to have these vestry meetings held in my study. This vestry should be composed, in my judgment, of men whom I can invite to my study, and who can help me to carry the heavy financial burden of the church. . . . The rector wants to democratize the church, and we agree with him and will help him as far as we can. But I do not want the vestry democratized. I want it to remain a body of gentlemen whom I can ask to meet me in my study."

With dismay Rainsford realized that if Morgan had his patrician way, the vestry would cease to represent the congregation in any true sense; they—and the church—would inevitably fall under Morgan's control. (Perhaps what Morgan had chiefly in mind was that he wanted a group of men so well heeled that he could pass the hat among them to meet the church's needs without being embarrassed by the presence of men who could not contribute their share; but if so, either he failed to make this point clear or Rainsford thought that anyhow it involved a distortion of the vestry's function.) He reminded Morgan that he, Rainsford, had long believed that the vestry ought to be, not reduced, but enlarged. As a matter of fact he had expressed this idea more than once at their after-breakfast sessions, only to be met with the silence with which Morgan customarily greeted an idea which he was not then willing to accept. Rainsford argued that the vestry ought to include at least one representative of the increasing number of wage-earners in the congregation; and he also had in mind particularly one man, H. H. Pike, who was largely responsible for the growth of the Sunday School and thus had come to know well a great many of the younger members of the church.

The issue was joined, and a long, embarrassing, and vehement debate followed. It was a fight—a lacerating one. It lasted from a little after nine o'clock until nearly midnight. Rainsford asked Morgan to withdraw his motion. "Do not let us divide!" said Rainsford. "We never have had a division on any serious question in this vestry since I sat at your head." Seth Low, subsequently Mayor of New York, who was among the vestrymen, joined Rainsford in asking that the motion be withdrawn. Morgan remained immovable.

Then another vestryman, "one of his oldest friends, one to whom in these financially troublesome times through which we were then passing Mr. Morgan had been of immense service (I did not know this till later), slowly rose. He was white to the lips, and turning to Mr. Morgan he said, 'Mr. Morgan, I am compelled to agree with our rector in this matter, and I move that this vestry be increased to eleven.' "

Mayor Low seconded this motion. Morgan could get no seconder for his. Thereupon the motion to enlarge the vestry was put and carried, seven votes to one.

For a moment the group of men sat very silent. Then Morgan got up and said slowly, "Rector, I will never sit in this vestry again," and walked out of the room and out of the building.

From this point on I shall quote Rainsford verbatim:

"Next day I had Mr. Morgan's written resignation, with a request to submit it to the vestry without delay. I acknowledged his letter, and nothing more, going to breakfast next week at 219 Madison Avenue as usual. As I expected he was very grumpy, and at the breakfast table conversation was limited to the weather. Next week I went again to breakfast. He had nothing to say to me at the table.

"As I asked for a cigar, in his study afterward, he said, 'Have you submitted my resignation?'

" 'I have not, and I will not.'

" 'Why not?'

" 'Because I will not now or ever put you in the position of going back on your pledge to the rector and the vestry of St. George's Church.'

" 'What do you mean?'

" 'You know what I mean. When I first came to you I came because you gave me your hand and your promise to stand by me in the hard work that lay ahead. I told you I was a radical. I told you I would do all I could to democratize the church. I am only keeping my word. I certainly shall not now, nor at any time, do anything to help you break yours.'

"Dead silence. So I lit my cigar and walked away.

"I think after that I went to breakfast three times before Mr. Morgan sailed for Europe. He never made another allusion to his resignation, nor did he enter into any private conversation with me. The day he sailed, I did what I had not done before, I went to the dock to bid him good-bye. On this occasion, in the days I am writing of, the late nineties, a rather miscellaneous crowd was wont to gather to bid him good-bye. It had become quite a function, and I did not usually care to take part in it. As I went up the gangplank, I saw Mr. Morgan standing at some distance surrounded by his friends. At the same instant he saw me and, coming out of the group, signed to me to follow him. He made for his cabin, entered quickly, without saying a word, and shut and bolted the door behind us. We never had another falling out."

What was said in that cabin Rainsford would not divulge. But Morgan remained senior warden the rest of his life.

4

A financial reporter and a clergyman having testified, let us turn to another phase of Morgan's life, introducing in due course other witnesses diverse in temperament and character. Morgan became the greatest collector of his time, and the way in which he did it throws light upon him from other points of the compass.

There was, of course, nothing new about the collecting of works of art as a hobby for men of wealth and power. Conquering kings had long been wont to regard masterpieces as a superior form of loot; rich nobles and bankers and merchants, traveling to far places, had brought home with them all manner of lovely objects which had caught their eye; and in the eighteenth and nineteenth centuries collecting had become one of the standard preoccupations of men of ample means both in England and on the Continent. Even in the United States, those who had been able to visit Europe or Asia and had been entranced by the exquisite workmanship achieved under older civilizations, had enjoyed bringing fine things back with them to their bleaker homeland, and many of these collectors had been men of real taste. All through the nineteenth century the auction notices in New York and other American cities had testified to the number and variety of private collections, whether of rare books, or of paintings, or of *objets d'art,* which had been accumulated by people of means. And when in the early eighteen-eighties William H. Vanderbilt installed in his new house on Fifth Avenue an art gallery full of readily comprehended and sentimental paintings from Europe, and cluttered the hallways of the house with a remarkable jumble of statues and tapestries and curios from all over the world, and an admiring writer proclaimed that now "wealth is first consenting to act the Medicean part in America, to patronize the inventors, to create the arts, and to originate a form of civilization," there was nothing especially new about what Vanderbilt did; he simply spent more money more grandly (and perhaps with less discrimination) than most of his American predecessors.

But as the century drew to a close, and American fortunes multiplied, the collectors became not only more numerous but more knowing. And there began a new period in which a swarm of American millionaires ransacked Europe for masterpieces, near-masterpieces, and pseudo-masterpieces of painting, sculpture, architectural accessories, and fine workmanship in all sorts of materials. This new surge of the collectors gathered momentum during the eighteen-nineties, rushed at full tilt from 1900 to 1914, and continued, though at a less sensational pace, after the First World War. It resulted in such extraordinary concentrations of fine objects from abroad as the Gardner, Huntington, Mellon, and Frick collections, to say nothing of those of John G. Johnson, Folger, Freer, Altman, Havemeyer, Widener, Nelson, Lewisohn, Bliss, Hearst, Bache, and a cluster of others. At the head and front of the company of American purchasers was Morgan, the pace-setter for them all.

This boom in collecting was a natural thing. The man who had accumulated great wealth sought both to establish or secure his place among the elect by indulging in those forms of "conspicuous waste"—to borrow Veblen's term—which found favor among the privileged, and to enrich his own life according to whatever tastes he possessed or could acquire. He tended, in Western civilization, to want to have his womenfolk admirably attired and outfitted; to want to have a fine house full of luxurious appointments and rare and lovely things; and to want to give magnificent parties. If he was susceptible to the English county tradition, he enjoyed having a country estate with well-cut lawns, prize animals, and prize crops and flowers. He might add a yacht, the very symbol of luxury. He wanted, perhaps, to visit the approved watering places at the approved seasons, have his own quarters set apart for him there, and even to buy or build extra residences for himself in these select areas. If his tastes were sporting, he could now engage in those forms of sport which traditionally required the most retainers, such as grouse shooting, or were expensively speculative, as was the maintenance of a racing stable. But none of these exercises of his wealth quite satisfied his sensibilities, if he had any; were there not in life things finer in quality than these? There were the arts.

In few cases could he practice the arts himself, even if this had occurred to him. But he could apply his money to them. In aiding contemporary artists? Not often did this occur to him either, especially if he were an American—for he supposed that there were almost no American artists worth supporting, and anyhow contemporary artists were reported to be absurd and troublesome people. But he could collect the well-certified art of the European past, thus simultaneously exercising the talent for acquisition that had made him rich, stimulating and satisfying his appetite for beauty, avoiding contact with the artistic temperament except through the medium of romantic legend, and appeasing his own sense of financial prudence (for what was he doing but investing in things which, if there came a rainy day, might be sold again?). And if he were an American, he could have as well the added inner satisfaction of bringing to American shores a treasure trove which he could vaguely dream of putting one day at the public disposal, for the enrichment of America's all-too-meager cultural life.

Of course the man of wealth could also give his money away, for the support of education, religion, or charity, thus putting into reverse, as it were, his acquisitive talent. And if it was hard for a man beset with suppliants for his cash to decide between them, he could set up a fund to be administered by special experts in giving. But it was not until after the turn of the century that the first great foundations were established by the two richest Americans, Carnegie and Rockefeller, and not until 1910 and 1911 that the Rockefeller Foundation and the Carnegie Corporation were respectively incorporated; and by that time the epidemic of collecting in Europe was already at its zenith.

It is odd to trace the chronological parallel between two of the foremost collectors of those furious years. Isabella Stewart Gardner, the famous "Mrs. Jack" of Boston, had loved during the eighteen-seventies and early eighties to buy beautiful things for her Beacon Street house, but as late as 1884, when she fell in love with the glory of the Renaissance painting in Italy, she brought home with her merely photographs of masterpieces. It was about 1886 that she acquired the collecting mania—and then she began with old and rare books. In 1888 she really began assembling old paintings; in 1892 this pursuit became with her a ruling passion; in 1896 she began seriously to think of amassing a real museum collection; in 1899 she bought the land on which Fenway Court was presently built. Morgan's time schedule was similar, with a slight lag at each point.

Morgan had always enjoyed bringing home with him fine things that caught his fancy, whether in New York or on his annual trips to Europe. As a youngster he had picked up numerous fragments of old stained glass which he had found on the ground beneath cathedral windows, and had carted to New York a crate of them. He had occasionally bought paintings that seemed to him adequate. When he moved into 219 Madison Avenue at the age of forty-five he was sufficiently vain of his books to engage one J. F.. Sabin to prepare a pamphlet *Catalogue of the Library of Mr. J. Pierpont Morgan*: this was the sort of thing that a gentleman of taste and means did. But an examination of the catalogue shows that the books themselves were, with very few exceptions, nothing special. Not yet had the collecting virus entered his system. It was not until 1888, when he was fifty-one, that he bought his first manuscript, two years after Mrs. Gardner had embarked upon book collecting; not until 1891, when he was fifty-four, that he began to concentrate passionate attention, while abroad, on the purchase in quantity of manuscripts, first editions, and old and rare and fine volumes generally; and it was only gradually, in the years that followed, that like Mrs. Gardner he shifted part of his attention from books to other lovely relics of the past. The century had almost turned, and he was already in his sixties, before he became a major assembler of an immense and widening variety of beautiful things, which in due time were to include paintings, bronzes, terra cottas, jades, ivories, enamels, crystals, glass, tapestries, bas-reliefs, miniatures, snuffboxes, watches, Bibles, Church of England rituals, autographs, and of course books and manuscripts. The twentieth century had arrived before he began making serious plans to construct the Library building next to his house, and it was in 1904, when he was sixty-seven, that he became the president, wholesale benefactor, and supreme ruler of the Metropolitan Museum.

How did he begin? Let us call as a witness his admiring son-in-law, Herbert L. Satterlee:

> It was really Pierpont's nephew, Junius S. Morgan, who interested him in collecting manuscripts and rare editions. Junius knew that a young friend of his, F. Wheeler, had acquired a Thackeray manuscript, but he himself could not afford to buy it; so he introduced Wheeler to his uncle at the latter's office. As far as we know, this is the first manuscript that Pierpont himself bought; and the interview (as Wheeler wrote it down) is characteristic.
>
> When young Wheeler was shown in, Pierpont asked, "What have you got to show me?"
>
> "A Thackeray manuscript which came to me from Thackeray's daughter, Mrs. Ritchie."
>
> Pierpont took it and turned over the leaves. In a moment he asked, "Are you sure that this is in Thackeray's own handwriting?"
>
> "Quite certain."
>
> "You are too young to be quite certain."
>
> "I think not, sir, because I have been dealing in manuscripts since I was seventeen."
>
> "Very well. What's the price?"
>
> "One hundred pounds."
>
> "Is that 'cash'?"
>
> "No, sir. Ninety pounds cash."
>
> "Very well. My secretary will give you a check. Let me know

if you get any more really good authors' manuscripts." That was the end of the interview.

Pierpont carried this manuscript uptown to his house and showed it to his family and friends. Eventually he put it into the little room in the basement which gradually became the storage place of many of the manuscripts and books that he bought during the next eighteen years. Before the Morgan Library was built the room became so crowded that it was difficult to get into it to find anything; books, pictures, and manuscripts were piled on the floor, after every table and chair had been filled.

There we have many of the elements of the Morgan collecting pattern: a chance beginning, through a family introduction; the briefest and sharpest of interviews; no haggling; and a satisfaction in acquisition even of an object that the purchaser could seldom if ever savor fully himself. But it throws little light upon either Morgan's motive or his method. Let us return witness Satterlee to the stand, to tell about Morgan's purchase, nineteen years later, of a Spanish painting, a "Portrait of a Child," which was submitted to him, in London, as a Velasquez. Remember as you read the Satterlee account of this episode that it took place in 1907, when Morgan was almost as famous for his huge-scale collecting as he was for his financial operations and influence:

At the time this picture was shown him he told the dealer to leave it until he could study it and consider the matter. This was quite according to his custom. The dealer left it on a chair at Prince's Gate [the Morgan town house in London]. There was no documentary evidence that went with it, but it was a charming little picture, painted undoubtedly in Velasquez's time. . . . Of course, when a picture like that was left for Mr. Morgan to consider, it was not hidden. The other dealers who came saw it in turn. One of them might say, "Oh, I know where that came from. I was offered that a year ago at such-and-such a price. It is not an original." Another would remark: "That picture was sold at Christie's ten years ago, but its authenticity is in question. I hope, Mr. Morgan, that you have not bought it as an original, nor paid much for it as a picture." And so on. Mr. Morgan always listened to it all without comment. Before he made up his mind whether he wanted the picture or not he would get someone from the Berlin Museum who happened to be in London, or an expert connected with one of the great London public galleries, to stop in and look at the picture. If it was not documented and the preponderance of the best opinion was against it, he rejected it.

In the case of this picture of the Spanish child, when the dealer came back and said, "Well, Mr. Morgan, what do you think?" he answered, "You cannot prove the picture is Velasquez's, and I feel quite sure it is not."

"All right," said the dealer. "I will take it away." And he started to pick it up.

"No," said Mr. Morgan. "Leave it right where it is. No matter who painted it, I have become very fond of it and I am going to keep it."

To this anecdote, which not only illuminates Morgan's method of collecting but suggests that he may have been moved by a personal love for exquisite things, whether or not attributable to recognized masters, Satterlee adds the unconsciously devastating comment, "It might be a Velasquez after all!"—thereby apparently demolishing Morgan the amateur and substituting for him Morgan the mere speculator in attributions, or at any rate Morgan the assembler of a collection which must carry the most imposing labels. Let us go a little further, and call the most adverse witness of all.

5

Roger Fry, who in his later years became famous as a critic and connoisseur of art, served as curator of paintings and then as European adviser on paintings for the Metropolitan Museum from 1906 to 1910, when his connection with the museum was terminated. According to

Virginia Woolf's life of Fry, it was terminated only because he tried to buy for the museum a picture which Morgan—who was then president of the museum—wanted for his own personal collection; and certain it is that during the summer of 1909 something happened which deeply offended Morgan. Only a few of the directors of the museum were told of this episode—whatever it was—and they considered it discreditable to Fry. Perhaps it is true that Fry had merely tried to buy for the Metropolitan a picture that Morgan wanted for himself, but that he had gone about the negotiation in a way that —rightly or wrongly—seemed to Morgan underhanded. But at any rate Fry had long tried the patience of the officers of the museum; his connection with it had been a chapter of misunderstandings, mistakes, differences of judgment, inefficiencies, and cross-purposes.

From the outset Fry had resented Morgan's vast influence at the Metropolitan. He had described him as "the most repulsively ugly" man, "with a great strawberry nose," and had said that he "behaved like a crowned head." Fry had written home from New York, "I don't think he wants anything but flattery. He is quite indifferent as to the real value of things. All he wants experts for is to give him a sense of his own wonderful sagacity. I shall never be able to dance to that tune. . . . The man is so swollen with pride and a sense of his own power that it never occurs to him that other people have any rights." And years later Fry, writing an account of a trip which he took with Morgan in Italy in the summer of 1907, described the financier with venom.

He recounted in detail how Morgan—who at the age of seventy was accompanied on his travels by his close friend, the "stately and enameled" Mrs. Douglas, by his sister, Mrs. Burns,* and by a courier, "a lank, hungry Italian cadger"—was beset by dealers and cringing aristocrats who had things that they wanted to sell him; how the banker was rude to two Italian ladies who wanted to sell him a service of majolica; and what lavish pains were taken by all and sundry to please Morgan in the hope that some of his money might be enticed in their direction.

I was asleep at the Grand Hotel in Perugia one morning in May 1907 [wrote Fry] when a knock at the door woke me and the Cameriera entered with a card. The Count Torelli urgently requested a short interview. I sent word I would be down soon, dressed, and went into an empty room on the ground floor where the Count, young, dandified, and weakly sympathetic, greeted me with anxious effusiveness. What did he want? I knew the answer beforehand—family heirlooms to be offered to Pierpont Morgan. . . . What were they? Chinese pictures rather recently imported and an immense eighteenth-century carpet spread all over the floor. The poor count had rushed from Rome to Perugia to catch some of the golden shower and there they were displayed. Would I do what I could? The family fortunes depended on his success. He would be eternally and even perhaps practically grateful if only I would intercede successfully with il Morgan. I could hold out very little hope but said I would see what could be done.

Before I could get away from him there jumped out from a dark corner of the room a little Levantine or Maltese gibbering in broken English and broken Italian. He had in his hands a large seventeenth-century crucifix which he handed me with feverish gestures. It was not a remarkable work of art and [I] was beginning the usual process of getting out when he whipped out a stiletto from the shaft of the cross. This was the *clou* of the piece and I knew my Morgan well enough to guess how likely he was to be taken by it. "Shows what the fellows did in those days! Stick a man while he was praying! Yes, very interesting." For a crude historical imagination was the only flaw in his otherwise perfect insensibility.

* Fry says his sister-in-law, Miss Burns, but on this point I follow Satterlee.

That is a damning judgment upon Morgan the collector. Its harshness may be attributed in part to the fact that Fry's employment by the museum had been from the outset uncomfortable; to the probability that Fry, a sensitive man not immune to self-pity, hated to be under the domination of a millionaire, who knew less about Renaissance art than he did; and to the fact that anyhow the two men were utterly dissimilar in temperament. Fry was complex, articulate, humorous, fastidious, and a student of *minutiae*; Morgan by contrast was simple, a man of a few short words, lacking in humor, and impatient of fine discriminations. One may guess that when Morgan asked for advice he wanted a plain yes-or-no answer, that Fry preferred to instruct him in historical backgrounds and aesthetic values, and that the conflict between them had in it something of the perennial conflict between the executive and the intellectual. Fry's judgment upon Morgan may therefore be likened to the judgment of a cavalryman upon a thirty-ton tank. Yet Fry was a genuine connoisseur who lived for art, and such explanations by no means explain his comment wholly away.

6

Perhaps the truth about Morgan the collector embraces both the Satterlee and Fry findings and also that of Edward P. Mitchell, editor of the New York *Sun*, who found in the banker "a genuine affection and hunger for the rarest and finest and most beautiful achievements in the arts." Unquestionably Morgan had such an affection and hunger. We need not doubt that his appreciation of the "Portrait of a Child" was real. He had in him nothing of the creative artist; though as a boy he drew a few graceful pencil sketches which showed a neat sense of form, there is no record of his ever having wanted thereafter to produce art for himself. Not even into the building of his Library, the apple of his eye, did he throw the sort of intense creative zest which Isabella Stewart Gardner threw into every detail of the planning and construction of Fenway Court. Nor did he take any noticeable interest in encouraging contemporary artists. He thought of art in the past tense, not the future.

Furthermore, when he approached the art of bygone days, he did not do so as a student; he did not even read much. He approached it, rather, as a venerator of old and choice and lovely things. What turned him to collecting was a romantic reverence for the archaic, the traditional, the remote, for things whose beauty took him far away from prosaic, industrial America—the same feeling, in essence, which made him delight in the ceremonies of the Church.

Morgan was also a man who did not do things by halves. (You may remember that in his earliest days in business, when he bought coffee in New Orleans, he bought the whole shipload.) Once he became enamored of collecting, he went at it in the same overwhelming way in which he went at a business reorganization. As the *Burlington* magazine said of him after his death, "Having become the greatest financier of his age, he determined to be the greatest collector." When Morgan decided to build a yacht, he wanted it to be the biggest one. When he bred collies, he wanted them to win the best blue ribbons. He was the sort of man who, when he takes up a sport, at once dreams of becoming the champion. When he went into collecting, nothing would satisfy him but the complete conquest of the marts of beauty—annihilating competition, taking his various objectives by frontal assault.

So completely did this ambition occupy him that, as

the *Burlington* said, he "had little leisure left for contemplation"—or even, one might add, for studious personal examination of works of art. He relied rather upon the quick verdicts of experts, upon his own instinct for quality (which seems on the whole to have become in time very good), and upon a strategy of concentrated attack—buying a whole collection rather than picking and choosing among its component parts, and coming instantly to his decision, cost what it might, without wearisome bargaining. For he had begun collecting late, and he had at his disposal less of time than money.

It may be that the editorial in the *Burlington* magazine was the soundest witness as to Morgan the collector:

> . . . In the world of art quite as much as in the world of finance, Mr. Morgan was above everything a man of action. His successful raids upon the private collections of Europe were organized and carried out with the rapid decisive energy of a great general. He believed in military methods; he regarded rapidity and irrevocability of decision as more important than accuracy of judgment; he considered discipline more effective than a nice discrimination. And in spite of many instances of failure it would be rash to say that for the end he had in view his choice of means was a wrong one.

7

Morgan never made money on any such gigantic scale as did John D. Rockefeller, who during his lifetime was able to give away something like 500 million dollars without by any means dissipating the family fortune; or as did Andrew Carnegie, whose benefactions totaled some 350 millions. Even so, when Morgan died in 1913 the public—which had thought of his wealth as limitless—was somewhat surprised at the comparatively modest size of the estate he left. If one excluded his art collections, which were variously estimated to be worth from 20 to

50 millions, the amount was only a little over 68 millions —a smaller amount than was left by Frick, or Harriman, or George F. Baker, or Richard B. Mellon, to name only a few of the multimillionaires of the time, and considerably smaller than the 135 millions left by Thomas Fortune Ryan in 1928 or the 186 millions left by Payne Whitney in 1927. For Morgan not only made less money than many other multimillionaires; he spent most of what he earned. He lived on an increasingly magnificent scale; his collecting during the last fifteen years or so of his life must have cost him millions a year; and he was also a lavish giver.

The nature and manner of his giving followed a highly personal pattern. In the first place, many of his gifts went quite unpublicized. (You may recall his setting up a trust fund for Dr. Rainsford and telling him to mention it only to Mrs. Rainsford.) None of them involved naming a building for him. Morgan felt that a gentleman should not advertise his benefactions. The chief reason why it is difficult for a biographer to estimate whether the total of Morgan's gifts was nearer five millions or ten is that so many of them were made so quietly.

In the second place, most of his gifts were closely connected with his personal loyalties and affections. He felt a close link with Hartford, where he had been born and brought up, and gave over a million dollars to its museum, the Wadsworth Athenaeum. He was long a vestryman and then senior warden of St. George's Church, and Rainsford was his loved and trusted friend; hence his gifts to it of a Memorial House, a building for its Trade School, a Deaconess House, a new organ. Another close friend was Dr. James Markoe; it was Dr. Markoe who aroused his intense interest in the work of the Lying-in Hospital, to which, after several previous gifts, he presented a million dollars (later increased to a million and a quarter) for the construction of a modern hospital building. He was an energetic Episcopal layman, zealous of the dignity of the Church's establishment; hence many large gifts toward the construction of the Cathedral of St. John the Divine and its Synod House. He was the president of the Metropolitan Museum; hence not only his many gifts to it of works of art, but his contributions toward its excavations in Egypt and other enterprises, and his plan (largely carried out after his death by his son) to turn over to it the bulk of his collections. There were quantities of other gifts—to the American Museum of Natural History, of which he was for fifteen years the treasurer; to the Metropolitan Opera, of which he was a director; to the American Academy in his beloved Rome; to St. Paul's Cathedral in London, the city where his father had lived and in which he had inherited his father's house and business; to a hospital in Aix-les-Bains, a resort which he enjoyed visiting; and so forth. Not all, but most, of these involved some tribute to loyalty.

But perhaps the most striking thing about Morgan's giving was the speed with which it was consummated. Unlike other men of wealth—especially today's men of wealth—he did not ask committees of experts to study appeals made to him. He had no truck with surveys of needs. Just as he hated haggling, so he hated undue deliberation. When he saw something worth giving to, he liked to do it without delay or ceremony.

To complete our brief triangulation of Morgan's nature, let us turn to Joseph B. Gilder's account, in the *Century Magazine*, of how Morgan made one of his major gifts. The story may be exaggerated, but at least it is characteristic.

Harvard University wanted to build a new group of buildings in Boston for its Medical School. Morgan liked the idea. Harvard was a good place; his son Jack had gone there and the results had seemed satisfactory. President Eliot was an excellent man. Medicine was a good thing, and the Harvard Medical School was well spoken of. So when Morgan was approached for a gift he said he would be glad to see the plans for the new group of buildings.

According to Gilder, John D. Rockefeller had taken six months to have the school's needs investigated. Morgan, when two or three representatives of the school came to see him at 23 Wall Street, and were shown into an inside room, walked in watch in hand.

"Gentlemen," said he, "I am pressed for time and can give you but a moment. Have you any plans to show me?"

The plans were unrolled.

Said Morgan, moving his finger quickly from point to point, "I will build *that*—and *that*—and *that*. Good morning, gentlemen." And he departed, having committed himself to the construction of three buildings at a cost of over a million dollars.

Chapter Nine

BILLION-DOLLAR ADVENTURE

DURING the summer and autumn of 1897 there came a change in the economic weather. It was something like the change which comes when, after many a day of rain and wind and fitful sunshine and renewed storm, suddenly the wind veers into another quarter, the clouds begin to break and scatter, patches of deep blue sky appear, and men and women walk with a fresh briskness. For more than four years America had been beset with depression, unemployment, unrest, and uncertainty. Brief recoveries had been followed by renewed distress. Now all at once men began to look ahead with lively hope. An immense change was beginning—a change which, in the words of the sober financial chronicler Alexander Dana Noyes, transformed within half a dozen years "the crippled industrial and financial state of 1894, with the country's principal industries declining, its great corporations drifting into bankruptcy, and its government forced to borrow on usurious terms from Europe to maintain the public credit" into "a community whose prosperity had become the wonder of the outside world."

On this new tide of confidence Pierpont Morgan was to rise to the crest of his power and prestige. Up to this moment, he had been an important figure in international finance, the most powerful of all bankers in United States Government finance, the greatest railroad reorganizer in the United States, and a mighty, if not determining, influence in the management of many

American railroads. But only in a limited way had he been concerned with manufacturing. He was now about to move into a new domain.

The prospect in the fall of 1897 was heartening for business men. The sober and conservative William McKinley, having demolished William Jennings Bryan the preceding autumn in a political campaign of unprecedented bitterness, now sat in the White House, with Mark Hanna, the friend of the corporations, at his elbow to guide him. The silver heresy was no longer a menace; the government's gold reserve was once again adequate; the world supply of gold was increasing and helping to lift prices the world over; a bumper wheat crop on the Plains was bringing good prices for export because of a wheat famine in Europe, and as the revenues of railroads and manufacturing companies and all manner of other businesses began slowly to swell, confidence at last returned. Plans for new enterprises were taken off the shelf where they had lain year after year because of the uncertain prospects for trade, and men began to sense that a new era of growth and activity for American business was beginning.

By today's standards, to be sure, the prosperity of this new era was singularly restricted. At the beginning of the twentieth century, while Andrew Carnegie was enjoying a personal income of something like fifteen million dollars a year (with no income taxes to pay), the mass of unskilled workers in the North were receiving less than $460 a year in wages, and in the South the figure was even lower—less than $300. According to Robert Hunter's study of *Poverty*, published in 1904, the wages of streetcar employees ranged from $320 a year to $460; a cotton-mill proprietor in Georgia testified before the Industrial Commission that the average wage paid to his employees was $234 a year; and the average wage in the anthracite district was less than $500. And this in a period when one millionaire's domestic staff was said to be ready at an hour's notice to serve a hundred guests; when another gave a dinner at Delmonico's at which seventy-two guests sat about a huge oval table in the middle of which was a contrived pond thirty feet long with four swans swimming in it; when a third was basking in a Scotch castle with forty guest suites, eight footmen whose sole function was to serve wine, and a personal bagpiper whose assignment was to march round the castle in the morning playing to wake the guests; and when a fourth was building a vast residence which was to contain a swimming pool, a gymnasium, a billiard room with ten tables, a private chapel with a marble altar weighing ten tons, a $50,000 organ, and a refrigerator large enough to hold twenty tons of beef!

Along with these wide contrasts went a state of mind which it is difficult for us, half a century later, to grasp imaginatively. When we go back today and read the polite journals of the eighteen-nineties, we find ourselves in a world of ideas in which there was only one group of people who appeared to matter much: ladies and gentlemen and those who aspired to be ladies and gentlemen (meaning the new rich and other imitators of the ways of the cultivated Eastern urban well-to-do). These journals took scant notice of the vast middle group of the population among whom Lorimer's *Saturday Evening Post* and Bok's *Ladies' Home Journal* were presently to recruit armies of readers, and who in subsequent decades would form the backbone of the audiences for the popular movies and radio shows—the proprietors of little businesses, the more successful farmers, and those hosts of small-salaried business employees and modest professional people whose unassuming and essentially democratic customs and manners William Allen White could celebrate so well. To the polite journalists of the eighteen-nineties, such men and women were untutored and negligible—except perhaps as aspirants to the genteel life. As for "the poor," the polite journalists referred to them almost as if they were residents of a foreign land. Occasionally one finds in these journals earnest studies of the plight of the poor, or amusing or sentimental accounts of their picturesque ways; but that the poor should themselves read the polite journals, or for that matter become consumers of any of the reasonable comforts of life (except by leaping out of their class, as many of them did, to join the ranks of the prosperous) did not seem to occur to editors or writers.

In part this curiously patrician attitude was due to the reign of genteelism in literary and artistic circles. (For example, business was not considered a suitable subject for general journalistic consideration. Although it was of course the central fact of life in the United States and the favorite topic for talk when men gathered by themselves, it was thought a little vulgar for ladies and gentlemen together; they might better improve themselves by discussing literature, preferably English, or art, preferably continental. Not until about the turn of the century did McClure, by turning his muckrakers loose upon the scandals and excesses of business, and Lorimer, by chronicling its wonders, begin to satisfy the innate interest of innumerable readers in the hard facts of the business world.) But in part the attitude of the polite journalists reflected also the actual conditions of American life under which they had grown up and the prevailing attitudes of the day.

Thousands of American communities west of the Alleghenies, and more especially west of the Mississippi, were only just outgrowing the crudities and isolation of frontier times. And as for the poor, they were—aside from the Negroes—mostly immigrants from Europe, who were then pouring into the United States by the hundreds of thousands each year and overflowing from the slums of the Eastern seaboard into industrial towns the country over; they spoke foreign languages, looked rough and ignorant and dirty to people of older American stock, and seemed destined in the nature of things to sweat for low pay and live in miserable slums. (Hence, perhaps, the long-continuing condescension of native-stock Americans toward the mass of Europeans.) If today, when you drive with an elderly man past a factory, he expresses astonishment at the number of cars jammed in the parking lot, that is because he half-remembers what industrialism was like when he was a boy, and is startled to be reminded how the United States has become democratized during the past half century.

Nor was there then any widespread realization of the existence of what we today call the national economy. Not that the statistics of business were not elaborately recorded. One can look back today in the financial journals of that time and find out exactly how much money a given railroad made in a given quarter of the year and exactly what were the totals of bank clearings, exports, imports, and sales of this commodity or that over a given period. One can find elaborate discussions of the condition of this industry or that, this company or that. But one looks in vain for any adequate measurement of the prosperity of the country as a whole, or for any suggestion—except in the writings of indignant radicals —that the prosperity of the country as a whole was anything but the sum of the prosperity of the various businesses which were conducted in it. Not for many years to come would Willford I. King produce the idea that there was such a thing as the national income.

2

But as business accumulated momentum during the McKinley days, an idea precedent to the idea of the national income, and immensely significant, did seize hold of the minds of business men with a vengeance: the idea of national—and even international—markets for individual businesses or combinations of businesses.

The concept was of course not new. Before the eighteen-nineties Rockefeller, for example, had spread the operations of his Standard Oil Trust so widely as to achieve something approaching a national monopoly, and of course many manufacturers—like the Singer Sewing Machine people, let us say—had sold their goods in so many areas of the country (to say nothing of other countries) as to conceive of the United States as a single market for their wares. And Pierpont Morgan, calling together the chief railroad presidents of the country, surely had had in mind at least a vague concept of all these separate lines making together something of a national pattern. But the vast majority even of good-sized businesses were local. Most pools and combinations in industry were apparently conceived more with the idea of holding up prices between competitors in a limited area than with the idea of controlling jointly a market stretching from coast to coast. The concept of national advertising was still in its infancy. Meanwhile during the depression of the mid-nineties almost all grand schemes for new business combinations had been held in abeyance or at least slowed down; the times were not propitious. Morgan, for example, had acquired his unique influence among the railroads of the East not by launching any magnificent plan for expansion, but by acting as receiver, as it were, for distressed corporations. But now, in 1897, ambition began to see its chance to make up for lost time.

The nation was now linked by railroads from Maine to California. The frontier was closed. The pioneer days were ending. The South was at last really recovering from the ravages of the Civil War. Manufacturers were learning the techniques of mass production. (Long before Henry Ford's business began to boom, Andrew Carnegie had demonstrated the validity of the principle of huge production at low cost and small profit per unit.) And now, all at once, among shrewd and well-heeled business proprietors, the idea spread like a wild epidemic that there was a national market awaiting them if only they could expand or combine to exploit it. And the easy victory of the United States in the Spanish War in 1898 encouraged an extension of this idea: why not an international market, for that matter?

American industry was abruptly—and feverishly—coming of age.

3

Yes, but how could a business or group of businesses grow so big as to capture the whole American market? The chief obstacle was not the Sherman Anti-trust Act, for although this act, passed in 1890, forbade combinations "in restraint of trade," the government had been singularly lax about enforcing it and the Supreme Court had shown considerable uncertainty as to what constituted restraint of trade. Apparently it was all right for a group of companies to join forces and achieve a near-monopoly in a given industry (provided their methods of eliminating their competitors were sufficiently discreet) *if* they could find a legal way of joining forces. Years before, Rockefeller had combined a lot of oil companies by getting the men who held stock in these companies to turn over their shares to a group of trustees to vote as a unit; hence the term "trust." But court decisions had made it clear that trusts in this strict or Rockefeller sense would no longer be permitted. How, then, could the thing be done?

As a matter of fact the answer to this question had already been found—found, indeed, before the Sherman act was even passed. The machinery for combining businesses had already been invented by a cheerful, rosy-faced New Jersey lawyer named James B. Dill.

On being asked in 1889 by the governor of New Jersey how the state's revenues might be increased, Dill had suggested passing a New Jersey law permitting one corporation to hold the stock of another corporation—a thing previously considered grossly improper, and only rarely sanctioned by special legislation. The law was accordingly passed, and New Jersey's revenues swelled as businessmen began to discover that now the door was wide open to perfectly legal combination. Did you want to combine ten companies into one? All you had to do was to go to New Jersey, incorporate a holding company under the New Jersey laws, make a series of agreements by which this company would buy the stock of the ten companies, giving its own shares in return—and the thing was done. The ten companies had now become in effect mere subsidiaries or departments of one big boss concern—which now might be big enough to capture the whole national market.

By the time the business tide turned in 1897, Dill's

invention had become very well known. Lincoln Steffens tells in his *Autobiography* how, when he was a financial reporter in New York, he was shocked to hear that all sorts of outrageous things could be done under the shelter of the New Jersey Holding Company Act, and went to see the author of the act, James B. Dill. Somewhat to his surprise, Dill appeared to share Steffens' dismay, told him that such abuses must be exposed and stopped, and provided him with even more scandalous facts than he had already gathered. Steffens wrote a detailed story and it was published. Not until some time later, when Steffens had got to know Dill really well, did the rosy little lawyer explain to him, with vast amusement, why he had been so helpful. "You thought that the things you were describing were dreadful," said Dill in effect. "But I knew that to a lot of business men they would look mighty inviting. I was advertising my wares and the business of my state."

The possibilities of the New Jersey law were certainly wonderful. How, you may ask, could anyone persuade the owners of, say, ten businesses to sell out to a new holding company? Well, suppose each of these businesses represented an investment of one million dollars. The promoter of the new holding company would offer the owners of each of them *two* million dollars' worth of the shares of the new company; that would bring them in all right. Yes, but would these new shares actually *be worth* two million dollars? Possibly not—but to the eye of optimism the advantages of monopoly or near-monopoly, plus the gain in efficiency that should come from integrating all these concerns, plus the appeal of a big and forward-looking scheme, would be very persuasive. What the promoters of the new holding company were doing was capitalizing, at one fell swoop, the prospects for the long future. Crazy? Perhaps. But was not America coming of age, and was not the future something to conjure with? As soon as the shares of the new holding company were launched on the Stock Exchange, the public swarmed to buy them; and the man who had sold his control of the Podunk Street Railway Company to a new Consolidated Traction Company, accepting stock in the latter as his payment, found he could sell this new stock at a fat price—and would be suddenly a rich man.

Not only that, but if the promoter, merging ten companies into one, was increasing their total capitalization from ten million to twenty million, why not increase it still more, say to twenty-two million, and award the additional stock to himself for his services in bringing the boys together and organizing the syndicate that would launch the new shares on the market? The idea began to get round that there was nothing so remunerative as promoting New Jersey holding companies. You could become a promoter without even learning much about the businesses you were combining; did not the Moore brothers, within the space of a few years, organize a combination of match companies, a combination of biscuit companies, and a combination of tin-plate companies, and profit preposterously thereby? What Dill had invented might well have been described as a device for the manufacture of millionaires.

Yet it was also a device for expanding and co-ordinating the industries of America to meet the conditions of a new day. A mature and united country offered a field for business operations on a national scale. And Dill's invention made such operations abundantly possible.

4

It was in the late summer of 1897 that Pierpont Morgan got his first real glimpse of the possibilities of combination in the great steel industry.

His life that year had been full of variety. Early in January he had given a million dollars to the Lying-in-Hospital for a new building. Then he had taken a short sub-zero winter holiday at his friend W. West Durant's camp in the Adirondacks, enjoying the place so much that he bought it the following year. In March he had promised to build a new rectory for the Church of the Holy Innocents at Highland Falls, of which he was senior warden (as he was of St. George's in New York). On March 24 he had departed from Wall Street and No. 219 Madison Avenue for his annual trip abroad, sailing this time on the *Teutonic* with his daughter Louisa. While in England he had supervised the affairs of his London banking house, had prepared the way among British investors for the refunding of the New York Central mortgage debt, and had also found time to make heavy purchases of objects of art, for himself and for the Metropolitan Museum, in which he was now taking an expanding interest. And returning from Europe in June, he had divided his summer attention between financial affairs and his plans for the annual regatta of the New York Yacht Club, of which he had recently been elected commodore.

They were big plans, for the new commodore liked to do things in a spacious way. The yachts were to assemble at Glen Cove, Long Island, proceed to New London and then Newport and then Vineyard Haven, and then go on the longest jaunt in their history—a race round Cape Cod and all the way to Mt. Desert, Maine. Morgan offered gold and silver cups for the winners. And at the beginning of August he filled his 204-foot black *Corsair* to capacity with guests and set out upon the festivities of regatta week.

The Yacht Club had never had such a gala cruise. When on the afternoon of August 4, the schooners and sloops and steam yachts slipped by twos and threes into Newport Harbor past the gleaming white warships of the Atlantic squadron, there was "a constant coming and going of launches and gigs filled with gay people, sunburnt yachtsmen and pretty women, carriages and traps bringing down favored ones for dinners on the yachts, and other favored ones driven off for dinners on shore"; after dusk fell, the harbor glittered with moving lights and on the shore there was a grand show of fireworks. And when, days later, the yachts had finished their long deep-sea race at Mt. Desert Light (*Vigilant* leading, followed in turn by *Colonia, Navahoe, Emerald,* and the rest of the long procession), they sailed round the lovely island to Bar Harbor, where Commodore Morgan gave a big dinner aboard the *Corsair* in honor of the winning captains; and again the night skies were bright with fireworks—furnished, of course, by the commodore himself, who had arranged to have a bargeload of them brought from New York.

It was not long after this regatta that he was waited upon in New York by Judge Elbert H. Gary, a Middle Westerner who had himself been vacationing that summer, in a somewhat less spectacular way—taking his first trip to England and dutifully doing the cultural round there, from Bunyan's grave and Dickens' "Old Curiosity Shop" to the British Museum and the Tower of London. Gary—whom Morgan had met before—had now come to New York on behalf of John Warne Gates, a rising manufacturer of barbed wire who had already, with Gary's help, combined a number of steel and wire companies into one, and who now wanted to combine a great many more—to form an eighty-million-dollar American Steel & Wire Company.

Charles Coster had already examined the data which Gary had brought with him, and had reported that the project was worth his chief's attention. Morgan talked with Gary, was favorably impressed, and gave his provisional OK to the ambitious project; and Gary and Gates thereupon went to work trying to line up the numerous manufacturers of wire for the great merger.

Morgan was dealing now with two quite different men. Gary, born and bred in an Illinois farm town, had become a leading Chicago lawyer, had been mayor of Wheaton, Illinois, had served two terms as a county judge, and had been president of the Chicago Bar Association; recently, as legal adviser for Gates, he had become an expert matchmaker among corporations. A shrewd, diplomatic man with the ability to frame a compromise which would satisfy both parties to a deal, Gary was aptly described by Herbert N. Casson as resembling, in appearance and manner, "a Methodist bishop—benign, suave, cordial, and earnest." But there was nothing about Gary's friend Gates that remotely resembled a bishop. Gates was a plunger, a gambler, a large, genial all-night poker player, once described by his secretary as a "great boy with an extraordinary money sense annexed." He had made his start in business as a barbed-wire salesman; had gone to San Antonio, rented a tract of land there, built a corral of his barbed wire, and challenged the ranchers to find a steer that could get out of it; and had triumphantly accumulated so many orders for wire that he abandoned his employer, went to St. Louis, raised some capital, and went into the wire business himself to fill those orders. Now he had become a big shot in the wire industry and was ready to become a bigger one. They called him "Bet-a-Million" Gates; he was said to have spent a rainy afternoon on a way train betting with a companion on which of the raindrops coursing down the windowpane would reach the bottom first—at a thousand dollars a race.

All that fall and early winter the negotiations over the proposed wire combine went on, but in February Morgan would go no further. What he said was that he was disturbed by the financial showing of one of the companies that was to be included in it. But there may have been other reasons. The American battleship *Maine* had just been sunk in Havana Harbor, and there was a threat of war with Spain; perhaps that fact contributed to Morgan's uncertainty. Or the main factor may have been distaste for Gates and the "Waldorf crowd" of speculative plungers who surrounded him. At any rate, Morgan would not say yes—whereupon Gates and Gary went ahead without him. The result was the formation, first, of a small combination, and then, a few months later, of a larger one called the American Steel & Wire Company, put together without aid from 23 Wall Street.

But Morgan had had his initiation into the steel industry. And he had found Gary both able and reliable. And so, in the summer of 1898—while the brief Spanish War was being won by the United States with one hand tied behind its back—he willingly embarked with Gary upon another combination scheme: a scheme for tying together the Illinois Steel Company, and an ore company, and several other concerns, to form what was to be known as the Federal Steel Company. And when, by

September, the job was done, he called Gary to his office and said, with his customary brevity:

"Judge Gary, you have put this thing together in very good shape. We are all very well pleased. Now you must be president."

Gary was amazed. He had had no inkling of any such plan. He said he couldn't think of it.

"Why not?" said Morgan.

"Why, Mr. Morgan, I have a law practice worth $75,-000 a year and I cannot leave it."

"We'll take care of that," said Morgan. "We must make it worth your while."

"But I must think it over," said Gary desperately.

"No, we want to know right now."

"But who are the directors to be?"

"You can select the directors, name the executive committee, choose your officers, and fix your salary."

Gary begged for a week to think the matter over. Morgan gave him twenty-four hours. Gary accepted.

And so, the following month, the Chicago lawyer came East at the behest of the New York banker to become the head of what had become the second biggest steel concern in the country. He was not a steelmaster, knew little about steel manufacturing. He was there because the banker trusted him.

Now Morgan was free to proceed to Washington, where, with a number of bishops as his guests at the Arlington Hotel, he spent several weeks attending the Triennial Convention of the Episcopal Church, at which there was especially vehement debate over the question whether a bishop, under certain carefully guarded conditions, might take "under his spiritual oversight" a "congregation of Christian people not theretofore in communion with this church."

5

So contagious did the idea of combining steel companies become during the next two years that it was as if a giant magnet had moved over the surface of the industry, pulling together into compact groups the innumerable separate particles of which it had previously consisted. Morgan himself helped to bring together two more groups—the National Tube Company and the American Bridge Company. And as for the Moore brothers, they worked with such diligence as to produce the National Steel Company, the American Tin Plate Company, the American Sheet Steel Company, and the American Steel Hoop Company. Each of these constituted a merger of a number of hitherto competing businesses; and each, as it acquired a partial monopoly of the operations in its special field of steel manufacture, lifted its prices sharply. The profits accordingly rolled in. During its very first year Gary's Federal Steel Company was handsomely in the black and paid dividends on its preferred and common stock, despite its heavy capitalization; early in 1900 American Steel & Wire paid a seven per cent dividend.

Inevitably, now, a new notion popped into many minds. *Why not combine the combinations?* Why not make them into a mammoth supercorporation, the biggest and most powerful thing of its kind in the world? Since the Spanish War, America had suddenly become conscious of being at last a world power; could not such a colossus of American steel capture the market not only of its own continent but of other continents, too?

But there was one thing which stood squarely in the way of such a dream. The biggest, most efficient, and most fabulously successful unit in the industry was the

Carnegie Steel Company, the control of which was held tightly in the hands of that twinkling little genius, white-bearded Andrew Carnegie. And while the new combinations which had been put together by Gary and Gates and Morgan and the Moores concentrated almost without exception upon making finished articles—wire, pipe, rails, girders, steel plate, etc.—Carnegie dominated the making of the crude steel from which they fashioned their wares. Obviously any supercombination must include Carnegie's company, or its life would be precarious indeed. Carnegie, who was in his middle sixties, was known to be looking forward to retirement. Perhaps he would sell. The trouble was that his company had become so incredibly prosperous, as the business boom of the late nineties continued, that men gasped at the size of the sum of money which would be required to buy out the principal stockholder. It would run into hundreds of millions.

Two of Carnegie's colleagues, Henry Clay Frick and Henry Phipps, toyed with various plans for buying Carnegie out. They engaged in a flirtation with the Moore brothers in the early months of 1899, and actually induced Carnegie to give them an option on the purchase of his company on behalf of some unidentified clients. (They did not dare tell Carnegie that the Moores were in on the deal, for if he had known it he would never have consented; he disliked everything that these speculator-promoters represented.) The scheme failed because too many other people distrusted the capacity of the Moores to manage such an undertaking; they could not get substantial financial backing. Morgan was among those who were approached, and would have none of any such deal. He too would not go into partnership with the Moores. Later, in the spring of 1900, Carnegie's chief aide, the brilliant Charles M. Schwab, went to Gary to propose that Federal Steel should buy Carnegie out, and Gary consulted Morgan. "I would not think of it," said Morgan; "I don't believe I could raise the money." He was well aware that so many New Jersey holding companies had been launched during the past two or three years—not only in steel but in other industries—with lavish issues of stock, that the stock market was suffering from what he called "undigested securities." Thus the matter rested. A supercombination seemed impossible.

6

Whereupon, in the summer of 1900, there began a ferocious struggle within the steel industry. The various new combinations which made finished steel products were conscious of the need for "integrating" their businesses—for producing their own crude steel and even acquiring if necessary their own sources of iron ore, so as not to be dependent for their very existence upon the whims of Andrew Carnegie. They were so prosperous that they could save or raise money for the installation of blast furnaces or the leasing of ore fields. And so they began to make themselves ready to go into the manufacture of crude steel, in the hope of thus achieving independence. On behalf of American Steel & Wire, John W. Gates sent word to the Carnegie Company that he was canceling his contract for crude steel; in the future he would make his own. The Moore brothers sent identical notices on behalf of Steel Hoop and Sheet Steel. And word came that National Tube and American Bridge expected likewise to stop ordering from Carnegie.

Carnegie was idling that summer at Skibo Castle in Scotland, but there was nothing idle about his reaction to these rebuffs. He had noted for several weeks that the orders from some of these concerns had been dwindling, and had written to his colleagues in Pittsburgh that if the Steel Hoop people stopped ordering crude steel, the Carnegie Company should reply by going promptly into the manufacture of steel hoops. Now, when the full scope of the impending crisis became clear, he decided on a full declaration of war. The Carnegie Company would go into making finished products of all sorts.

"No use going halfway across a stream," Carnegie wrote; "should aim at finished articles only; it is coming to this in all branches." And again he cabled: ". . . Urge prompt action essential; crisis has arrived, only one policy open: start at once hoop, rod, wire, nail mills; no halfway about last two. Extend coal and coke roads, announce these; also tubes . . . have no fear as to the result; victory certain. . . ."

Schwab, who was Carnegie's right-hand man, went over to Scotland to visit him, bringing plans for a great new steel works to be constructed at Conneaut on Lake Erie. "How much cheaper, Charlie, can you make tubes than the National Company?" asked Carnegie. Schwab said he could save at least ten dollars a ton. "Go on and build the plant," ordered Carnegie, the fire of battle in his eyes.

The prospect that this decision opened up was staggering. All the steel combinations that had been effected during the past three years were in deadly peril. For Carnegie could produce steel more cheaply than anyone else on earth. He had immense resources. And he didn't mind stopping dividends entirely in order to pour the earnings of his company into new construction. If there were a lethal price war, could he not cut and cut his prices until his heavily capitalized rivals were doomed?

Morgan was uneasy; and not on the score of Carnegie's steel operations alone. For Carnegie had declared war on the Pennsylvania Railroad too. The Pennsylvania had raised Carnegie's freight rates, and now in answer to this move the little warrior was negotiating with George Gould for the building of a new railroad link to connect the Western Maryland with Pittsburgh, thus destroying the Pennsylvania's monopoly of freight traffic between Pittsburgh and the seaboard. This new threat carried Morgan's mind back to the conference on the *Corsair* fifteen years earlier, when he had negotiated peace between the New York Central and the Pennsylvania, and thus had stopped the building of the South Penn. Was that episode going to have to be repeated? "Carnegie," he was heard to say, "is going to demoralize railroads just as he has demoralized steel." Morgan tried to get Schwab to come and see him for a talk. Schwab did not come. Carnegie drove ahead with his plans. Apparently there was no stopping him.

7

But on the evening of December 12, 1900, two New Yorkers, J. Edward Simmons and Charles Stewart Smith, gave a dinner to Schwab at the University Club; Morgan accepted an invitation to attend, and was seated next to Schwab; and after dinner Schwab, who had a fine voice and was something of an orator, made an extraordinary speech on the future of the American steel industry. He told how the demand for steel was growing, and how America could dominate the steel trade of the entire world, if only the industry could be fully integrated for complete efficiency: if inadequate or badly situated plants could be abandoned, new plants could be built in the right places, every unnecessary mile of transportation could be eliminated, and every cost-cutting measure could be taken. Only a single corporation which could carry the manufacture of steel through every stage from the mining of the ore to the completion of the finished product could accomplish this, said Schwab. And so great would be the economies such a company could achieve, that it would not have to hoist prices to prosper, as had the recent combinations; it could even cut prices and still make millions.

Morgan was vastly impressed. The picture that Schwab had drawn was of an orderly and disciplined industry, at peace with itself; how much better than this crazy, wasteful warfare! And the idea was big, very big indeed. Morgan liked things big. "After the cheers had subsided"—I quote from Burton J. Hendrick's life of Carnegie—"he took Schwab by the arm and led him to a corner. For half an hour the two men engaged in intimate conversation. The banker had a hundred questions to ask, to which Schwab replied with terseness and rapidity." Then Morgan went home to No. 219, and Schwab took the night train for Pittsburgh. But in the days that followed it was clear that Morgan was thinking long and hard about Schwab's idea, and was wondering how it could be turned into a reality. He would have to negotiate with Andrew Carnegie. How could this best be done?

He sent for Bet-a-Million Gates, who even if unreliable surely knew his way round, and asked whether Gates thought there was a chance that Carnegie would sell. Gates thought he might. Morgan suggested that perhaps the first thing to do would be to talk with Frick. Gates, surprised that Morgan did not realize that Carnegie and Frick were then on bad terms, said this would never do; Schwab was the man to work through. All right, said Morgan; can you arrange this? Gates thereupon called up Schwab on the long-distance telephone and suggested that he come on to New York for a talk with Morgan.

Schwab didn't like the idea of talking with Morgan without telling Carnegie in advance; but Gates persuaded him that there would be no disloyalty to Carnegie if he, Schwab, were to happen to go to Philadelphia on a certain day and Morgan just happened to be there—say at the Hotel Bellevue. The date was accordingly set, and Schwab went to Philadelphia—only to find, instead of Morgan, a message to the effect that Morgan was laid up with a cold, and wouldn't Schwab be so good as to go on to New York and talk with Morgan that evening at No. 219? Schwab politely agreed to do so, and took the train to New York.

Whereupon there began, that very night, a momentous conference in the high-ceilinged, mahogany-paneled library at No. 219 that lasted until daylight. Four men took part in it: Morgan; his handsome and substantial partner Robert Bacon; the knowledgeable, easygoing Gates; and the young, self-made, energetic Schwab. They discussed what companies ought to be included in a merger, what companies omitted. Gates, who knew the whole map of the industry, explained why certain concerns such as Bethlehem and Cambria and Jones & Laughlin should remain independent. Gradually the picture of a new giant steel company began to take shape. Morgan asked Schwab whether he thought Carnegie would consent to sell; Schwab said he couldn't be sure, for the Scotchman was changeable, unpredictable. But Morgan had made up his mind to try. When the night-long session came to an end, Morgan asked Schwab to convey a firm proposal of purchase to Carnegie and to ask his price.

8

Schwab was a little uneasy at the prospect of confronting his chief with such a proposal, and asked Mrs. Carnegie's advice as to how to proceed. She suggested that a game of golf might put her husband in the most approachable humor; and so Schwab challenged the older man for a match the following morning at the links of the St. Andrews Golf Club in Westchester County. The two men played round the wintry links, and adjourned for lunch afterward to Carnegie's stone cottage on the hilltop above the club. There Schwab broke the news of Morgan's offer.

Now it must have occurred to the reader—it has occurred to a great many people—that possibly Carnegie had all this time been playing an elaborate game with a view to inducing just such a result as the Morgan offer: that his announced invasion of the territory of the other steel companies, and his threat to do battle with the Pennsylvania Railroad, had been conceived to this very end, and that he had concocted the idea of the Simmons-Smith dinner, and of getting Morgan to attend, and of turning loose upon him some carefully contrived oratory of the sort at which Schwab excelled. Perhaps; but there is no evidence of anything quite so Machiavellian. Like many men who one moment dream of retiring and then the next moment are filled with the lust of activity, Carnegie wanted to be bought out and yet didn't. And so when, after the round of golf at St. Andrews, Schwab finally broke the news, Carnegie at first was dismayed. But presently he realized that the time had at last come. This was it—the inevitable and desirable end of his years as a steelmaster—the moment when he could satisfy his long-standing wish to stop making money and begin making a career of giving money away.

On a slip of paper he jotted down in pencil a few figures. He gave the slip to Schwab and asked him to present it to Morgan.

What Carnegie proposed was that for every $1,000 in bonds of the Carnegie Company there should be exchanged $1,000 in securities of the new corporation which was yet to be formed; that for every $1,000 in stock of the Carnegie Company there should be given $1,500 in securities of the new corporation; but that he would take his own personal payment wholly in bonds. (Carnegie distrusted the stock of these new supercorporations; he thought there was much too much of it. And besides, if he were really to retire, it would be better not to have any responsibility for the new concern, but to be simply its creditor.) To Carnegie himself, who owned some fifty-eight per cent of Carnegie Company stock, this would mean a payment in bonds to the amount of no less than $225,639,000 (par value). For all the bonds and stocks of the Carnegie Company, it would mean a payment of bonds and stocks to the amount of $400,000,000—later increased by throwing in some extra common stock for Carnegie's partners, so that the total reached $492,556,766 (par value). A huge transaction.

Schwab took the slip of paper to Morgan. Morgan glanced at it and said, "I accept."

Not only was there no bargaining over terms, but it was not until weeks later, when Morgan was drawing contracts with the other concerns in the deal, that he suddenly woke up to the fact that he had no signed agreement from Carnegie at all—nothing but those penciled figures on a slip of paper. Suppose Carnegie should drop dead? Or utterly change his mind? Hurriedly Morgan sent for Stetson and for Carnegie's lawyer, and they prepared a suitable letter which Carnegie obligingly signed.

During this interval of time it occurred to Morgan that he and Carnegie had not met for a long time and that perhaps they should have a friendly chat. Being accustomed to meeting people on his own ground, he called up Carnegie and suggested that he come down to 23 Wall Street for a visit. Carnegie replied that since the distance from Wall Street to Fifty-first Street was no greater than the distance from Fifty-first Street to Wall Street, and since he, Carnegie, was the senior of the two, perhaps Mr. Morgan would care to call upon him. Morgan at once went, and the two men talked together in a closed room for just fifteen minutes; after which Morgan departed, saying as he shook his host's hand, "Mr. Carnegie, I want to congratulate you on being the richest man in the world!"

To this remark there is a postscript to be added. A year or two later the two men met on shipboard. Said Carnegie, "I made one mistake, Pierpont, when I sold out to you."

"What was that?" asked Morgan.

"I should have asked you a hundred million more than I did."

"Well," said Morgan, "you would have got it if you had."

9

Matters now proceeded at a rapid pace. The heads of one big company after another were called into conference and the terms worked out for its acquisition.

There were, of course, difficulties. John W. Gates proved to be one of them, though he had been present at the four-man conference at which the basic plan had been worked out. All the stockholders of the various constituent companies were going to be paid at a high rate in stock of the new company; but Gates, representing American Steel & Wire, demanded what seemed an altogether impossible sum. According to Gary's subsequent account of the negotiation, Gates held out through hour after hour of fruitless bargaining in a room at 23 Wall Street. Morgan was not present at this session, but was sitting outside, at his desk in the front office; and as the afternoon wore on, he sent word in to Gary that he wanted to go home. Gary asked him please not to, and he remained. Finally Gary slipped out of the conference, went out to Morgan, and suggested that presently he should come into the conference room and issue an ultimatum. Whereupon in due course Morgan entered the room and said sternly, "Gentlemen, I am going to leave this building in ten minutes. If by that time you have not accepted our offer, the matter will be closed. We will build our own plant." And he left the room.

Said Gates, uncertainly, to a colleague, "Well, William, I don't know whether the old man means that or not." Gary assured him that Morgan did mean it. "Then I guess we will have to give up," concluded Gates.

Morgan was sent for and was told that his proposition had been accepted. "Now let's go home," said he, and—according to Gary's description—went uptown "as happily as a boy going home from a football game."

The Rockefellers were difficult too. It had been decided that the new supercorporation should acquire also the Lake Superior Consolidated Iron Mines, which controlled the largest deposits of ore in the great Mesabi Range; this concern was owned by John D. Rockefeller. Carnegie had leased these properties from Rockefeller—but with Carnegie out of the picture, would not ownership of them be safer? Gary felt sure of this. Morgan at first was doubtful. "We have got all we can attend to," said he. Gary insisted, outlining his reasons in full, and Morgan was impressed.

"How are we going to get them?" he asked finally.

"You are to talk to Mr. Rockefeller," said Gary.

"I would not think of it," said Morgan.

"Why?"

"I don't like him."

"Mr. Morgan," argued Gary, "when a business proposition of so great importance to the Steel Corporation is involved, would you let a personal prejudice interfere with your success?"

"I don't know," said Morgan.

But the next morning—according to Gary's account—he met his right-hand man excitedly, throwing up his arms in exultation as he cried, "I have done it!"

"Done what?"

"I have seen Rockefeller."

"How did he treat you?"

"All right."

"Did you get the ore lands?"

"No. I just told him that we ought to have them, and asked him if he would not make a proposition."

Rockefeller had proved very coy. When Morgan had asked to see him, he had replied that he was quite out of business but would be glad to have a purely personal chat with Morgan at 4 West Fifty-fourth Street, his home. When Morgan got there and began to talk business, Rockefeller told him that the man to see on business matters was his son. But not long afterward the son—young John D. Rockefeller, Jr., then only twenty-seven years old—showed up at 23 Wall Street accompanied by Henry H. Rogers, one of the head men of Standard Oil.

When they came in, Morgan was deep in talk with his partner Charles Steele and seemed entirely oblivious of their arrival. When the conversation was completed and Steele left the room, Rogers introduced young Rockefeller.

Said Morgan in a stern voice, "Well—what's your price?"

Rockefeller mustered courage to say firmly, "Mr. Morgan, I think there must be some mistake. I did not come here to sell. I understood you wished to buy."

For a moment Morgan glared. Then, as usual when his brusqueness was boldly met, he thawed, and the negotiations began in a more friendly vein.

There was disagreement over the price to be paid for the mines; Frick had to be called in as intermediary; and the price which was finally set seemed to Gary beyond all reason. A few days earlier it had been Gary who had insisted on the purchase of the mines; now, when the issue had become merely one of price and not of dealing with a man he didn't like, it was Morgan who was insistent. "Judge Gary," said he, "in a business proposition as great as this would you let a matter of five million dollars stand in the way of success?" And he accepted the Rockefeller price. Clearly the amount of capital stock which the new concern would have to issue to take care of all these payments would be enormous. But he would rather drive ahead than haggle.

And so there appeared in the newspapers of March 3, 1901—less than three months after the Simmons-Smith dinner—a large advertisement announcing that under the laws of New Jersey there had been organized the United States Steel Corporation, which would acquire not only the outstanding stocks and bonds of the Carnegie Company but also the preferred and common stocks of Federal Steel, National Steel, National Tube, American Steel & Wire, American Tin Plate, American Steel Hoop, and American Sheet Steel. To these, a little later, were added the Lake Superior Consolidated Iron Mines and the American Bridge Company. This new concern would embrace under a single management and control roughly three-fifths of the steel business of the entire country; and its total capitalization would reach—at par value—the altogether astonishing, altogether unprecedented figure of $1,402,846,817—nearly a billion and a half dollars!

10

At the news there arose a great outcry of wonder and dismay—with the dismay at first predominating. Some newspaper editors expressed the fear that such concentration of power in Wall Street would lead the public to welcome socialism as the lesser of two evils. The Philadelphia *Evening Telegraph,* for instance, said that if a "grasping and unrelenting monopoly" should be the outcome of the current trend, it might provoke "one of the greatest social and political upheavals that has been witnessed in recent history." President Hadley of Yale said in a speech in Boston that unless trusts were regulated by a really effective public sentiment, there would be "an emperor in Washington within twenty-five years." The London *Chronicle* was especially sharp in its comment. "It is little less than a menace to the commerce of the civilized world," said the *Chronicle*; "it sets the seal to the triumph of the millionaire."

William Jennings Bryan's *Commoner* struck a note of unexpected humor as it commented, " 'America is good enough for me,' remarked J. Pierpont Morgan a few days ago. Whenever he doesn't like it, he can give it back to us." And as usual Finley Peter Dunne's "Mr. Dooley" put into the mouth of an Irish saloon-keeper sentiments which suggested what millions of people were vaguely feeling:

> Pierpont Morgan calls in wan iv his office boys, th' prisidint iv a national bank, an' says he, "James," he says, "take some change out iv th' damper an' r-run out an' buy Europe f'r me," he says. "I intind to re-organize it an' put it on a paying basis," he says. "Call up the Czar an' th' Pope an' th' Sultan an' th' Impror Willum, an' tell thim we won't need their savices afther nex' week," he says. "Give thim a year's salary in advance. An', James," he says, "ye betther put that r-red headed book-keeper near th' dure in charge iv th' continent. He doesn't seem to be doin' much," he says.

Assuredly the new corporation represented a very large gesture of faith. For not only did it issue its own stock on a lavish basis to the owners of the constituent companies in order to induce them to come in, but almost all of these constituent companies had already issued their own stock equally lavishly to the owners of still smaller concerns. According to the Bureau of Corporations, the Steel Corporation's investment in tangible property alone, as indicated by historical analysis, was $676 millions; the value of all property, tangible and intangible, as indicated by market prices of securities of constituent concerns, was $793 millions; and yet the total capitalization amounted to $1,402 millions. Even making due allowance for the integration, increased efficiency, and increased bargaining power which such an enormous corporation supposedly could command, how on earth could it expect to pay dividends upon such a mass of securities? And, for that matter, would the investing public be able to digest such a great issue of stock? Large numbers of the stockholders of the constituent companies, finding themselves the startled possessors of Steel Corporation stock in amounts beyond their wildest dreams, would hasten to cash in on at least part of the bonanza: could the market absorb their sales?

These latter questions were soon answered. James R. Keene was engaged by the Morgan syndicate to make a market in Steel Corporation stock; and so actively did this skilled operator keep the market churning, and so mightily did the chance to invest in the biggest company on earth appeal to buyers' imaginations, that the preferred stock, starting on the Stock Exchange at a price of 82¾, soon went to 101⅞, while the common stock, starting at 38, rose to 55—amid a burst of speculative enthusiasm which astonished the elders of Wall Street.

A great many of the chief beneficiaries of the mighty prices paid for the stock of the constituent companies were Pittsburgh steel men, and now Pittsburgh witnessed a carnival of spending such as it had never known before. According to Herbert N. Casson, one of the sudden millionaires in Pittsburgh "ordered a special brand of half-dollar cigars made in Cuba, each with his name and coat of arms on the wrapper"; another "had his wife's portrait painted by every obtainable foreign and American artist"; the city became "a Klondike for artists, book agents, curio dealers, and merchants who had expensive gewgaws for sale. A young [Carnegie] partner would say: 'See that painting? Cost me $22,000; but I could get $28,000 for it. Have a cigar. Fine brand. Seventy-five cents apiece wholesale.' "

The Morgan syndicate, for that matter, did very well indeed; here, too, Mr. Dill's device for the manufacture of millionaires worked beautifully. The syndicate had been paid for its services in launching the new combination with a big block of stock, amounting to nearly

1,300,000 shares. When this stock had been "distributed" —sold on the Exchange during the speculative excitement—the syndicate's profit, including the managers' fee, came to $57,515,000, plus some preferred stock and the right to participate in a subsequent U. S. Steel Retirement Syndicate, which increased the total to $60,000,000 or more. The House of Morgan's share in these profits—its fee for managing the syndicate—came to $11,503,000, again plus stock and participation in the new syndicate; this enabled the firm, at the close of the year 1902, to transfer to profit and loss the sum of exactly $12,000,000. It had been an enormous and highly risky operation, completed with rich success.

11

Morgan himself remained in New York for a month after the great announcement. By that time he felt assured that all was well. The reliable Gary was going to be chairman of the board of the Steel Corporation; Schwab was going to be president; Bacon, head of the finance committee. He felt he could trust them all; Gates he vetoed even for membership in the board of directors. Whatever the future might hold for the new corporation, it was off to a very favorable start. On April 4, well satisfied, he sailed for Europe on the *Teutonic,* accompanied by his sister, Mrs. Burns.

Wherever he went, now, crowds gaped at him. He slipped aboard the *Teutonic* by the second cabin gangway to outwit the reporters and photographers; when he reached Euston Station in London there was another small army of them and another great crowd of the general public. He forced his way through them, hating their curiosity and their interference with his privacy. He could not learn to stomach the staring and crowding and reportorial inquisitiveness that must now be the lot of one of the mightiest personages in the world. It was said that certain English brokers were taking out insurance policies on his life, paying premiums at the rate of £30 on the £1000 for three months to protect their American investments if he should die while overseas. And why not? Was there not much truth in what John Brisben Walker had written in the *Cosmopolitan* (which was then a magazine containing much serious political discussion) for April: that "the world, on the 3rd day of March, 1901, ceased to be ruled by . . . so-called statesmen," and that now "the world's real rulers" were "those who control the concentrated portion of the money supply"? Perhaps; but Pierpont Morgan was tired, and he wanted to settle down quietly in his great house at Prince's Gate and enjoy the beautiful things that the dealers would bring him to see.

And so he did. Within a very few days he had bought Gainsborough's famous portrait of the Duchess of Devonshire.

Chapter Ten

POMP AND CIRCUMSTANCE

IT IS doubtful if any citizen of the United States ever led—or ever will lead, for that matter—a life more regal than that of Pierpont Morgan during the early years of the twentieth century, when he was in his sixties and seventies. Not that he led all comers in wealth; for although he made, on the average, several million dollars a year, nevertheless, if it had been possible to compile each year an accurate rank-list of American incomes in order of size, probably Morgan's would usually have stood well below the top. Nor did he lead in lavishness, for there have been plenty of more extravagant spenders and certainly innumerable flashier ones; Morgan, a publicity hater, never spent for mere show. Nor was he preeminent in the world of fashion, for he went his way with contemptuous indifference to the glitter of social pretension. What set him apart from all others was a combination of large wealth, large spending, social assurance, international social experience, love of grandeur, and restrained taste.

Once in a conversation with that Prince of Wales who later became Edward VII of England, Gambetta remarked that if the French Republic were to make noblemen of successful business men, as did Britain, "the Duke of Rockfount would never rub shoulders with the Duke of Industry." The phrase is apt: Morgan was by nature a duke of industry, pursuing the life of an unostentatious gentleman on a majestic scale.

His home base during these years continued to be No.

219 Madison Avenue. It was a very ample house in which his family enjoyed the ministrations of some twelve servants (including a butler, two or three other menservants, a lady's maid, a cook, two kitchen maids, two chambermaids, a laundress, and a gardener) but it was by no means palatial. Fashionable society had for many years been gravitating farther uptown; the Murray Hill region where Morgan remained, and the house itself, represented not fashion, but rather the strict brownstone tradition of conservative Manhattan respectability. He kept accumulating property in the neighborhood: some lots on Thirty-sixth Street for houses for his children, a lot on Thirty-fifth Street for a new stable, the big brownstone Phelps Stokes house (still standing in 1948) at the corner of Madison and Thirty-seventh for a residence for his son Jack; and enough land just to the east of No. 219, on Thirty-sixth Street, for a separate lawn-surrounded building in which he could house the books and manuscripts that had long since overflowed the storage room in his basement.

Upon this Library building—definitely projected in 1900 and completed in 1906—he lavished loving pains. He chose as his architect Charles F. McKim, the leading practitioner at that time of the art of adapting classical and Renaissance designs to practical American purposes; there was no better guarantee of order, restraint, and a severe beauty quite detached from the American scene. Though brownstone was quite all right for domestic purposes, art, it was thought, deserved a more exquisite setting; and so McKim produced a one-story white marble building in early sixteenth-century Italian Renaissance style, with an arched entrance, a large central hall, a great east room lined with books to the ceiling, a small north office room, and a large west room which had the air of a gentleman's capacious and beautifully appointed living room. The white marble blocks of which the Library was built were set in place without mortar, after the ancient Greek practice, despite the extra polishing—and extra expense—which this involved. From the day the building was completed to the end of Morgan's life, he spent more and more of his time in its big west room. Its grandeur, its masculine comfort, the Florentine paintings that hung on its red walls, the statuette of Eros that stood on a pedestal by the fireplace, the other bits of choice craftsmanship that decorated it, all satisfied him completely.

There was also the Morgan country house, Cragston, at Highland Falls on the Hudson—another old-style place, in a resort progressively abandoned by fashion. Cragston embodied simplicity on an ample scale, with half a dozen or so guest rooms, small detached cottages for the staff, cattle barns, a dairy, and kennels for fifty or more of Morgan's prize collies, which monotonously carried off blue ribbons at the dog shows. Here Mrs. Morgan spent most of the time between April and mid-autumn, and here Pierpont Morgan came when the opportunity offered, which in his later years was not very often, so very widely did his activities range.

For winter holidays he had also a thousand-acre place in the Adirondacks, Camp Uncas; for less spartan intervals in the cold months, a furnished apartment in the building called "Sans Souci" at the Jekyll Island Club, on a piny island on the Georgia coast; and, for stopovers when his yacht was in Narragansett Bay waters, a small "fishing box" at Newport, with an expert cook in readiness to satisfy the palates of his guests. (He seldom if ever fished there; a picture of him, in yachting costume, sitting beside a string of remarkably large bass was staged as a joke by his friend Charles Lanier; the fish had been caught by others.)

In London his headquarters was the big double house at Prince's Gate which had formerly been his father's town residence. This, too, was unpretentious in aspect; but very few unpretentious houses contain paintings by Rubens, Rembrandt, Hobbema, Velasquez, Gainsborough, Reynolds, Constable, Turner, and other artists of wide renown, or for that matter contain a special room designed to display a series of Fragonard panels. And outside London there was Dover House, a comfortable country seat so satisfactorily equipped with gardens, orchards, and a dairy farm that when Morgan ended his English visit in 1902 his special railway carriage, attached to the boat train for Southampton, was piled high at one end—according to Herbert Satterlee's account—with "the boxes from Dover House that contained melons, hot-house grapes, peaches, nectarines, and bottles of cream sufficient for the voyage," these supplementary provisions being taken along because, in Satterlee's matter-of-fact words, "the menu of even the best transatlantic liner was much more simple then than it is today."

In Paris, Rome, and watering places such as his favorite Aix-les-Bains, Morgan needed no private property, for he always had his pick of accommodations; in the Hotel Bristol at Paris and in the Grand Hotel at Rome there were special suites set aside for his use whenever he came.

2

But the finest of his residences was none of these which I have mentioned, but the *Corsair*. Not *Corsair II* now, for that vessel had been sold to the government for use in the Spanish War, where it saw service as the *Gloucester* (and was hit in the mast by a Spanish shell), but *Corsair III,* which was completed at the end of 1898 to take her place. The new vessel was very large: 302 feet long, as against 204 for *Corsair II* and 165 for *Corsair I.* There have been larger private pleasure craft, but not many of them, and none of such regal dimensions are produced today; the Fleischmann diesel yacht pictured in *Life* in 1947 as the "first big luxury vessel since the war" was a mere 168-footer.

When Morgan decided to build *Corsair III,* he specified to his friend Beavor Webb, who took charge of her construction, that she must be much larger than *Corsair II* but that her interior fittings must be identical. (Thus was conservatism combined with a love for bigness.) His insistence on close resemblance to *Corsair II* raised a number of difficult problems. It was found, for example, that the kind of carpets that had been bought for *Corsair II* were no longer made. But that did not bother Morgan; he ordered the old patterns set up on the looms and new carpets especially made for him with exactly the old design.

The graceful black steamer served many uses. She could ferry him up the Hudson to Cragston. When he was working in Wall Street during the summer months, he could dine and sleep and breakfast aboard her between week ends. A launch would meet him and his friends at the dock at West Thirty-fifth Street and take them across the river to where the *Corsair* lay at anchor off the Jersey shore; in the morning they would return, after a monumental breakfast at which astonished guests would watch Morgan work his way through a menu of fruit, porridge, eggs, hash, fried fish, and sliced tomatoes. Or the party would board the *Corsair* at the East Twenty-third Street landing of the New York Yacht Club, and she would take them through Hell Gate to an anchorage off Great Neck in Long Island Sound; in warm weather this was pleasantly cooler than the Hudson, and in the evening the *Corsair* might steam slowly up and down the Sound, while the company sat in wicker chairs on the deck and conversed, Morgan perhaps dozing off as they did so, his cigar between his fingers.

The *Corsair* also could be packed with guests for a cruise of the New York Yacht Club, of which Morgan was commodore in 1897-99, and for whose new clubhouse in West Forty-fourth Street he had donated the land; and it was from her deck, in 1901 (the year when he formed the Steel Corporation), that Morgan watched the first of the races for the America's Cup between Sir Thomas Lipton's *Shamrock II* and the American defender, the *Columbia*. Morgan had a special concern over this contest because he himself had headed the syndicate which had built the *Columbia* and thus the lovely racing yacht was virtually his personal property. But he couldn't see the later races because he had to take a special trainload of bishops and other guests to the San Francisco Convention of the Episcopal Church—a convention during which his attention was from time to time divided between the ecclesiastical debates and a series of telegrams recording the leg-by-leg progress of *Shamrock II* and *Columbia* as they raced off Sandy Hook, with *Columbia* winning.

Morgan could also use the *Corsair* from time to time as a conveyance and a haven on his travels abroad, for she was seaworthy enough to cross the ocean, albeit uncomfortably, and thus could serve him as a floating residence in the quiet waters of the Mediterranean. And if he himself never ventured to make the crossing in her, that mattered hardly more than the fact that she could not ascend the Nile. In the last years of his life he engaged Thomas Cook and Sons to build for him a private all-steel Nile steamer, the *Khargeh,* with paddle wheels; and as for his voyages across the Atlantic, in a sense he had his own ships for those too. For did he not nearly always travel by the ships of the White Star Line, and was not the White Star Line a part of the great ship combination, the International Mercantile Marine, which he himself organized in 1902? And was he not therefore treated on board the *Oceanic* or the *Germanic* almost exactly as if he were the owner of the line and of all the ships that carried her flag? (It was said, for example, that before the ill-fated *Titanic* had even been built, he had been shown the plans and had picked out which was to be his suite aboard her.)

As one of these White Star liners, bringing Pierpont Morgan home from Europe, approached New York, the *Corsair* would steam down the bay to meet her, festive with pennants from stem to stern, while Morgan responded to her salute by leaning over the rail and swinging a handkerchief from side to side; then after the liner had been warped into her dock, the yacht would take him on up the river to Cragston. What grander welcome could there be to one's native shores?

There was one occasion when it was not Pierpont but Mrs. Morgan who was arriving, and he not only went out in the *Corsair* to meet her liner, but climbed into a launch as the liner paused at Quarantine, and then—as soon as the health officer had gone down the liner's side by rope ladder—swung his launch alongside the great ship, grabbed the ladder, and climbed up the full sixty perpendicular feet to the liner's deck—a cigar in his mouth and a straw hat on his head. At this time he was sixty-two years old and entirely unaccustomed to exercise, and the long climb was difficult for him. "The time was long enough," says Satterlee, "for the sporting element on the decks of the *Oceanic* to make bets as to whether he would ever reach the rail. If he should fail, there was very little chance of doing anything for him in that tideway. When his face, dripping with perspiration, appeared over the rail, and he got where he could throw his leg over it, he waved aside all the outstretched hands and asked, 'Where is Mrs. Morgan?' and without pausing followed the steward down to her cabin."

A frequently quoted remark of Morgan's about the proprietorship of a great pleasure vessel like the *Corsair* deserves repetition here despite its familiarity. Some successful man who was thinking of buying a steam yacht asked him about the cost of maintaining it. Said Morgan, shortly: "Anybody who even has to think about the cost had better not get one."

When traveling within the United States, Morgan customarily used a private car. He did not own one; he would simply use one of those owned by one of the railroads in which he was influential. And on occasion he used a special train, as when he took the large party of bishops and laymen and other guests to the San Francisco Episcopal Convention in 1901, putting them up for the duration of the convention at the large Crocker residence, to which he had sent in advance Louis Sherry and a catering staff; and afterward conveying them home by a roundabout route which included a stop at Seattle, where Morgan took his guests to a fur store and invited them to pick out fur rugs or fur collars or gloves as keepsakes from him. On another occasion, some years later, he was in a hurry to get back from a business trip to Chicago and made the trip home by New York Central special train with the track cleared ahead; time from Chicago to New York, sixteen hours and three-quarters, which in 1908 was pretty sensational.

The wife of a Morgan partner said, much later, that her most vivid recollection of a trip she made on a Morgan private car was of the entranced expression on the porter's face when the banker tipped him with a hundred-dollar bill.

3

Morgan once remarked that he could do a year's work in nine months; but not in a year; and after he reached the age of sixty he was usually absent from the office routine for some three or four months of each twelve. Usually he would leave New York for England in March or thereabouts, and from then until June or July would divide his time between London—where he kept in touch with the office of J. S. Morgan & Co.—and the Continent. Wherever he was, whether at Prince's Gate or Dover House, or at the Bristol in Paris, or at Aix-les-Bains, or at the Grand Hotel in Rome, or journeying about to inspect works of art, or taking a look at the excavations conducted in Egypt by the Metropolitan Museum, he was in touch with his office by coded cable; either he would be accompanied by a secretary with a code book, or he would rely upon J. S. Morgan & Co. or Morgan, Harjes & Co. to decode the messages that came from New York, usually several a week. A message might say, for example, something like, "We have concluded a Burlington bond issue on such-and-such terms and unless we hear from you to the contrary will proceed," and he would cable his assent. But on these holidays he liked to throw off responsibility, leaving the conduct of affairs wholly to his associates; it was seldom that his return message counseled caution or delay. Part of the time in London he might be busy with banking consultations, but much the largest part of his time was given to the art dealers who day after day besieged Prince's Gate or his suite at the Bristol, bringing paintings or porcelains or miniatures or rare books or manuscripts for his inspection. After his return to New York there might be a few other interruptions of the working routine—a voyage up the coast in the *Corsair*, a Yacht Club cruise, a church convention trip, or during the winter a few days in the Adirondacks or at Jekyll Island.

So accustomed was he to vacationing on this generous scale that it was not always easy for him to understand that such a life was not possible for a great many people. When one of his young partners-to-be, preparing to enter the firm, said he would like to be able to manage his work so as to get three months off each year, Morgan was all affability: "Why certainly. Of course. Let's see: you're coming in January first—why don't you pick up your family on February first and take them up the Nile? Have you ever been up the Nile?" The young man demurred. He and his wife had young children. He doubted if this would be possible. (Privately, of course, he was meanwhile wondering what sort of impression it would make in the Street if he went off on a long holiday at the end of his first month at the Corner.) But Morgan made light of his doubts. "Nonsense. Take a couple of nurses. Take a doctor if you want to." It was all very simple to him and he was cordial and enthusiastic, planning a trip which—as the young partner later said—"of course never came off."

4

Morgan was very loyal to family ties and family rituals —the Sunday-evening hymn singing (at which he loved to hear, and sometimes to sing in a voice of uncertain pitch, old favorites such as "Blest Be the Tie That Binds," "The Church's One Foundation," "Rock of Ages," or "Jesus, Lover of My Soul"); the family Thanksgiving dinner (with four kinds of pie); the Christmas festivities (a tree for the grandchildren, an expedition in a cab to leave presents at friends' houses, and a big Christmas dinner with the choir of St. George's Church to sing for the company, with the famous Negro baritone Harry Burleigh as soloist). When he was at breakfast at No. 219, he liked to have one of his daughters, usually Louisa Satterlee, with him, because Mrs. Morgan had her coffee upstairs; and nothing pleased him more than to have one or two small grandchildren playing about in the dining room. With Mrs. Morgan he was always affectionate and deferential. But she was seldom with him on the *Corsair* or on the European trips of his later years; when she traveled abroad, she went separately. Being shy, domestic by taste, and in increasingly uncertain health, she became increasingly settled in the habit of remaining behind at No. 219 and at Cragston while he with his overpowering energy and hunger for human society roamed widely.

Usually on his voyages abroad it was a daughter who accompanied him—again most likely Louisa; and since he loved to have many people about him and had at his disposal big houses, a very big yacht, and almost unlimited means, he was accompanied wherever he went by considerable parties of friends. Once he remarked that no man who did not number among his close associates several men who would be willing to spend much time with him, ought to consider having a yacht: otherwise he would find it the loneliest place in the world. The frequent presence of attractive women in the party on his trips abroad or on the *Corsair* caused systematic gossip, especially as he liked nothing better than to escort one of them to the jewelers' shops in the Rue de la Paix and ask her to choose what she liked. Exactly how much fire there was behind the smoke of continuous rumor is a matter of conjecture; without doubt there was some. But as I have already remarked in a preceding chapter, it must be remembered that in a puritanical society rumor always puts the most extreme construction upon any companionship that looks at all unorthodox, especially if a man of note is involved.

Naturally, too, Morgan's lamentable nose was attributed by some people to high living. As a matter of fact, he drank very moderately: ordinarily nothing before dinnertime (it was before the era of the inevitable cocktail); some wine at dinner and perhaps a cordial afterward; nothing in the evening. He smoked perpetually; or rather, there was usually a cigar between his lips or between his fingers from breakfast until bedtime, though it was often unlighted for considerable intervals. He breakfasted hugely, but lunched lightly; in the office he would have a chicken or turkey sandwich and perhaps a slice of pie set out for him in the back room, where he ate it alone; or perhaps, in summer, nothing but a plate of sliced peaches which he would bury in sugar. No coffee, no milk; just a glass of water. In his last years, when he came to the office only briefly, he would sometimes arrive about half-past twelve and join the partners for lunch in the building; on one or more such occasions, a partner recalls his choosing a somewhat startling, if small, repast—a dozen raw oysters and a slice of mince pie.

But if his lunch was usually light, he enjoyed dining largely and well; and dining largely and well, during the first decade of the twentieth century, was among people of means a formidable thing indeed. Those were the days of multicourse dinners—six or eight or ten courses. Morgan belonged to a small dining group who called themselves the Zodiac Club; they met from time to time at the house of one or another of the members, or at a club, and vied with one another in offering sumptuous meals. Here is the menu of one Zodiac dinner, given at the University Club; Satterlee, from whose book I quote it, swears that it was devised to be eaten right through from start to finish, though he imagines that most members preferred to let one or more of the dishes pass untasted:

Amontillado Sherry
Cotuit oysters
Bisque of crabs à la Norfolk
Consommé de volaille Sévigné
Hors-d'oeuvres variés
Rhine Wine, 1893
Soft clams à l'ancienne
Château-Latour, 1878
Saddle and rack of spring lamb
Mint sauce
Peas à la Française
Bermuda potatoes rissolées
Moët & Chandon, 1893
Terrapin, Maryland Club
Grapefruit au Kirsch
Clos-Vougeot, 1893
Canvasback ducks
Fried hominy
Celery à l'université
Parfait noisettes
Cheese
Fruit
Coffee
Cognac, 1805

5

Whatever Morgan did, he did in a big way, whether it was organizing a party or buying masterpieces. When Herbert Satterlee and Morgan's daughter Louisa were about to be married in 1900, their first idea was that they would prefer a modest service in the little church at Highland Falls, followed by a reception at Cragston. But Morgan took over the planning, and the result was that the ceremony was held at St. George's in New York, with cards of admission because the church would hold only fifteen hundred people; for the reception, Morgan had a large ballroom temporarily erected behind No. 219 to hold the twenty-four hundred guests who came. As for his purchases of art, they were made on such a scale that an annual worry at 23 Wall Street at the year end, when the books of the firm were balanced, was whether Morgan's personal balance in New York would be large enough to meet the debit balances accumulated through the year as a result of his habit of paying for works of art with checks drawn on the London or the Paris firm.

There is a story—probably apocryphal but nevertheless suggestive of Morgan's purchasing methods—to the effect that once two men who owned a steel mill decided, as they approached Morgan's office, that they would be willing to take five million dollars for it but might as well begin by asking for ten; whereupon Morgan said to them abruptly as they entered, "Now, I don't want to hear any talk from you men; I know all about your plant and what it's worth; I haven't time for any haggling; I'm going to give you twenty million dollars—now take it or leave it." Often art dealers got much more money from him than they had dreamed of getting. On more than one occasion, finding that some object of art that appealed to him was part of a large and varied collection, he said to himself, "What's the use of bothering about one little piece when I might get them all?" and promptly made a large offer for the whole collection. Nor did he like to waste time. Once he was just getting into his automobile to take the steamer for Europe when a dealer came along and told him that such-and-such a collection was for sale. It was a collection which Morgan knew all about. "Very well," said he, "if you are authorized to negotiate for it, you may buy it for me"—and drove off without another word.

The Rigbys, in their entertaining book on collectors and collecting, produce two other equally characteristic anecdotes. One is to the effect that George S. Hellman once brought Morgan a Vermeer to look at, and found to his surprise that "the great Dutchman's name was strange to the Morgan ear." Thereupon Hellman delivered a brief lecture on Vermeer, his place in the history of art, and the value set upon his work in recent sales.

"Morgan gazed at the picture; abruptly asked the price.

" 'One hundred thousand dollars,' said the dealer.

" 'I'll take it,' snapped Morgan, and the deal was concluded."

The Rigbys' other story is to the effect that after Morgan had bought the famous Garland Collection of Chinese porcelain, he remarked to Duveen, the dealer who had acted for him, "I understand that Mr. Garland did not complete the collection." That was true, said Duveen. "Then," said Morgan, "I shall be glad if you will complete it for me"—an instruction which, in view of the expense of Chinese porcelains, was enough to take a dealer's breath away.

He showered the Metropolitan Museum with gifts in

great variety; in 1906, for example, when he bought the great Hoentschel collection of eighteenth-century French decorative art and also of Gothic decorative art, he gave the eighteenth-century part of it to the museum outright, and announced that he would deposit the entire Gothic part of it on loan. He filled his new Library with beautiful things, he filled Prince's Gate, he loaned treasures in quantity to this museum and that, yet still the works of art piled up in storage—and he could not stop, had no idea of stopping. Edward P. Mitchell, editor of the New York *Sun*, sketched him briefly as he sat in the West Room of his Library about 1910, an old man, yet still burning with the collector's fever:

> The lesser monarchs of finance, of insurance, of transportation, of individual enterprise, each in his domain as haughty as Lucifer, were glad to stand in the corridor waiting their turns like applicants for minor clerkships in the ante-room of an important official, while he sat at his desk in his library room within, looking through a pile of newly bound volumes which the binder had sent for his inspection, giving a three-seconds glance at some treasure of printed or manuscript literature which was to go instanter to the shelf or safe in that incomparable storehouse, probably never to be seen again by the eyes then contemplating the acquisition.

Mitchell ended his description with the comment, "It was *his* possession now and Mr. Morgan was pleased." That was true; but that, I think, was not all. He was engaged in assembling a big thing—as big in its way as the Steel Corporation—every bit of which was to him beautiful; and he must make it bigger still, the very biggest aggregation of lovely things that there was or ever could be.

6

After breakfast at No. 219, and perhaps a business conference or two or a call from an art dealer, Pierpont Morgan would proceed downtown in a horse-drawn box cab which he hired from the New York Cab Company; or, in his very latest years, in a large automobile. Arriving at the Drexel Building—which occupied the site of the present Morgan headquarters at Broad and Wall—he would establish himself at a corner desk on the Broad Street side of the ground-floor banking rooms; there was a glassed-in place behind him which was occupied by secretaries. He dressed severely in a dark suit, with a wing collar and an Ascot tie which filled almost completely the V of shirt front at the neck; he had a taste for fancy waistcoats, which people liked to give him for Christmas, but those were for the *Corsair* or for traveling; he wore to the office an old-fashioned square-topped derby hat, or in summer a wide-brimmed Panama. At intervals he would retire from his desk in the front office to a back room which was in the adjoining Mills Building; he had another desk in this room, and his partner Charles Steele had one, and there was a pleasant open fire; here he could work more comfortably and quietly, out of sight of people who came to ask for him. There was, of course, a stream of these, some of whom had no idea of being granted an audience but came in merely in order to be seen going in and out of the building; there was even one occasion on which a broker carefully dropped on the steps of 23 Wall Street an unsigned buying order for securities, in the hope that passers-by might pick it up and the report might go about that the great House of Morgan was interested in the stock.

At some time between twelve and three o'clock, "the Senior," as they called him in the office, would make a tour to look at the books. First to the stock desk, then to the security department, then to the general books, beginning with the cash position and going on to the ledgers which showed the balances of all depositors. It was a nervous moment for the clerks, for his searchlight gaze seemed to be able to take in a whole page of figures in an instant and catch any irregularity; if a clerk had put down a 4 per cent bond as 4½ his eye would pick up the error without fail. His manner was ordinarily quiet and kindly, but if he found something that he disapproved of, he would shout out something like "Who gave that order, Kinnicut?" in a loud deep voice—and if he caught a mistake that he attributed to sheer carelessness he would thunder. He often took his sandwich lunch in the back room as late as two or even three o'clock; by four or thereabouts the box cab would be waiting outside the door—often to remain there hopefully for an hour or two; finally he would be through for the day and would be off in the cab, to proceed to his beloved Library or to drop off at a friend's house for a call on the way home.

7

That his mien could be frightening—as Steffens has so well made clear—is undeniable. When people first met him the one thing they saw was his nose; trying not to look at it, they met his blazing eyes, and were speechless. One woman who came to know him very well said that for the first few weeks of her acquaintance with him she was terrified; only gradually did she come to realize that behind his alarming front were courtesy and kindness. Edward Steichen, who took the great photograph of him which appears as the frontispiece of this book, says that meeting his gaze was a little like confronting the headlights of an express train bearing down on one. If one could step off the track, they were merely awe inspiring; if one could not, they were terrifying.

His gestures were abrupt. In the office he would snatch up a piece of paper as if pouncing on it with a claw; he would glance at it and either lay it down or crumple it up so suddenly that one who did not know him would have thought him angry. Yet to people who did not catch him off guard, or who did not seem to him to be trying to take advantage of him, he was truly courteous; it is characteristic that while almost everybody who has written about him has applied to him the word "brusque," people who worked with him daily emphasize the graciousness of his manners and say that everybody in the Morgan organization worshiped him.

He was given to sudden acts of good will. There was, for example, the time when a reception was being held at the Metropolitan Museum, with ladies and gentlemen in evening dress filing up in a long line to meet the president of the museum. In the line was a young woman in plain attire with a baby in her arms; and some of those about Morgan, overtaken by the contemptible sense of the proprieties which afflicts small-minded people, wondered whether she should not be asked to step out of line. Not so Morgan; he greeted her affably and then, as she went on, whispered to Robert W. De Forest, who stood beside him: "Quick—get that baby's name, so that I can make it a life fellow of the museum."

"That will cost you a thousand dollars," said De Forest.

"So much the better," said Morgan. Nor did he forget. The woman proved to be the wife of a new museum attendant; at the next meeting of the museum board, her baby was formally elected a life fellow, and Morgan footed the bill.

There are many other stories of friendly acts: of his lending a million dollars to a wealthy friend who had had great losses during the grim days of 1893, and, when the friend asked what collateral he would want, saying, "You may need your collateral with the banks—I am lending you the money on your business record and on what I know your character to be"; of his getting word of the business failure of a man who had been a companion of his earliest years in New York, and at once writing to him, "Why didn't you let me know?"; of his taking great pains to concoct a job for an elderly lady which would give her a sense that she was earning her way.

In his life of Henry P. Davison, Thomas W. Lamont tells of an incident that happened on the very first day when he reported for work as a partner—January 2, 1911. The Carnegie Trust Company in New York was in trouble, and by a process of contagion, runs had started on two other small banks in poor neighborhoods in uptown Manhattan. Representatives of these two banks came to see Lamont and another Morgan partner, William H. Porter, to see if the House of Morgan could be persuaded to stand behind the banks in their emergency. An examination of the last balance sheets of the banks indicated that this would be risky, and the young partners were inclined to say no; but Porter called up Morgan, who was at his Library, to get his advice. Whereupon—according to Lamont—Morgan, learning that the two banks had some thirty thousand depositors and that they were mostly poor Eastsiders, said, somewhat to Porter's amazement: "Well, some way *must* be found to help those poor people. We mustn't let them lose all they have in the world. Suppose that, at worst, we were to guarantee the payment of these deposits in full. You say the total is only six million dollars? That means that the firm can't lose more than six million dollars, doesn't it?" The firm thereupon backed the two banks, and—partly because of the fact that its great prestige restored confidence in them—escaped with a limited loss which according to Lamont amounted in the end to about $190,000.

That anecdote has always roused in me considerable skepticism. I have found it hard to believe that in the banking world anybody would think or talk in those terms; and I still think that in reporting the dialogue Lamont sentimentalized the language used. Yet whatever words Morgan actually chose, the incident did happen. And it was characteristic. No competition was involved. Nobody could be trying to get the better of Morgan. And under such circumstances he could astonish people with his openhandedness.

8

He could also surprise them by his readiness to pay heavy tribute to the principle of fiduciary responsibility. There was one year in which the House of Morgan ran at a loss; the reason was that in 1905 Morgan had purchased, as agent for the Erie Railroad without commission, a controlling interest in a small railroad line known as the Cincinnati, Hamilton & Dayton, and then had discovered—after he had turned over the stock to the Erie—that the figures which had been shown him, and on the basis of which he had made the purchase, did not show the true financial condition of the line, which was actually in very bad straits. As one partner later said, "It was incredible to him that anyone would show him false figures." Thereupon he at once bought back the line from the Erie at the same price that the Erie had paid for it—about twelve million dollars—and put it into receivership, at what proved to be a virtually total loss to J. P. Morgan & Co.—a loss of so many million dollars that it translated a year of lucrative business into a year of deficit. Morgan would not let it be said that his firm did not stand back of whatever responsibilities it had undertaken on behalf of other institutions, even if its only fault was that it had allowed itself to be deceived.

He had a way of saying to partners entering his firm that he wanted its business done "up here" (raising his hand high in air) "not down there" (dropping his hand near the floor). It was as if an old king were instructing his young princes in the moral responsibilities attending the royal function. For kingly Morgan was—in the range of his possessions, in the splendor of his journeyings, in the bigness of his plans, in the weight of his presence. And kingly he was too in his limitations. His royal manner of living and of traveling insulated him from the great mass of men and women; and though he might by an impulsive act of kindness make connection with them, most of the time they were to him creatures apart. Legislation designed to give them a greater share in the fruits of the national economy seemed to him unsound—an affront to the thrift and sagacity upon which national prosperity must be founded. He believed it was the lot of such improvident or inexpert or unlucky people to go their way unaided except by private charity—charity to which he would be one of the first to contribute.

When Morgan thought of industry, he thought of it not in terms of the thousands of workers whose sweat made its production possible, nor even in terms of the engineering advances which contributed to its efficiency, so much as of the investors whose money supported it, and of the officers and directors whose duty it was to protect and enrich the investors. For these officers and directors his standards were both stern and aristocratic: they had better be honest, and it was preferable that they be gentlemen. He would have liked to see the United States run by gentlemen. That these gentlemen, too, might be insulated from their fellow men, and might like to run things in whatever way proved most comfortable for themselves, and might have swollen ideas of their proper share of the fruits of industry, did not apparently occur to him; if you had suggested such an idea to him he would probably have replied promptly that certainly the politicians liked to run things to *their* own advantage. In short, though he was unswervingly loyal to the United States and believed in its government, his ideas were kingly, like his conduct of life; the idea of democracy evaded him.

In a society sufficiently equalitarian to hate to see great luxury existing side by side with great poverty, such a way of life as Morgan's is out of place. Even in his own lifetime it was out of place. But after his special kingly fashion, he played his part in the grand manner.

Chapter Eleven

THE LIMITS OF TRIUMPH

TRIUMPH invites challenge; and Pierpont Morgan's pre-eminence, heightened by his success in launching the biggest corporation the world had ever known, was to be put to a series of tests. The first challenge arrived promptly—and inopportunely.

It was on March 3, 1901, that the newspapers carried the first announcement of the formation of the Steel Corporation. On April 4, convinced that the corporation was off to a promising start, Morgan had sailed for Europe, going first to London, then to Paris, and then to Aix-les-Bains in the hills of southeastern France. It was on Saturday, May 4, that his holiday ease was broken by the arrival from New York of a cablegram of disquieting import.

The message told of a swift surprise attack upon him in a sector where he had felt secure. Morgan the peacemaker, who had come to believe that the only way to maintain peace among the American railroads was to see that they were held in "safe hands," had almost lost control of the Northern Pacific Railroad in a raid without warning by a man whom he considered unsafe.

The raider was Edward H. Harriman, a shrewd little man with sharp bespectacled eyes and a drooping mustache, a stockbroker turned railroad manager. Harriman had crossed swords with Morgan in earlier years; back in 1887, as I have already recounted in Chapter Six, he had taken control of the Dubuque & Sioux City Railroad in Iowa by a trick that Morgan regarded as crafty. Some years later, when Jacob Schiff of the New York banking firm of Kuhn, Loeb & Company had been trying to reorganize the Union Pacific Railroad, and had found that somebody—he didn't know who—was trying to upset his reorganization plan, Schiff had suspected Morgan and had called him up. Morgan had replied that he himself was not interested in the Union Pacific, but that he knew who was throwing the monkey wrenches into Schiff's plans. "It's that little fellow Harriman," said Morgan. "You want to look out for him." Schiff had thereupon conferred with Harriman, and had made with him a treaty of peace by which Harriman would have a part in the new Union Pacific management. So well did Harriman play his cards and so able did he prove himself at practical railroad management that presently he was not only running the whole Union Pacific Railroad, with Schiff as his firm backer and ally, but was brilliantly transforming a run-down property into an efficient, up-to-date, and highly profitable one. The little man with the spectacles was a genius, equally adept at rebuilding a railroad across the Rocky Mountains and at conducting a foray on the New York Stock Exchange. He was also a man of Napoleonic ambition, ready to challenge Morgan's pervasive influence. His moment for attack came in the spring of 1901.

To understand what happened you must realize that Harriman's Union Pacific reached no farther east than Omaha, and had no access to Chicago. And also that the rival Northern Pacific, which was controlled by Morgan and James J. Hill, reached no farther east than St. Paul and Duluth, and likewise had no access to Chicago. The managements of both the Union Pacific and the Northern Pacific cast longing eyes upon a third road which not only had access to Chicago—and to St. Louis as well—

but also was the most important road in the Iowa region; this was the Chicago, Burlington & Quincy, known for short sometimes as the C.B. & Q. and sometimes as the Burlington. Both the Union Pacific and the Northern Pacific wanted to buy control of the Burlington for the sake of the useful connections it would give them. And in March 1901 the Morgan-Hill group, representing the Northern Pacific, got it—purchased a large majority of the Burlington stock and thus achieved what looked like a secure grasp. Apparently Harriman had lost his chance for the Burlington.

But Harriman would not accept defeat. What he thereupon did, with the aid of ample credit from Schiff and other bankers, was astonishing. He tried to buy, not the Burlington, but the *Northern Pacific itself,* his rivals' own line, right out of their grip.

Morgan and Hill and their friends owned considerably less than half of the stock of the Northern Pacific. In ordinary cases such a minority holding was sufficient to guarantee control of a large corporation. But in this case it gave Harriman his opportunity. Acting through Schiff, he began to buy Northern Pacific stock heavily right on the open market, through the Stock Exchange. The moment was auspicious for such a maneuver, for the launching of the Steel Corporation had set off a furious stock-market boom, speculative pools were active, and stocks were gyrating; Harriman rightly reasoned that if his heavy purchases caused the price of Northern Pacific to rise, people would simply assume that speculators were responsible. Harriman bought and bought and bought. The price of Northern Pacific climbed. Yet for many days nobody seemed to realize what was happening.

At the end of April old James J. Hill, who was out in

Seattle, decided that the rise in Northern Pacific shares must be investigated, and set out for New York by special train. On Friday, May 3, he arrived in New York, went to see Schiff, and learned to his amazement that Harriman and Schiff had already succeeded—or almost succeeded—in buying control of the road. He at once reported the situation to Morgan's partners, who were thunderstruck.

In Morgan's absence, Robert Bacon was in charge at 23 Wall Street. (Coster, the great authority on railroad finances, had died a few months earlier.) Bacon and his colleagues had been caught sound asleep at the switch. They were aware that the Harriman group were buying, and thought this was being done with a view to gaining representation on the Northern Pacific board of directors, but they had no idea of the scale of the operation. It seemed incredible, but it was true.

As a matter of fact, Harriman had not yet quite succeeded in getting a sure majority. In the Northern Pacific, both the common and the preferred stock had the right to vote. Of a total of 750,000 shares of preferred, Harriman had got hold of 420,000—well over half. But of the 800,000 shares of common, he had thus far acquired only a little over 370,000—not quite half. Of the two classes of stock combined, that gave him a little over fifty per cent —790,000 out of 1,550,000. But in a pinch the common stock might be more valuable, since the preferred was subject to retirement; and of the common he still lacked a majority, though he was mighty close to achieving it.

The shocked Morgan partners conferred—and Bacon sent off a cable to his senior partner in Europe asking for authority to buy 150,000 shares of Northern Pacific common.

2

Of Morgan's reaction when he received the news at the Grand Hotel in Aix-les-Bains there is no record, but it must have been blazing. He cabled the authority to buy. As he later testified, "When I heard that, I felt in this position. We had reorganized the Northern Pacific. We had placed all the securities of the Northern Pacific. . . . I feel bound in all honor when I reorganize a property, and am morally responsible for its management, to protect it, and I generally do protect it; so I made up my mind that it would be desirable to buy 150,000 shares of stock, which we proceeded to do, and with that I knew we had a majority of the common stock, and I knew that actually gave us control, and they couldn't take the minority and have it sacrificed to Union Pacific interests."

But it was only by what looked like an accident, and may have been one, that the Morgan purchases—which did not begin until Monday—prevented a Harriman victory. For on Saturday morning, probably at just about the moment when Morgan was getting the news from New York, Harriman decided to buy 40,000 additional shares of Northern Pacific common to make his own position unassailable. He called up Schiff's office and put in the buying order. It couldn't be executed because Schiff, a devout Jew, was at the synagogue.

Was it simply devoutness that took Schiff there, or had he decided that enough was enough, and that further purchases might cause trouble? If so, he was quite right. For when, on Monday, May 6, the Morgan buying orders poured into the market through broker after broker, they caused something that a man as knowledgeable as Morgan must have foreseen if he had not been three thousand miles away. They caused a panic.

For what Harriman and Morgan had succeeded in doing, between them, was to buy more Northern Pacific common shares than there were in the market. (Remember that there were 800,000 in existence, of which many thousand must have been in the hands of people remote from the news of Wall Street. Harriman held over 370,-000; Morgan's order would bring the number that he and Hill and their friends held to some 410,000. That would make the total of shares going into the strongboxes of the two groups at least 780,000, leaving very few of the 800,000 for anybody else.) What happened, of course, was that the Morgan brokers were buying, in part, stock that didn't exist. Traders who saw the price of Northern Pacific rising beyond all reason, and who had no idea of what was happening, were selling the stock short—selling stock that they didn't own, in the hope of buying it later at a lower price to make delivery. And having sold this nonexistent stock, they were finding to their dismay that there was little stock to borrow and almost none to buy.

On Monday the Morgan brokers in New York bought no less than 127,500 shares of Northern Pacific, and the price climbed from 114 to 127½. On Tuesday they continued buying, and it touched 149¾. On Wednesday they had stopped buying, but it reached 180. And on Thursday, May 9, it leaped wildly all the way to 1,000—while the price of all other stocks cascaded furiously downhill, as brokers who realized that their inability to deliver the Northern Pacific shares that they had sold might make them liable for terrific sums of money sold everything they could lay their hands on to escape bankruptcy.

3

The Northern Pacific panic was brief. For that very Thursday the Morgan and Harriman forces made an agreement by which the short-sellers were saved from destruction. And presently they made a treaty of peace. They agreed that Morgan, who now held a clear majority of Northern Pacific common, would name the new board of directors and give Harriman some places on it; that they would consider setting up a new concern—a New Jersey holding company—to hold securely the shares of both the Northern Pacific and Hill's Great Northern (with of course indirect control of the Burlington); and that in this new concern, which would be called the Northern Securities Company, Harriman as well as Morgan would have representation. Thus at last "community of interest" would be achieved. The Northern Pacific battle was over.

Morgan had repelled Harriman's challenge. He did not have to return at once to the United States. He remained for several days at Aix-les-Bains, where the Grand Hotel looked out upon a pleasant little park, and the sulphur baths were soothing to the skin, and the views across the Lac du Bourget were enchanting, and his company of friends was congenial; then he returned to Paris, where the art dealers set siege to the Hotel Bristol, and to London, where with a deputation from the New York Chamber of Commerce he went out to Windsor Castle in silk hat and frock coat to pay respects to the new King Edward VII, and then—in due course—to New York, where the *Corsair* steamed out to meet his liner with all her pennants flying. He had won at least a partial victory, and new and impressive projects occupied his mind. But his prestige had suffered a heavy blow.

For not only had his organization been caught napping, not only had his position of supremacy in American railroading been rudely challenged by a rising power, but his headlong reaction to Harriman's attack had been a financial barrage so destructive to innumerable bystanders as to outrage public opinion. Is this, people asked, the way in which the monarchs of American finance preserve order and peace in the business community?

The setback was sharp. And presently Morgan would have to face other challenges still more severe, and of another sort entirely.

4

"On the afternoon of September 14 [1901]," writes Herbert Satterlee, "Mr. Morgan had just finished his day's work and was getting ready to go down to Great Neck. I was going with him on his yacht. He had put on his hat and we were both just starting to the front door of the office, when half a dozen newspapermen rushed in. The first one cried out, 'Mr. Morgan, President McKinley is dead.' He turned and went back to his closed desk, took off his hat, and sat down heavily as if he were very tired.

"The newspapermen gathered around, and nothing was said for a full minute. Finally the spokesman of the group said, 'Mr. Morgan, what have you got to say about the news I gave you?'

"Again there was a long pause. Then Mr. Morgan got up and, looking at the reporters, said, 'It is the saddest news I ever heard. I can't talk about it.'

"Putting on his hat, he went out, drove in silence up to the yacht landing, and hardly spoke during the run down to Great Neck. Once down there, with the [Satterlee] baby in his arms, he brightened up, and during the evening he talked a great deal about President McKinley's fine character and ability, and how really fond of him he had grown, and what a great loss the country had suffered."

The loss was more than personal. For the death of McKinley at the hand of the assassin Czolgosz, and the arrival in the White House of Vice-President Theodore Roosevelt, might mean the end of an era.

Behind the amiable McKinley had stood the forthright Mark Hanna of Ohio, chief of the bosses of the Republican party, who believed that whatever was good for the big corporations of the country was good for the country; with the unpredictable Roosevelt in power, who could tell what might happen to Hanna's influence and policies? Hanna himself, when he received the same news that had just reached Morgan, exclaimed to his friend Kohlsaat, "And now look—that damned cowboy is President of the United States!"

Morgan had felt he could rely on Hanna. He had met him in 1896, before McKinley's election; had had him out on the *Corsair* for dinner, and as the two men sat smoking on the yacht's afterdeck, looking over the waters of the North River to the lights of Manhattan, Morgan had argued to him that at all costs the Republican party must back the gold standard. It had done so, and had won; and from that time forward Morgan had felt that the government in Washington was as sound as any government made up of politicians could be. But this young Roosevelt was an upsetter of applecarts. As governor of New York he had on occasion brashly resisted the advice of boss Tom Platt, who knew what was sound for business. Platt had thereupon helped to get him kicked upstairs into the Vice-Presidency of the United States—with unforeseen results. Could one be sure that he would be any more amenable to Mark Hanna's counsel than to Platt's? Roosevelt came of a fine old New York family; in Morgan's view, he ought to be aware of what sort of people were best fitted to run things in the United States. During his

Vice-Presidency he had been sufficiently conscious of the value of maintaining friendly relations with men of substance to give a dinner for Morgan, and in fact had written to Secretary of War Root that this dinner represented "an effort on my part to become a conservative man in touch with the influential classes." But Roosevelt was headstrong and sometimes said wild things. Could one be sure that he would not become the instrument of some of the popular discontent that was so strangely rising even when prosperity was high and wide?

That discontent was rising was quite true. Partly it was a delayed reaction from the suffering caused by the depression of the mid-nineties—following the rule that it is not when men are terrified by adversity that they listen to radical ideas, but when their confidence has returned and yet the memory of adversity is still strong in them. Partly it was due to the fact that a group of journalists—the "muckrakers," as Roosevelt was later to call them—were beginning to report, in lurid detail, facts about business excesses and political corruption of which the public had previously been only vaguely aware. Partly it was a natural consequence of the sudden spectacle of unbridled wealth which had attended the big holding-company promotions of the late nineties—men making millions at a stroke when the average American wage earner's family was struggling along on less than a thousand dollars a year. Partly it was due to the fact that many of these promotions of what were loosely called "trusts" unquestionably brought about monopoly—followed by rising prices—and to the average American, monopoly and "the trusts" had long been fighting words. And finally the discontent had been sharpened by the spectacular news of the formation of a "trust" of unprecedented size—the Steel Corporation—and by the coming of the Northern Pacific panic as the result of a battle between two giants of finance.

In that very summer of 1901 a steel strike had been called—to which the board of directors of the new Steel Corporation had replied with a resolution "that we are unalterably opposed to any extension of union labor and advise subsidiary companies to take a firm position when these questions come up, and say that they are not going to recognize it." The strike was broken, but many people who then learned for the first time about the twelve-hour day in the steel industry sympathized with the strikers. Many more were to sympathize with the anthracite miners when they struck in 1902. Newspaper cartoonists—especially those who worked for Pulitzer and Hearst—had long been fanning the popular feeling; sometimes, in their caricatures, the big man with the dollar mark on his waistcoat who represented the "money power," or the "trusts," or the "interests," looked like Mark Hanna; sometimes he bore an unmistakable resemblance to Pierpont Morgan. The reform spirit which was rising, and would continue in strength for well over a decade, was essentially a rebellion of the American conscience against gross inequality, corruption, and greed. And inevitably, after the manner of such rebellions, it lumped together as ogres all the men who seemed to it to typify the power which it distrusted.

Up to now this rebellion had lacked an effective leader or mouthpiece. During Theodore Roosevelt's seven and a half years in the White House he was destined to be only intermittently and uncertainly its leader, for after every sally against big business he would go back to touch base with the conservative leadership of the Republican party. But he became and remained its most enthusiastic mouthpiece. And sometimes he not only talked but acted with decision, as Pierpont Morgan was soon to note.

At first, however, Roosevelt was very cautious. His first message to Congress, written and revised after consultation with many notables of the party, succeeded in facing both ways simultaneously on the issue of business combination. As Finley Peter Dunne described it in the person of "Mr. Dooley," " 'Th' trusts,' says he, 'are heejous monsthers built up by th' inlightened intherprise iv th' men that have done so much to advance progress in our beloved counthry,' he says. 'On wan hand I wud stamp thim undher fut; on th' other hand not so fast.' "

But only a few weeks later the blow fell.

5

One evening in February 1902, Morgan was at dinner at No. 219 when he was called to the telephone by a newspaper friend who told him that the Attorney General of the United States was about to prosecute the Northern Securities Company for breach of the Sherman Anti-trust Act of 1890. The Northern Securities Company, you will recall, was the holding concern which Morgan had just set up in order to settle in an orderly way the Northern Pacific dispute with Harriman, and to prevent any further stock-market raids upon the northwestern railroad properties.

When the news of the government's action came out the next day, the financial world was aghast, and there was frightened selling on the Stock Exchange. So seldom had any corporation been prosecuted under the Sherman Act that it had come to be regarded almost as a dead letter; and anyhow the best lawyers—following the decisions of the United States Supreme Court—had long since made up their minds that a combination brought about through a holding company was immune. Such holding companies were innumerable; did this mean that they were *all* to be in danger of attack from Washington? Morgan's own reaction, when he got the news that February evening, has been well described by Mark Sullivan:

> Morgan turned from the telephone to his associates at the dinner table, his countenance showing appalled dismay, but little anger. In telling the news to his guests he dwelt on what he felt was the unfairness of Roosevelt's action. Roosevelt, he said, ought to have told him, ought to have given him a chance to make over the Northern Securities Company, if necessary, so as to conform to whatever Roosevelt thought was right. Or, if the company must be dissolved, Roosevelt ought to have given him an opportunity to dissolve it voluntarily. . . . He had regarded Roosevelt as a gentleman. . . .

Morgan went to Washington and had an interview with Roosevelt, in the presence of Attorney General Knox, who had brought the government's suit. He protested that Roosevelt might have shown him the courtesy of advance warning.

"That is just what we did not want to do," said the President.

"If we have done anything wrong," persisted Morgan, "send your man to my man and they can fix it up." (He meant the Attorney General and one of his own lawyers, presumably Stetson.)

"That can't be done," said Roosevelt. To which Knox added, "We don't want to fix it up, we want to stop it."

Morgan wanted to know whether the President was going to attack any of his other interests, such as the Steel Corporation. "Certainly not," answered Roosevelt, "unless we find out that in any case they have done something that we regard as wrong."

Morgan left, so angry that according to one of his lawyers he later sat down at his hotel and wrote to Roosevelt a long and irate letter, which he was with difficulty persuaded not to send.

After Morgan's departure from the White House, President Roosevelt said to Knox, "That is a most illuminating illustration of the Wall Street point of view. Mr. Morgan could not help regarding me as a big rival operator, who either intended to ruin all his interests or else could be induced to come to an agreement to ruin none."

That was almost, but not, I think, quite true. Morgan was angry that he who had once before visited the White House to help another President preserve the country from what he regarded as dishonor—he who was convinced that the Northern Securities Company was the straightforward and constructive and aboveboard answer to the problem of bringing about community of interest among the railroads—should be attacked as if he were some sort of a crook. And also he thought Roosevelt was behaving as no gentleman would behave. If a gentleman thought a friend of his—a man for whom he had once given a dinner—was doing something out of bounds, he told him so, and gave him a chance to adjust his course. Only if the man continued wilfully to offend did he go to law. The curse of politics, in Morgan's view, was that it glorified behavior which no gentleman would countenance. Things were coming to a sad pass when politicians could upset the enterprises of men of honor, and win public applause by so doing.

Most lawyers felt the government's case against the Northern Securities Company was doomed to defeat. But they were wrong. A change was taking place in the climate of opinion, and it reached even the judiciary. Not until March 14, 1904—two years later—did the Supreme Court say the final word on Northern Securities; then, reversing its former position on holding companies, it voted, five to four (with Chief Justice Fuller and Justices White, Peckham, and Holmes dissenting) that the company was illegal: that in the words of Justice John M. Harlan, "No scheme or device . . . could more effectively and certainly suppress free competition."

6

But before that decision had been handed down Morgan had been thrust into another dispute in which the President and public opinion were factors to be reckoned with. This was the anthracite coal strike of 1902—a rebellion of the miners, under their idolized leader, the eloquent and persuasive John Mitchell, against the virtually feudal conditions of work imposed by the mine operators headed by George F. Baer, who as president of the Reading Railroad was subject—in certain financial matters at least—to Morgan's authority.

During that year Pierpont Morgan had been spending an exceptionally long time overseas. In the spring, in London, he had completed the arrangements for combining the White Star, American, Red Star, Leyland, Atlantic Transport, and Dominion lines into a new big shipping combine which was to be called the International Mercantile Marine. This was a project in which he took delight. It would mitigate, he thought, the mutually damaging competition between transatlantic steamship lines, providing a more orderly and convenient and profitable way of distributing international traffic. It would associate Englishmen and Americans harmoniously, under American leadership, in a sort of enterprise for which, as an annual transatlantic traveler, he had a sentimental regard. It was big, too, very big; the combined fleet numbered over 120 steamships. And if the investing public would buy the new shares of International Mercantile

Marine at solid prices, the profit to his firm would run high into the millions.

Many Englishmen were disturbed at the news that so large a shipping combination would be under the aegis of an American; was Britain to be no longer mistress of the seas? Questions were asked in the House of Commons, to which Prime Minister Balfour replied that Mr. Morgan did not intend to injure British shipping and would meet the British on any point where their shipping interests were likely to be imperiled. But the uneasiness remained in a good many British minds, and it was accentuated by the further fact that Morgan had taken half of a British government loan of thirty-two million pounds for the account of his own firm, the Rothschilds, and the Barings, and that he was trying (unsuccessfully, as it turned out) to develop a plan for the financing of the London underground railway system. Peddlers on the London streets were selling for a penny a "license to stay on the Earth," signed by "J. Pierpont Morgan."

But Morgan didn't mind much; he was having a gay time in England, giving large dinner parties at Prince's Gate and Dover House and making lavish purchases of works of art; and soon he was off on a real holiday round—a voyage on the *Corsair* from the Riviera to Venice and back to Brindisi; another voyage to Kiel, where Kaiser Wilhelm of Germany came aboard for luncheon; an expedition to Berlin in the private railway car used by members of the Imperial family, with Albert Ballin, the German shipping magnate, as the Morgan party's host; and finally, attendance at the coronation of King Edward VII in Westminster Abbey. It was not until late in August that he returned to the United States, to find the coal-strike problem awaiting him.

Ever since May the anthracite miners had been out on

strike. They would not return unless the coal operators would negotiate with their union, the United Mine Workers, which represented both anthracite and bituminous miners. The operators were adamant; they would talk with their own men, they said, but not with the union; their position was set forth—and unintentionally caricatured—in the famous reply of George F. Baer of the Reading Railroad to a letter from one Mr. Clark of Wilkes-Barre, to whom, with magnificent ineptitude, he wrote: "... I beg of you not to be discouraged. The rights and interests of the laboring man will be protected and cared for—not by the labor agitators, but by the Christian men to whom God in His infinite wisdom has given the control of the property interests of the country. . . ." The strike went on and on. Morgan, on his grand tour of Europe, had been kept informed of events, but had refused to do anything, feeling that labor relations lay outside the range of his authority or influence over the Reading and the other railroads which controlled most of the anthracite mines; and after his return to New York he still saw no chance for active intervention. The acute shortage of coal for consumers troubled him, and he contributed twenty thousand dollars toward the maintenance by Nathan Straus of a coal depot on Grand Street, in New York's East Side, where poor people could buy coal at low cost. But he felt that he could not lay down the law to Baer and the other operators.

By the first of October matters had reached such a pass that President Roosevelt intervened. (It is interesting today to note that to the editors of many conservative newspapers his intervention seemed outrageous interference—what business of the President's was a labor dispute?—and that Roosevelt himself was acutely conscious that he was without authority to act.) He called

John Mitchell and the chief operators to the temporary White House on Lafayette Place (the Executive Mansion was being repaired). Mitchell promptly agreed to accept the findings of an arbitration commission appointed by the President, whatever these might be; Baer and the other operators not only refused, but insolently told the President that "the duty of the hour is not to waste time negotiating with the fomenters of this anarchy" and asked if the operators were being expected to "deal with a set of outlaws." Roosevelt's effort had failed.

It was at this juncture that Elihu Root, the Secretary of War, had a brainstorm. He thought he could see a formula for bridging the gap, and he also thought he knew who would make the operators see reason. With Roosevelt's enthusiastic approval he got in touch with Morgan, and at the latter's invitation he went to New York by train, clattered in a cab to the landing at West Thirty-fifth Street, and was taken by launch to the *Corsair*, lying at anchor in the North River. There he talked for hours with Morgan. Once again the yacht was the scene of a peace conference.

Under Morgan's eye Root wrote out, on a piece of note paper bearing the legend "On board the *Corsair*," a brief memorandum to be adopted by the mine owners for settlement. Then he and Morgan went ashore and drove by cab to the Union Club, where some of the operators had gathered at Morgan's request. Morgan got out and went into the club; Root went on to take a train back to Washington.

The essence of the memorandum was that the operators would not negotiate with the union but would submit to impartial adjudication. At the session in the Union Club, and in a meeting the next day with Baer, who came on to New York from Philadelphia, Morgan secured acceptance of the memorandum with a few changes. After much conferring and long-distance telephoning, Morgan boarded a special train late on Tuesday, October 14, and rushed to Washington, accompanied by his partner, Bacon, who had been a classmate of Roosevelt's at Harvard. They went to the Arlington Hotel, where they were joined by Secretary Root; then the three men proceeded to the temporary White House in Lafayette Place. They brought a specific proposal for settlement of the strike.

It was a strange experience for Morgan. Only a few months before he had faced Roosevelt as a man accused of the offense of setting up machinery to bring peace among warring railroad companies; this time he faced him as an ally in setting up machinery to bring peace between railroad companies and organized labor.

7

The specific proposal, signed by Baer and the other operators, was for arbitration of the strike by a commission to be appointed by the President, this commission to consist of an engineer officer of the Army or Navy, an expert mining engineer, one of the federal judges in eastern Pennsylvania, "a man who by active participation in mining and selling coal is familiar with the physical and commercial features of the business," and finally "a man of prominence eminent as a sociologist."

Roosevelt was delighted. Morgan had certainly brought the operators a long way from their previously haughty position. He submitted the proposal to the miners, who accepted it, but made the natural suggestion that the commission should include a representative of organized labor, and further that, since most of the miners were Catholics, the presence of a Catholic bishop on the commission would tend to win their approval of its findings.

On the evening of the following day, Morgan having returned to New York, Bacon and his partner George W. Perkins (another friend of Roosevelt's), sat for hours at a telephone in the temporary White House, trying to win the operators' consent to these revisions, which Roosevelt thought should be granted. No luck—the operators would not accept a board on which sat a representative of organized labor. It was late at night before Roosevelt suddenly discovered that they were quite willing to accept, as a member of the board, the Grand Chief of the Order of Railway Conductors, *provided he was labeled "a man of prominence eminent as a sociologist."* With that ludicrous face-saving arrangement made, the operators said yes—and the strike was settled.

To all of this a footnote should be added. When Morgan was accused in the press of having intervened simply because he had a personal financial interest in stopping the coal strike, John Mitchell came to his defense in an interview in which he was quoted as saying:

> To my personal knowledge Mr. Morgan had been trying to settle the coal strike ever since he came back from Europe two months ago. If others had been as fair and reasonable as Mr. Morgan was, this strike would have been settled a long time ago. I know nothing about Mr. Morgan's financial interests compelling him to seek settlement of the strike, but I am informed that he keenly felt his responsibility to the public in connection with the fuel famine, and has done his best to bring about the end. Both Mr. Morgan and Mr. Cassatt of the Pennsylvania Railroad were working for a settlement when President Roosevelt made his last and successful move. Mr. Morgan could not very well have been forced to do something which he had been trying to achieve for several weeks. I make this statement in justice to Mr. Morgan. We have no quarrel with him and wish none; we do not fear him, but prefer his friendship if he is willing to give it to us. I am credibly informed that he is friendly to organized labor. As an organizer of capital he concedes the

right of labor to organize also and when labor organizations are fair and conservative he believes in dealing directly with them for the advantage of both employers and employees. It is this relationship which the United Mine Workers of America seek in the anthracite field, and we invite Mr. Morgan to co-operate with us in securing a permanent and scientific solution of the labor problem in this region.

In the latter part of Mitchell's statement there may have been a certain amount of wishful thinking combined with diplomatic suasion. The issue was one with which Morgan seldom had to deal, and certainly many of the corporations in which he had influence—such as the Steel Corporation—were hostile to the last degree. But at any rate he had shown himself, in this bitter coal controversy, far more conciliatory than the stiff-necked operators.

8

From this time on there was a sort of armed truce between President Roosevelt and Morgan. To the Republican campaign fund of 1904, when Roosevelt was up for election, Morgan and his partners contributed $100,000, and toward the New York State campaign fund in that same year an additional, last-minute $50,000 (given at Harriman's special request); but although, as the campaign approached, Roosevelt had prudently become more discreet in his references to business, it may be guessed that Morgan made these contributions less out of enthusiasm for the President than out of a sense that a Republican Administration was best for business even if led by a man of unfortunate tendencies. And years later, testifying before the Clapp Committee investigating campaign expenditures, Roosevelt asserted that he had not known of the Morgan contributions at the time, and had been surprised to hear of them later. "I knew that Mr. Morgan had felt very much aggrieved over the bringing of the Northern Securities suit, and I understood, though I cannot say that I knew it—I understood that he had expressed himself in very strong terms over the action which I took during the anthracite coal strike; and I had not known—I had supposed he was hostile to me—I had not known that he had contributed to my campaign fund."

During 1905 and 1906 Roosevelt, safely secured in the White House by a landslide victory at the polls, resumed his forays against business excesses. He fought energetically, and successfully, for the passage of the Hepburn Bill, which would widen the powers of the Interstate Commerce Commission over the railroads and give it authority to fix maximum rates; and in the course of this battle he said a great many severe things about big business men. And when, on January 27, 1907, Roosevelt and his arch-enemy Senator Foraker both spoke at a Gridiron Club dinner in Washington, and Roosevelt in the course of a bitter attack upon Foraker again denounced the forces of wealth, some reporters thought that as he did so he looked directly at Morgan, who was present at the dinner, sitting next to H. H. Rogers of Standard Oil. But Morgan's friends later insisted that Roosevelt could have had no such intention; that if he was looking at anybody, he was looking at Rogers; and that anyhow the President was too nearsighted to distinguish faces at such a distance. Only six weeks later the banker visited the White House to urge Roosevelt to receive a committee of railroad presidents, and the meeting of the two men was apparently amiable. And the following autumn, at the climax of the Panic of 1907, Roosevelt (as we shall see) accepted the implicit advice of Morgan's emissaries in approving the purchase of the Tennessee Coal & Iron Company by the Steel Corporation. There was never an open break between the two men. Nevertheless the relations between them were not easy.

For although Roosevelt was held in leash by the necessity of holding together the conservative Republican party with its superconservative financial backers, the truth was that when he spoke—or more rarely acted—to keep the growth of the power of big business within bounds, he represented a very large body of increasingly influential American opinion. And the further truth was that Morgan was building up a sphere of influence, financial and industrial, so very much more formidable than that of any other individual or group in the business world, that no one could speak of keeping the power of big business within bounds without thinking of him. The two men had become symbols—Roosevelt, of the authority of the government; Morgan, of the authority of private business. Roosevelt had dared to challenge Morgan's authority, and henceforth Morgan must never forget that what had happened once could happen again.

9

Another set of difficulties confronted Morgan in these years of his mature power—economic difficulties. He faced the limitations of the methods with which he had chosen to reorganize the railroads and amalgamate industrial corporations.

When Morgan reorganized a railroad, as we have seen, he had to make his plan palatable to the creditors and stockholders of the road while reducing its fixed debt. This meant issuing stock lavishly. When he pulled together a group of corporations to make a supercorporation like United States Steel, again he had to make the arrangement palatable to the owners of the constituent companies. And this too meant issuing stock lavishly.

The result was that, in terms of stock, both the reorganized railroads and the newly organized supercorporations were overcapitalized; such quantities of shares in them had been issued that only if these concerns achieved high success could they pay adequate dividends. And sometimes they could not achieve it.

In the case of the Steel Corporation, the results were good—but only after some periods of anxiety. During the "rich men's panic" of 1903—a time when there were so many "undigested securities" on the market that all values fell on the exchanges—dividends on the common stock had to be interrupted and their price fell all the way to 8¾. How Morgan felt when this happened he hinted long afterward, at the Pujo inquiry of 1912, when Samuel Untermyer asked him whether, when he launched the Steel Corporation in 1901 and made J. P. Morgan & Co. its depository, he had thought this would be a good stroke of business. Morgan answered that at that time he had not known whether it was going to be good business or not.

"It proved pretty good?" asked Untermyer.

"It did," replied Morgan; "very good indeed, sir."

"You did not think you were taking many chances on its being good business when you took it up, then?" pursued Untermyer.

"No," said Morgan, "but I began to have doubts when the stock went to eight dollars a share afterwards."

"Your doubt did not interfere with your buying heavily?"

"No; I bought all I could. . . ."

"You were getting the advantage of other people's doubts at that time?"

"Nobody ever sold it at my suggestion, sir."

"No; I did not mean to assume that," said Untermyer,

realizing that he had touched Morgan's sense of fiduciary responsibility.

"I know," said Morgan.

"My question does not imply that," said Untermyer in further reassurance.

"I know," said Morgan again.

"It only implies your confidence in the company at that time."

"I always had it, sir."

Slowly the Steel Corporation pulled out of the doldrums; for not only had the amalgamation permitted some economies in production, but also the steel industry was still young enough to be capable of great growth. When the International Harvester Company of New Jersey was incorporated under the Morgan aegis in 1902—pulling together the McCormick Harvesting Machine Co., the Deering Co., and three other rival concerns, and thus assembling into one enterprise some eighty per cent of the harvester trade—it was a full success, acquiring as it did a partial monopoly of a young and lusty industry. But the International Mercantile Marine, that combination of shipping companies, British and American, for which Morgan had cherished such high hopes when he brought it together in that same year 1902, proved a grievous disappointment. There was such a dismally small public demand for its securities that in 1906, after the life of the stock-distributing syndicate had been twice extended, the Morgan firm had to report to the syndicate participants that "the prices at which the Company's securities ruled in the market have been so low that we have not felt justified in attempting to dispose of those held for the account of the Syndicate"; the participants had to pay up their subscriptions in full and receive in return I.M.M. bonds and stock of limited value. And the company itself, beset by tribulations such as the *Titanic* tragedy, did not prosper.

10

But the most dismaying of Morgan's ventures, in its results, was his attempt to expand the New York, New Haven & Hartford Railroad into a great integrated New England system. How sadly this plan of his was destined to miscarry he did not live to know; only after his death did the drama reach its climax.

Morgan had a sentiment for the New Haven road, as an old Hartford boy whose grandfather had invested in one of the little lines out of which it was pieced together. When in 1892 he became a member of its board of directors, he began to try to build it into a real system; and when President McLeod of the Reading invaded its territory in 1893 he fought back lethally, as we have seen. A decade later, in 1903, President Charles S. Mellen of the Northern Pacific was induced to take over the management of the New Haven, and with Morgan's active and continuing encouragement Mellen embarked upon a still more ambitious—and costly—plan of expansion.

Some steamship lines which plied on Long Island Sound, carrying passengers and freight from New York to Fall River and other points, appeared to menace the New Haven Shore Line by offering low rates which undercut those of the railroad. Very well, those steamship lines must be bought by the New Haven or put out of business. Another menace was the rapid growth of interurban trolley lines, which were then the very latest thing in transportation; people—and goods too—could travel imposing distances by transferring from one to another of these careening, cross-country electric car lines. Very well, the New Haven must buy up all the competing trolley lines. There were other railroads in New England which, if acquired by the New Haven, might extend it into a great all-New England system. Very well, the New Haven must buy control of the Boston & Maine and bring other lines into alliance. Some New York men had acquired franchises for two little lines which it was thought might carry commuters from the New York suburbs as far as the Bronx terminal of the New York subway, thus competing with the New Haven's suburban service. Very well, these projects must be bought up and the New Haven must build such a suburban line of its own.

For every one of these ventures a persuasive argument could be advanced. But together they cost so much money as to strain the resources of the New Haven very severely. Too many men had decided that when Morgan set his heart on a project his men would pay through the nose for something he wanted; too many men got the bright idea that in the complicated purchase deals which were put through they could grab some boodle for their own pockets. As Morgan confidently moved issue after issue of stocks and bonds to pay for the expansion, the total capitalization of the railroad climbed from 93 millions in the middle of 1903 all the way to 417 millions in the middle of 1913. Such aggressive purchasing in New England by the "foreigners" of the New Haven management provoked legal and political opposition, led by the Boston lawyer Louis D. Brandeis, and this both delayed the fruition of the plans and weakened public confidence in the New Haven. Brandeis contended that it was trying to bite off more than it could chew, and he was right. Disaster followed in due course. In 1913, shortly after Morgan's death, affairs had come to such a pass that Mellen was forced out of the presidency of the road by Morgan's own firm; presently the New Haven passed its dividend; it never recovered its former standing. But that was not all. In two investigations the Interstate Commerce Commission disclosed gross scandals in the management of the line.

The investigations—like many others conducted by government commissions or congressional committees to this day—were one-sided; some men who were eager to testify were not permitted to take the stand. But certain facts that were brought out seemed too damaging to be explained away. It was disclosed, for example, that one director, in whose name the New Haven had for a time carried its Boston & Maine holdings of stock, had profited by $2,700,000 without spending a dollar of his own money; that newspapermen and a Harvard professor had been paid for respectful treatment of the New Haven in their dispatches and lectures; and that over a million dollars of the money expended on the new suburban line —the New York, Westchester & Boston—had apparently been paid out in political graft and could not be accounted for, some of the books which might have thrown light on these payments having been foresightedly burned. The history of the New Haven expansion made a very shabby story indeed.

Mellen regarded Morgan as his boss. In 1911 he told Clarence W. Barron of the Boston *News Bureau,* "I wear the Morgan collar, but I am proud of it." In 1912 he was quoted in a magazine article as saying, "If Mr. Morgan were to order me tomorrow to China or Siberia in his interests, I would pack up and go."

And in the hue and cry that took place after Morgan's death, Mellen claimed, not too creditably, that in this whole campaign of expansion he had been following Morgan's lead and acceding to his wishes. When asked in the investigation whether he had been "Morgan's man," he answered, "I have been called by the newspapers his office boy." When asked how important the rest of the directors were as compared with Morgan, he said that there were other strong men on the New Haven board, but that he "could not recall anything where Mr. Morgan was determined, emphatic, insistent . . . where he did not have his way." To Barron he said in October 1913, "I took orders from J. P. Morgan, Sr. I did as I was told, and when Morgan, Sr., who always sat at my left hand in the meetings of the board, desired the approval of his directors, he got it, and don't you think he didn't! When he wanted their negative vote, he got that just as quick!" In another part of his examination by the I.C.C. in 1914 Mellen, who prided himself on his picturesque language, declared that the record of the New Haven, without Morgan, would have been "as tame and uneventful, as devoid of interest and incident, as would the record of a herd of cows deprived of the association of a bull."

Not only that, but Mellen testified, apparently correctly, that the New York, Westchester & Boston project —which up to 1914 had cost over 36 million dollars and had resulted in a suburban line only 18.03 miles long which was losing money at the rate of over a million dollars a year—had been pushed through the board of directors by Morgan; that he, Mellen, had been skeptical about it; that he was never given an adequate account of the way in which millions of dollars were spent for it out of a bank account at J. P. Morgan & Co. called "Special Account No. 2"; and that when, after a directors' meeting, he had complained to Morgan about the vagueness of a report upon it, Morgan had rebuffed him by saying, "Didn't Stetson draw that report? . . . Well, doesn't Stetson know more about how it should be drawn than you do?" Mellen complained on the witness stand that if anything went wrong with the New York, Westchester & Boston scheme he could see then that he himself would be "the goat." "I was a president," he testified, "and I knew, if trouble came, that lots of people would go to Carlsbad or some other place where they would be inaccessible, and I would have to stay and fight it out."

Despite these insinuations, we may dismiss any notion that Morgan had any direct part in any of the financial irregularities of the New Haven. That he even had any direct knowledge of them is highly unlikely. He was a man of many and diverse affairs, absent from his desk for months at a time and preoccupied with large decisions. His way was to pick a man, trust him, and leave everything to him. If Stetson drew a report, it was all right. If Mellen said there was nothing to Brandeis' charges that the New Haven was overextended, that was enough. Morgan's judgment of men was not always reliable; he once confessed to Rainsford, "I am not a good judge of men. My first shot is sometimes right. My second never is." He had left too much to Mellen and Mellen's henchmen.

In his later years, when he had dealt successfully with so many vast projects that almost anything bold and big appealed to him, his judgment of enterprises such as the New York, Westchester & Boston was likewise not always reliable. The idea of rounding out the New Haven system came as naturally as the idea of rounding out the Garland art collection; and if it cost a few extra millions, what did that matter? He may have gathered that some of the money would have to go in the payment of graft for the rewriting of franchises; if so, he may have dismissed this as the sort of thing you could not escape when you had to deal with such reptiles as politicians. But it was not his way to look into details—except on the books of his own firm. It was totals he dealt with. The details were up to the men he trusted.

But for the totals he was indeed responsible, in large part; and the downfall of the New Haven road emphasized the economic lesson that some big projects will not pay out. The purchase of steamship lines and trolley lines and all the rest did not increase the New Haven's earnings adequately. A railroad operating in New England, a part of the country that had reached high noon in its development, could not, at high noon for the railroads in general, win enough new business to justify such headlong expansion. In this case the irresistible force of Morgan's desire to do things in a big way, regardless of cost, had come face to face with immovable economic facts. An aging man could not repeat indefinitely the triumphs of his prime.

Chapter Twelve

ROCK OF DEFENSE

PIERPONT MORGAN was seventy years and six months old when, in the autumn of 1907, his influence was put to its most inexorable test.

He had been taking business much less strenuously that year, as befitted his age. During the winter and early spring of 1907 he had often been absent from 23 Wall Street, preferring to remain uptown in the big red-walled West Room of his recently completed Library, where he could interview business callers or art dealers at leisure, feast his eyes upon newly acquired books and paintings, or sit quietly for long intervals at his solitaire. In March he was off to Europe, to be gone no less than five months—shuttling back and forth between London and Paris, visiting Rome, Florence, and Aix, cruising briefly in the Adriatic on the *Corsair*, assembling a yacht-load of fashionable friends for the Cowes Regatta, and, as always, collecting indefatigably. Not until August 19 was he back in New York.

He arrived to find the business situation threatening. There had been minor panics abroad; the New York stock market had been subject to sinking spells since early in the year; new issues of securities had languished in an obviously glutted market; commodity prices were sagging; and there was an ominous feeling in many minds that an economic storm was brewing. But still Morgan was intent upon leaving as much work and responsibility as possible to his younger partners, while he himself remained half withdrawn from active affairs;

and since the triennial Episcopal Convention was scheduled to be held at Richmond, Virginia, during the first three weeks of October, and it had become his invariable custom to attend these assemblages of the bishops and leading clerics and laymen of the Church, he set out as usual. Two special cars took him and his guests—who included three American bishops and the gaitered Bishop of London—to Richmond, where they took up residence in the Rutherford house on Grace Street, which Morgan had engaged for the occasion, with Louis Sherry once more serving as major-domo. And for three weeks he threw himself energetically into the business of the convention, which debated such questions as whether to accept the wording of a proposed preamble to the constitution of the Church, whether to reduce the number of delegates which the various dioceses would send to future conventions, whether there should be separate bishops for the Negro race, and whether the Revised Versions of the Bible should be permitted to be used in the reading of the lessons.

During the last few days of the convention it was noticed that Morgan began to receive messages from New York with increasing frequency. One morning he was closeted with an emissary from 23 Wall Street. Telegrams kept coming to him, and they appeared to be long and urgent. As Bishop Lawrence of Massachusetts later wrote, "If one came during a meal, he tore it open, read it; then putting the palms of both hands on the table, a habit of his, he looked ahead with fixed eyes and deep thought for a few minutes. One day a member of the party said, 'Mr. Morgan, you seem to have some bad news.' He shot his eyes across the table at the speaker and said nothing. No question of that sort was asked again. The fact was that we were so busy in our convention work, we were not aware of the clouds gathering in New York and the country which were to break in the great financial panic of October 1907."

2

In New York those clouds were piling up swiftly. A group of speculators headed by a swashbuckler named F. Augustus Heinze made a disastrous attempt to corner the stock of the United Copper Company, and went to the wall. Heinze was also head of a bank, the Mercantile National, and naturally rumors began at once to fly about that the bank might have been involved in his speculations. A run on the bank began. Short of money with which to pay depositors, the bank appealed to the Clearing House for aid. (There was at that time no Federal Reserve System, and therefore the Clearing House—an association of banks set up for the clearing of checks—was the logical agency to turn to if one's bank was in trouble.) Among Heinze's associates in his stock-market adventures had been two other speculators, Charles W. Morse and Edward R. Thomas, who likewise headed banks; and presently these banks, too, were beset by whispers of suspicion. Whereupon the conservative bankers who headed the New York Clearing House, deciding that the situation called for prompt and drastic surgery, demanded the resignation of Heinze, Morse, and Thomas from all their banking connections. The Clearing House announced simultaneously that these men's banks had been examined and found to be in sound condition, but by now the rumors of trouble to come were redoubled.

Especially people began to question the reliability of a certain type of bank. For several years before 1907 there had been an epidemic of setting up trust companies, which were permitted by law to engage in banking operations almost as if they were national banks, but without being subject to the strict regulations with which national banks were surrounded. A good many plungers and stock-market operators had got into the managements of some of these trust companies, whose funds could be invested in enterprises more adventurous—and more risky—than ordinary banks were permitted to engage in. Might some of these newfangled banking institutions be headed for the rocks?

Investors, speculators, and bank depositors began to run for cover—selling stock, calling loans, drawing their funds out of suspect banks. The whispers multiplied. "You say your company's funds are deposited in the Knickerbocker Trust Company? Better watch out; didn't you know that Charles Barney, the president of Knickerbocker, was mixed up in deals with Morse?" "What, you're holding three hundred shares of Union Pacific on margin? Sell. Get out of the market. In a few days more, the way things are going, some of the biggest brokerage houses will go under—and then wait and see what happens to prices! I tell you, there's nothing like a safe-deposit box full of cash these days."—"You say your bank account's in the Lincoln Trust Company? Well, I guess it's all right, but a lot of that Waldorf crowd have been tied up with that bank."—"Did you realize that these trust companies don't belong to the Clearing House, and have to rely on a national bank to clear their checks for them? Well, suppose the national bank gets cold feet and decides it won't do this any more? That will be nice for the trust company's depositors, won't it?"—Thus the talk ran. It was the beginning of panic.

Some of Morgan's friends wanted him to come back from Richmond. He was the central figure in American banking, was he not? And the banking world was imperiled. Surely he should be in Wall Street, to rally the forces of confidence. But Morgan and his partners thought he had better remain in Richmond, lest his return be taken as a sign of alarm. So remain he did, until the convention broke up on Saturday, October 19. Let Bishop Lawrence's diary take up the story:

"As I was going out of the door [of the Rutherford house] to the House of Bishops on Saturday morning, Mr. Morgan called me into his room and said, 'Bishop, I am going back to New York on the noon train.' I said, 'Why do you do that?' He answered, 'They are in trouble in New York: they do not know what to do, and I don't know what to do, but I am going back.' I replied, 'Why do you go back at noon? You will arrive in New York in the middle of the night. Why not get Mr. Sherry to have your two cars hitched onto the early evening train tonight? We will all pack up and go with you.' He said, 'I had not thought of that: I do not believe it can be done, but I will try.' It was done, and off we went by the evening train. Still, there was no suggestion of care or anxiety on his part, indeed rather the contrary: he was in the best of spirits. Held at Washington for an hour at midnight, he sat on the rear platform smoking until the train should start.

"Sunday morning, as we ran into Jersey City, we went again into Mr. Morgan's car for some bread and coffee before arrival, and found him sitting at the table with a tumbler turned upside down in each hand, singing lustily some tune which no one could recognize."

Arriving at the ferry house in New York, Morgan escorted his guests to cabs. When some of them asked if they would see him at St. George's Church, he said, "Perhaps so." But after driving his daughter Louisa Satterlee to the West Shore ferry so that she could proceed to Highland Falls, he then went on by cab, not to St. George's, but posthaste to his Library. No. 219 was not open, for Mrs. Morgan was at Cragston, so he expected to have to live at a hotel for the next few days. But Herbert Satterlee, hearing from Louisa of her father's fears, set out at once from Highland Falls for New York to open up the Satterlee house, the big stone house just east of the Library. It was there that Morgan would sleep during the next few nights—when there was time for sleep.

But he was not thinking of that now, as, like a general arriving at the headquarters of a beleaguered army, he climbed the steps of the Library and entered its massive doors.

3

He spent the rest of that Sunday, until after midnight, studying the problem which confronted him—talking with partners and friends, with bank presidents, with trust-company heads; hearing about the demoralized condition of the Stock Exchange, the widespread calling of loans, the runs on bank after bank; looking at financial statements; listening to the appeals of men who wanted him to lend cash to this institution or that. His own banking house was secure—or rather, would be secure unless everything went. What concerned him now was the general situation, the general mood of panic. Everybody seemed to look to him for leadership in averting disaster. But how could that leadership best be applied? Morgan listened, considered, played solitaire, was uncommunicative. He did not yet know what the situation demanded. Reporters took up their watch in Thirty-sixth Street outside the Library gate, and noted who arrived and who left, but there was no news. The commander of the forces of defense had not decided where or how to draw up his battle lines.

The next morning—Monday, October 21—Morgan made a first move. He asked Satterlee to get in touch with some able young bankers—such as Thomas W. Joyce of the House of Morgan, Richard Trimble of the Steel Corporation, Henry P. Davison of the First National Bank (subsequently a Morgan partner), and Benjamin Strong of the Bankers Trust Company (subsequently head of the Federal Reserve Bank of New York)—who could go about and assemble figures and facts for him, and if necessary could make rapid examinations of the condition of a bank which applied for aid. Then he went downtown. Among the banks which appeared to be headed for trouble was a very big trust company, the Knickerbocker, whose fine main office was conspicuously situated at what was then the chief crossroads of the city, the corner of Fifth Avenue and Thirty-fourth Street, opposite the grand brick-and-sandstone pile of the Waldorf-Astoria. Some of the Knickerbocker's funds were said to have been dubiously invested and depositors were beginning to draw out their cash. After banking hours a committee of the Knickerbocker's directors came to see Morgan. They reported that because the name of the popular and amiable president of the Knickerbocker, Charles T. Barney, had been too closely linked in the public mind with those of Heinze and Morse, they had called for Barney's resignation. That very afternoon the National Bank of Commerce, which customarily cleared checks for the Knickerbocker, had sent word that it would do so no longer. The committee appealed to Morgan for help for the bank.

Morgan would promise nothing. He was a stockholder in the Knickerbocker himself, some of his own firm's money was on deposit in it, and he had a sentimental attachment for it because it had been founded by an old school friend of his; but he doubted if it could be saved. And anyhow he had too little precise information about its condition to offer help. There would be no sense in throwing valuable funds into a sinking institution. He advised the committee to assemble at once a meeting of all the directors of the Knickerbocker and to see whether they themselves could devise a plan to prevent its downfall.

The Knickerbocker meeting was held that evening—at Sherry's restaurant, in a room so lamentably unprivate that strangers wandered in and out, picking up fragments of the talk, telephoning their friends, spreading the news that the Knickerbocker was in jeopardy. That evening Morgan remained by the fire at Satterlee's house. Not yet had he decided where the lines of defense could be drawn. He went to bed after midnight, with a cold coming on—a tired and uncertain man.

Tuesday, the 22nd, came; and with it the expected run on the Knickerbocker, as depositors swarmed to Fifth Avenue and Thirty-fourth Street to draw out all their funds. Benjamin Strong, one of Morgan's team of examiners, had been making a quick examination of the Knickerbocker's condition, and his report, while incomplete, was unfavorable. There was nothing to be done. The run continued—and at two o'clock in the afternoon the Knickerbocker came to the end of its cash. It suspended payment. It had failed.

The news of the failure of this large and important and widely known bank came like a thunderclap in the midst of a gathering storm. Every banker, and especially every trust-company president, knew that he faced the possibility of a run on his own bank the next day. The Secretary of the Treasury, George B. Cortelyou, sped to New York to see what use could best be made of such government funds as were available. Again Morgan conferred with anxious financiers half the night. "It was at this time," says Satterlee, that he "organized the group or committee of bankers who voluntarily submitted their statements to him and permitted him to allocate to each one the sum of money which he felt was appropriate and necessary to make up the total amount needed to carry the weaker institutions through the panic." He tried to get the heads of the trust companies, too, to organize for mutual aid, but failed. Not until after three o'clock in the morning did he turn in, still miserable with the heavy cold that had fastened itself upon him.

4

Where would the lightning strike next? As a matter of fact, the direction it was to take was largely determined by something that happened on that very evening of Tuesday, October 22—an episode that was subsequently to become a subject of furious controversy.

Among the bankers who discussed possible plans of action that night with Secretary Cortelyou in his rooms at the Hotel Manhattan was George W. Perkins, one of Morgan's partners. When the session was over the reporters clustered round, and Perkins attempted to brief them on the situation to date. As a result there appeared the next morning in the *New York Times* and *Sun* a statement that "the sore point" was now the Trust Company of America (which was located in Wall Street not far from the House of Morgan). The statement added that the Trust Company of America had applied for help, but that provision had been made to supply it with all the cash it might need the next morning, and that it was sound and would pull through.

That statement, centering as it did the attention of frightened men on a single bank, was so injudicious, to say the least, that the Associated Press refused to send it out. Under the circumstances it was not surprising that, although there were runs on many institutions the next day, by all odds the worst one besieged the Trust Company of America.

Oakleigh Thorne, the president of that particular trust company, testified later before a congressional committee that his bank had been subjected to only moderate withdrawals on Tuesday (one and a half million dollars, as against thirteen million on Wednesday), that he had not applied for help, and that it was the "sore point" statement alone that had caused the run on his bank. From this testimony, plus the refusal of Morgan to help the Knickerbocker, plus the disciplinary measures taken by the Clearing House against the Heinze, Morse, and Thomas banks, plus other fragments of supposedly pertinent evidence (even including Bishop Lawrence's account of Morgan's cheerful singing in the dining car on Sunday morning), certain chroniclers have arrived at the ingenious conclusion that the Morgan interests took advantage of the unsettled conditions during the autumn of 1907 to *precipitate* the panic, guiding it shrewdly as it progressed so that it would kill off rival banks and consolidate the pre-eminence of the banks within the Morgan orbit. To this hypothesis the most obvious answer, given over and over again by bankers, is that no banker in his senses encourages a bank panic. That would be like dropping a match in a powder keg; he would be too likely to go up in the explosion himself. Nor does this hypothesis accord either with Morgan's character or with subsequent events, as we shall see. And Thorne had undeniably been consulting with Perkins that evening, whether or not he had specifically asked for help. There is, however, some ground for believing that Perkins, who later denied having given out any "sore point" statement but admitted that he had given the reporters such information as he thought it was "proper to give, of a reassuring and helpful nature," may have felt that by directing attention to one bank he would be helping to localize the panic, and perhaps to keep it from enveloping other institutions whose safety he rightly or wrongly regarded as more essential. (Which, incidentally, raises the question, what would *you* do if called upon to give out news to reporters during a panic? Tell them nothing at all? Rumor thrives on ignorance. Tell them everything? That, in a panic, would be inflammatory to the last degree. Merely utter soothing generalities? That would convince nobody.) But let us see what happened after that statement appeared in the *Times* on the morning of Wednesday, October 23.

5

On that Wednesday morning "Morgan could not be waked up." (I am quoting Satterlee, at whose house on Thirty-sixth Street he was staying.) "If he could not be aroused, the consequences were too serious to contemplate. He seemed to be in a stupor. I finally got him to open his eyes and answer my questions. His cold had made fast progress owing to his fatigue. He could hardly speak above a whisper. Dr. Markoe was summoned by telephone and came down provided with sprays, gargles, etc. After half an hour's heroic work Mr. Morgan dressed and went down to breakfast."

A cup of coffee appeared to revive him, and after a few conferences in the Library he went downtown by cab.

His voice was hoarse and his eyes wept so that it was hard for him to read, but there was no staying home that day. When his cab turned into Wall Street he found the place full of crowds, gathered as if to watch a fire; and outside the door of the Trust Company of America there was a long line of depositors reaching down the street and round the corner into William. President Oakleigh Thorne of the Trust Company had opened seven paying tellers' windows that morning instead of the customary one window, hoping thus to reduce the crowd of panicky depositors, but this had had no appreciable result. Two members of Morgan's team of examiners were inside the bank, appraising hurriedly the securities in its vaults; they had been there since four o'clock that morning, but as yet had not finished their survey. Morgan could not yet know whether the bank was worth saving.

Meanwhile he invited the presidents of all the other trust companies to meet in his office—discovering to his dismay that many of them had to be introduced to one another—and urged them to organize a committee to get together funds to help such of their own group as might, like the Trust Company of America, be in trouble. And he also asked the two most important national bankers in the city, George F. Baker of the First National and James Stillman of the National City, to meet with him. The hour for decision was approaching, and he needed their aid and counsel. They joined him in one of the back rooms of the Morgan office—while frantic messages came from Thorne that the cash in the tills of the Trust Company of America was dwindling fast.

At about half-past twelve Morgan knew that he could wait no longer; so he sent for the men who had been examining Thorne's bank. One of them, Willard King, went into the meeting of the trust-company heads to make a report. The other, Benjamin Strong, joined Morgan and Baker and Stillman in the back room. Morgan sat and listened while Strong consulted Baker and Stillman as to the value of certain securities on which their judgment would be valuable. It was a slow business. Minutes dragged by—half an hour, three-quarters of an hour. Morgan was well aware that meanwhile Thorne's cash was getting lower and lower. Finally Morgan asked Strong whether he believed the Trust Company to be solvent. Yes, said Strong.

"This, then, is the place to stop this trouble," said Morgan.

At once, with the aid of Baker and Stillman, he made cash available to Thorne's bank. It arrived in the nick of time, and the Trust Company of America did not close.

6

It was a very tired man of seventy who heaved himself into a cab on Fifth Avenue late that evening and rode home to the Satterlee house. He had spent the entire evening at the uptown office of the Union Trust Company, at Fifth Avenue and Thirty-eighth Street, in a prolonged session with the committee of trust-company presidents which he had succeeded that day in getting organized. He had told them that the panic was now a trust-company panic, and that they positively must subscribe among themselves a fund of ten million dollars which could be used for the support and rescue of their weaker brethren such as the Trust Company of America. Secretary Cortelyou was going to put federal funds at the disposal of certain of the national banks, which would pass them on to the trust companies; but there was no time now to wait for that. They must act themselves, at once. The talk had been interminable, and at one time

Morgan had dozed off for half an hour or so, his cigar out, his head down on his chest. But at last they had subscribed up to eight and a quarter million, and he had told them that his firm and the leading national banks would be responsible for the remaining million and three-quarters; and then he had left for home.

All in all, it had been a terrible day. The Westinghouse Company had failed. The Pittsburgh Stock Exchange had suspended. Western banks which had money on deposit in New York were drawing it away, for the panic was now national. No one could tell what turn it would take next. But here in New York disaster had been halted, at least for the moment. And it looked as if the forces of defense were at last getting organized. So far, so good. Morgan played a last game of solitaire and went slowly up to bed.

7

But Thursday and Friday proved to be even worse.

At about ten o'clock Thursday morning, Morgan drove downtown with Satterlee "in the Union Club brougham drawn by the white horse and driven by the faithful Williams." Satterlee has given an account of that ride: "The newspapers had been carrying his picture on the first page, and his name had been biggest in the headlines. All the way downtown people who got a glimpse of him in the cab called the attention of passers-by. Policemen and cabbies who knew him well by sight shouted, 'There goes the Old Man!' or 'There goes the Big Chief!' and the people who heard them understood to whom they referred and ran beside the cab to get a peep at him. Near Trinity Church a way through the crowd was opened as soon as it was realized who was in the cab. The crowd moved with us. . . . All this time he looked straight ahead and gave no sign of noticing the excitement, but it was evident that he was pleased. Wall Street and Broad Street were filled from curb to curb with an excited throng through which messengers forced their way. As Mr. Morgan got out of the cab and hurried up the steps into his office the hubbub ceased, and there was a moment's pause; and then the struggling mob fought their way on, all looking up at the windows of J. P. Morgan & Co."

There was new aid available now for the forces of defense. John D. Rockefeller had put up ten millions to aid the trust companies. Cortelyou stood ready to follow the leading bankers' advice as to where the United States Government's money should be applied. But the bank runs continued, especially at the Trust Company of America; and the ten-million-dollar fund which had been subscribed the preceding evening had been "swallowed up . . . so quick you couldn't tell where it went to," as Perkins later testified. And now the storm center had shifted to the Stock Exchange, which was feeling the full brunt of the universal urge to turn anything and everything into cash. Prices were tumbling; that morning Union Pacific fell from $108\frac{1}{2}$ to 100, Reading from $78\frac{5}{8}$ to $70\frac{1}{2}$, Northern Pacific from 110 to $100\frac{1}{2}$; and what was much worse, there was practically no money at all available to lend on the Stock Exchange floor for the purchase of securities. Toward the end of the morning, sales had almost stopped—there was no money with which to buy stocks. President Thomas of the Stock Exchange thereupon crossed the street to 23 Wall.

The accounts of what happened next vary somewhat, for it was a confused time and memories of it were jumbled. According to Thomas' own testimony before the Pujo Committee some years later, he went to the Morgan office and waited twenty minutes; then Morgan came out of an inner office with some other men and said, "We are going to let you have twenty-five million dollars. Go over to the Exchange and announce it." Satterlee's version is different. According to it, Thomas walked right into the back room where Morgan was talking with some men, and said to him:

"Mr. Morgan, we will have to close the Stock Exchange."

"What?" said Morgan, turning sharply.

Thomas repeated his statement. He didn't see how the Exchange could be kept open till the regular closing time of three o'clock.

" 'It must not close one minute before that hour today!' said Morgan, "emphasizing each word by keeping time with his right hand, the middle finger of it pointing straight at Mr. Thomas." And at once he sent for the presidents of all the national banks in the neighborhood. Some of Cortelyou's federal funds were available. From these and other sources he raised within a few minutes the twenty-five million dollars to be lent on the Exchange. And the Exchange did not have to be closed that day.

But how long could such rescue operations continue to be carried out? The next morning, Friday, at six o'clock, Secretary Cortelyou and George W. Perkins were sitting on the edge of Cortelyou's bed at the Hotel Manhattan and turning over the facts of the crisis as these had developed to date; and according to Perkins' subsequent testimony there seemed to be "not a ray of hope in the situation." But Perkins went on to see Stillman, who had been enlisting the help of John D. Rockefeller, and gathered that Rockefeller's aid could still be counted on. Once more, as the day went on, there was a total shortage of cash on the Stock Exchange; once more Morgan had to call upon the bank presidents to meet with him and take up a subscription. This time the meeting was held, not at 23 Wall Street, but at the office of the Clearing House; it produced, not the fifteen millions that Morgan had considered vitally necessary, but thirteen—which might or might not be enough to save the day.

As things turned out, it *was* enough. Just. As Perkins later testified, "If twenty millions had been needed that day, the Stock Exchange and a hundred or more firms would have gone up, it was just that close. It was touch and go." But the Exchange stayed open.

"Anyone who saw Mr. Morgan going from the Clearing House back to his office that day will never forget the picture," writes Satterlee. "With his coat unbuttoned and flying open, a piece of white paper clutched tightly in his right hand, he walked fast down Nassau Street. His flat-topped black derby hat was set firmly down on his head. Between his teeth he held a paper cigar holder in which was one of his long cigars, half smoked. His eyes were fixed straight ahead. He swung his arms as he walked and took no notice of anyone. He did not seem to see the throngs in the street, so intent was his mind on the thing that he was doing. . . . The thing that made his progress different from that of all the other people on the street was that he did not dodge, or walk in and out, or slacken his pace. He simply barged along, as if he had been the only man going down Nassau Street hill past the Sub-treasury. He was the embodiment of power and purpose. Not more than two minutes after he disappeared into his office, the cheering on the floor of the Stock Exchange could be heard out in Broad Street."

8

Night after night there were conferences at the Morgan Library. On Thursday evening the presidents of the banks and of the trust companies gathered in the lofty East Room, planning the disposition of financial forces for the morrow, while Morgan sat in the West Room at his little card table, smoking a cigar and playing solitaire. On Friday the scene was repeated. One of the main subjects of discussion Thursday evening was whether a scheme could be worked out for supplementing the meager supply of cash in the financial markets of the nation. Would Clearing House certificates serve the necessary purpose? Or was there some sounder method? The bankers would work out a scheme, and one of them would cross the marble hallway to the West Room and tell Morgan about it, and he would listen, and say briefly, "No, that won't work," and continue with his cards until they arrived at a solution which his instinct and experience told him was practicable.

The setting was a strange one for the discussion of a currency problem. The West Room of the Morgan Library was walled with red silk damask, patterned with the arms of the Chigi family of Rome. On the walls hung splendid Florentine masterpieces of the fifteenth and sixteenth centuries. Upon the bookshelves stood a bust by Michelangelo and a rock-crystal bowl said to have been mounted for Queen Christina of Sweden. The mantelpiece and the gilded ceiling had been made for great Italian houses. Morgan sat in a red plush armchair by the fire in this great room, with a Madonna and Child by Pinturicchio looking down over his shoulder, and Fra Filippo Lippi's altarpiece of St. Lawrence and Saints Cosmo and Damian facing him from the opposite wall. There was a card table before him; and here—while elsewhere in the Library the other financiers who had become his lieutenants in the struggle against the panic labored at the making of battle plans—he concentrated on the cards before him, slowly puffing his black cigar as he carefully placed the five of clubs on the two, and the eight on the five, and the jack on the eight.

A delegate from the East Room would enter the room and present a new scheme. "No," Morgan would say shortly; and the delegate would retire again, and the game of solitaire would continue under the watchful eyes of the Madonnas and the great ladies of Florence, until at last the conclusion which Morgan could accept had been reached and the immediate objective in his battle gained.*

9

At last the week came to an end. The Trust Company of America had not failed; the Stock Exchange had not closed; the decision had been made to put into circulation Clearing House certificates; and it looked as if the worst might be over. The newspapers talked, with laudable if synthetic optimism, as if the panic were a thing of the past. Theodore Roosevelt, who had so often berated "malefactors of wealth" that half the men in Wall Street believed him to be personally to blame for what had happened, gave out a confident statement in which he praised "those influential and splendid business men . . . who have acted with such wisdom and public spirit." Clergymen of all faiths were asked by a committee of bankers to make reassuring statements to their congregations, following the line that Morgan himself had set in a brief interview earlier in the week: "If people will keep their money in the banks, everything will be all right." And Morgan himself, whose cold had fortunately moderated, went off to Highland Falls by train Saturday afternoon—

* The two preceding paragraphs follow closely a description of the same scene in a previous book of mine, *The Lords of Creation*, pp. 134-135.

sleeping most of the way there—and got a few hours of rest.

Yes, the worst seemed to be over. But the crisis continued. Still there were runs on banks and trust companies; still there had to be night session after night session at the Library. And there were two moments of acute danger.

The first came when officials of the City of New York approached Morgan to report that the city needed thirty million dollars at once, to pay off some short-term obligations that were coming due; that in the disordered state of the money market, there was no way of borrowing thirty million after the normal fashion; and that therefore they must imperatively have an emergency loan lest the city go bankrupt. Morgan took two days to consider the matter, and then acted with his customary boldness. On the afternoon of Tuesday, October 29, the mayor of New York and other city officials came to the Library; and Morgan, sitting at his desk in the West Room, wrote out by hand, in his flowing script, a commitment to buy thirty million dollars' worth of six per cent New York City bonds. How on earth his firm could sell those bonds no one at the moment could be sure. But if conditions improved, of course they could; the rate of interest would be attractive to anyone who had any money to spare. Morgan simply took a chance on the coming of more orderly conditions in the markets of the nation, and thereby not only saved the credit of the City of New York, but advertised his own confidence as no words, however eloquent, could have advertised it.

The second crisis was even more severe. It came to a head on the following Saturday and Sunday—the 2nd and 3rd of November.

10

This second crisis—the final one of the acute stage of the panic—has been the subject of sharper controversy than any other. I shall try to explain it as simply as possible, but it was undeniably complicated.

It came about from the fact that a prominent firm of brokers, called Moore & Schley, was in danger of collapse. This firm had borrowed a lot of money on time loans which would presently fall due, and it was short of cash with which to meet them. Now it happened that the head of this firm, one Grant B. Schley, was also a member of a syndicate of wealthy men who owned, between them, a large majority of the stock of one of the lesser steel companies, known as Tennessee Coal & Iron. They had bought this Tennessee Coal & Iron stock through the firm of Moore & Schley—had bought it with money largely borrowed through Moore & Schley, which accordingly held a great many of the Tennessee Coal & Iron stock certificates as collateral against these loans. Moore & Schley had in turn been borrowing money from various banks for the financing of its various operations, and had used some of these Tennessee Coal & Iron certificates as collateral to secure the loans to it from the banks. And now some of the banks were getting restive; for Tennessee Coal & Iron stock, whatever its normal value might be, was a very inactive security; the last recorded price for it had been well over 100, but if a block of it were suddenly thrown on the market during panic times, it might wait long for a purchaser, and then fetch no more than 60 or even 50 or less. Meanwhile Moore & Schley desperately needed cash. So somebody—probably Colonel Oliver Payne, who along with Grant B.

Schley was a member of the syndicate which owned this Tennessee stock—had a brainstorm.

The Tennessee Coal & Iron Company, he reflected, was a competitor in the steel business—though a small one—of the United States Steel Corporation. There had been some previous talk of the possibility of the Steel Corporation's buying control of Tennessee, though Morgan, when the proposition had been put up to him, had turned it down flatly, saying that the price of the Tennessee shares was too high. But perhaps the Steel Corporation would not be wholly uninterested now. And if the Steel Corporation should buy control of Tennessee Coal & Iron by exchanging its bonds for Tennessee stock, the results would be wonderful. Steel Corporation bonds were practically as good as cash. They could be substituted for the Tennessee stock as collateral in the banks. The credit of Moore & Schley would at once be restored. And, what was more, the rescue of Moore & Schley would have been accomplished without tying up cash for any long period, at a time when every penny of cash was needed elsewhere. Those Steel Corporation bonds would turn the trick.

The crisis in the affairs of Moore & Schley, and the fear that it might set off a chain reaction of brokerage failures, had already been a matter of anxious discussion for twenty-four hours when on Saturday morning, November 2, Morgan was visited at the Library by Lewis Cass Ledyard, who was attorney for Colonel Payne. Ledyard explained this ingenious scheme to Morgan, who at once embraced it and set about putting it into effect.

That it was a peculiar scheme there is no denying. For one thing, none of those Tennessee shares was actually owned by Moore & Schley; and it would seem possible that the plan which Ledyard proposed had been originally devised less for the relief of Moore & Schley than for the comfort of the wealthy men who belonged to the Tennessee Coal & Iron syndicate. This plan, if carried out, would restore Moore & Schley, to be sure; but it would also be a direct boon to those men. And except for Schley himself, they were mostly men who needed no relief at all in this crisis. Also it has been argued subsequently, with some plausibility, that the plan offered the United States Steel Corporation a wonderful chance to swallow up a lively competitor, while wrapping itself in the cloak of public spirit. To be sure, Gary testified before a congressional committee that the Steel Corporation did *not* want Tennessee Coal & Iron, and that he himself consented to the purchase during the panic only because Morgan, with his immense influence, insisted that the deal must go through in order that Moore & Schley might be saved and a new outbreak of disasters in the stock market might be prevented. But how much weight to give to this testimony of Gary's it is not easy to say. One has to balance the word of an interested party against the theories of men who could not know what was going on in Gary's—or Morgan's—mind; and one has to consider, too, the confused atmosphere of those days of uncertainty, the difficulty of getting detailed information quickly, and the difficulty of weighing the exact effect of any action proposed.

My own inclination is to believe that Morgan—when Ledyard told him that Moore & Schley were almost over the edge of the dam, and that if they went, other firms would go with them, and that this Tennessee scheme would save the day—said to himself: "This is our chance. There may be some other way of saving Moore & Schley, but this one will work anyhow. It can be put through quickly—and time is short. Besides—who knows?—it may turn out to be a good stroke of business in the long run for the Steel Corporation. Gary will consent to it if I tell him to. Let's go ahead."

The people immediately involved in this plan were no strangers to him. Schley was George F. Baker's brother-in-law. Ledyard was one of his own kind, the sort of man he instinctively trusted; it was Ledyard whom he later chose to draw his will. He felt he didn't have to inquire further.

And once having grasped the idea—whatever its origin—he drove ahead with it relentlessly, summoning Gary and the finance committee of the Steel Corporation and sweeping them into acceptance of the plan.

11

On that evening—Saturday, November 2—the battle against the panic came to its climax in another memorable session at the marble Library. Morgan had conceived a plan. The trust companies were still having trouble; in the West Room he assembled their presidents once more. In the East Room were the heads of the national banks and other assorted financiers. He himself, with Gary and a few other men, had withdrawn for the occasion into the librarian's office, a small room opposite the Library entrance. During the evening his plan developed: he would undertake to see that the Steel Corporation bought Tennessee Coal & Iron (meanwhile obligating his own firm, temporarily, for the twenty-five millions or so that this would require)—thus saving Moore & Schley and removing the immediate pressure of danger from the stock market—*if* the trust companies would raise among themselves a further fund of twenty-five million dollars to meet their own emergencies.

It was an exhausting evening, at the end of an exhausting fortnight. These men had been brought together again and again, in this very Library, and had been compelled, against all the dictates of prudence, to subscribe money which they felt their banks could ill spare. Again and again the meetings had lasted till long after midnight. There was hardly a man among them who did not feel at the end of his tether. How much longer must this recurring nightmare continue among the rare editions and the gorgeous tapestries and the Renaissance masterpieces? Late that evening Benjamin Strong, sitting next to James Stillman on a lounge in the East Room, dozed off to sleep. Stillman asked him when he had last been to bed. "Thursday night," said Strong; all Friday night he had been hard at work re-examining the financial condition of the still-besieged Trust Company of America. At last he was called into the librarian's room to make his report to Morgan; and then, feeling that he might reasonably leave, he went to the front door to go home. It was locked. Morgan had the key in his pocket; this was a conference which no one must dare to walk out on until the problem had been solved.

The trust-company heads, in the West Room, were reluctant to put up another twenty-five millions. They were disturbed about their inability to consult their directors, about the huge responsibility they would be shouldering, about the necessity of conserving all their assets. The talk went on and on. At last Morgan walked into the West Room and confronted them. He had with him a document which provided that each trust company, according to its resources, would put up its share of the twenty-five million dollars. One of his lawyers read it aloud, then laid it on the table.

"There you are, gentlemen," said Morgan.

No one stepped forward.

Morgan put his hand on the shoulder of Edward King, the dean of the group. "There's the place, King," he said firmly. "And here's the pen." And he put a gold pen in King's hand.

King signed. Then they all signed.

Morgan had carried the day. It was a quarter to five in the morning.

12

The crisis was not yet finished. The conferences on the terms of the purchase of Tennessee by the Steel Corporation went on late into Sunday night; and then—because Gary refused, without consulting the President of the United States, to consent to a purchase which might make the Steel Corporation subject to government prosecution under the Anti-trust Act—Gary and Frick made a night journey by special train to Washington to talk with President Roosevelt. They met the President Monday morning after breakfast and gave him a quick—and rather vague—summary of the situation; and Roosevelt said he would interpose no objection (thus setting off another future controversy). It was not until three or four minutes of ten on Monday morning, November 4, that Perkins, sitting in the Morgan office with a telephone line open to the White House, heard Gary's voice telling him that it was all right, the President had said OK. The announcement of the Tennessee deal could now be made just as the Stock Exchange opened.

The news had the expected effect. The market rallied.

Not for a long time yet would the financial markets of the country return to normal operations. There would still be runs on banks, and minor bank failures; and the aftermath would follow—a short, but emphatic, slump in American business. But the corner had been turned. Now one could honestly say that the panic was over.

13

The lesson of the Panic of 1907 was clear, though not for some six years was it destined to be embodied in legislation: the United States gravely needed a central banking system, which could build up reserves to be disposed where they were most needed. The significance of Morgan's role during the panic was likewise clear. To the extent that a single man could exercise the functions of a central banking system, Morgan had done this. He had been, as it were, a one-man Federal Reserve Bank.

Where, the present-day reader may ask, was the President of the United States during such a public emergency? Where was the Secretary of the Treasury? Where were the governor of the state, the mayor of the city? They were either inactive in the crisis, or following Morgan's guidance, or looking to him for aid. Morgan was the leader.

Not by reason of the wealth of his firm; for though this was great, it could meet only a small fraction of the gigantic demands which developed. Not by reason of any special inventiveness on Morgan's part; other men worked up the tactical plans while he sat at his card table. His unique power in the crisis derived partly from the sense in the back of men's minds that if his leadership failed, the whole financial world would go to ruin, whereas if it succeeded, one would probably prosper much better if Morgan remembered one as an ally in time of need, than if he marked one down as an objector. It derived partly from his organizing ability; partly from the fact that men trusted him to work for the general interest as they would trust nobody else of remotely comparable authority; partly from the compulsion in his very glance; but mostly from his courage. At a time when the almost universal instinct was to pull one's own chestnuts out of the fire, to escape new commitments, to dodge responsibility, he risked everything, again and again, on the success of his campaign. It is said that one banker came to 23 Wall Street during the panic and said, "I am very much disturbed; I am below my legal reserve." Said Morgan, "You ought to be ashamed of yourself to be anywhere near your legal reserve. What is your reserve for at a time like this except to use?" Thus he bludgeoned other men into displaying the courage that was his own supreme contribution.

Chapter Thirteen

ENVOI

AFTER the Panic of 1907, Morgan's retirement from active business was progressive. His annual absences abroad, which for several years had averaged four or five months in length, were now sometimes extended to six months or more. Not that his European sojourns were inactive. He liked to be on the move, and would shift back and forth between London, Paris, Aix-les-Bains, Rome, and perhaps Monte Carlo or Venice, spending a few days in each place and then going on to the next. More than once he extended his tour to Egypt; once the *Corsair* took him to Greece. As always, he enjoyed having a party with him, including usually one of his daughters or some other relative, along with a variety of men and women friends. The overtones of grandeur still sounded: in Rome he had audiences with the Queen Mother of Italy and with the Pope, in England Queen Alexandra came to Prince's Gate to inspect his art collection, at Kiel the German Kaiser came aboard the *Corsair* for lunch. An aging international personage, Morgan liked to surround himself with companions, old or new, familiar or glittering, though often he said little at the gatherings he had assembled, preferring to smoke and listen and perhaps doze while the others talked; one reason why he appreciated the company of Salvatore Cortesi, the Associated Press correspondent in Rome, was that Cortesi could drive with him for hours about the streets of Rome without feeling any necessity to say or hear a word.

But it was at home in the United States that Morgan's

withdrawal from affairs was most apparent. He spent less and less time at 23 Wall Street, or at the office high up in the Bankers Trust Building which was set aside for him while the Drexel Building was being demolished to make way for the present Morgan headquarters; mostly he remained in his Library.

If you would see the Morgan of those last years in your mind's eye, picture a somewhat bulky old gentleman, six feet tall, seating himself in an armchair in a European hotel suite, and pulling toward him a card table on which is a silver box containing two packs of cards. He is rather formally dressed for a gentleman on holiday, with a wing collar, Ascot tie, and white waistcoat. He sits solidly, his weight rather forward on his two feet, his toes turned out. Chun, his Pekinese dog, is curled up close to him. For background, imagine a Grand Hotel sitting room of the early years of this century, with the French windows open and the street sounds drifting up from below; with innumerable obsequious servants ready to come at the sound of a bell, to fetch trays to the occupants of the Morgan suite, or to call the carriage and pair that stand waiting not far from the hotel door, in case the old gentleman should put on his hat and take up his gold-headed cane to go driving.

Or picture him in London, wearing a silk hat and a velvet-collared overcoat, entering the Bond Street galleries, where there has been set out for his inspection a diverse assortment of objects of art, including a famous panel of Flemish tapestry. Morgan looks them over carefully and takes the dealer's breath away by saying, "How much for the stack?" The dealer names a sum in six figures, to which Morgan simply replies, "Right," and not only the tapestry but all the other exquisite things are his. . . . Or, by contrast, see him, again in London, talking with James Henry Duveen, nephew of the Henry Duveen who was for several years Morgan's most trusted dealer. Says the younger Duveen, bringing out a photograph, "This is a picture of the vases about which I wrote you, Mr. Morgan." Morgan grabs at the print—pounces on it. "How much?" "Twenty-two thousand pounds." "Much too dear." And he walks away. . . . Or watch Morgan sitting with Cortesi in the anteroom of the Borgia apartment at the Vatican, waiting for a talk with the Papal Secretary of State, Cardinal Merry del Val. The cardinal keeps them waiting half an hour, but Morgan does not mind; now for once he talks volubly and eloquently, pointing out to Cortesi the masterly handling of light and shade in the frescoes by Pinturicchio which adorn the room. A messenger from the cardinal comes in with apologies for the delay; Morgan sends word that the cardinal must not mind, that he is perfectly happy where he is, and only wishes that he had a bed so that he could lie on his back for hours and study the frescoes the better.

Or, better still, you might hold in your mind's eye a glimpse of Morgan at home, in the West Room of the Library, going over the morning's mail at the desk and sorting it into two piles, the letters that must be attended to, and those that can wait. Belle da Costa Greene, the devoted young librarian, remonstrates with him at the size of the pile of letters that can wait. He answers that he has found that if you leave letters alone long enough, they "die out." After a while he asks Miss Greene to read aloud to him from the Bible as he sits in the red plush chair in the corner, and specifically requests the story of Jonah and the whale. She asks him if he really believes it. He answers stoutly that he does; that if the time ever came when he could not believe every word in the Bible, he could believe none of it. . . . At times he sits motionless in the stuffed chair, doing nothing, while cigar ashes fall unnoticed on his waistcoat and the cigar at last goes out; the minutes go by and still he does not move; his eyes are far away as he sits there lost in who knows what thoughts.

In the very last years he would often visit the office only to talk with his partners for a few minutes and then lunch with them. More and more he was leaving to them the conduct of banking affairs. His son Jack—J. P. Morgan, Jr.—would one of these days be taking over the senior partnership, with Charles Steele as elder adviser, young Henry P. Davison (who joined the firm in 1909) as a brilliant and rising associate, Thomas W. Lamont (who succeeded Perkins in the firm in 1911) as a sagacious and diplomatic junior aide, William H. Porter (formerly of the Chemical National Bank) as an expert in bank management, and a group of other able partners; and Jack must be given a spreading responsibility.

2

There were no grand feats of organization, no new major crises to command his attention during those last years, but the influence of the firm became even more pervasive than before 1907; and partly as a consequence of Morgan's acknowledged leadership in the panic, and of the co-operative mood established then, it was in the field of banking that the lines of influence were most firmly extended.

For a generation Morgan and George F. Baker, the bewhiskered chief of the First National Bank, an inexorable and competent student of money and what could be done with it, had been hand in glove. After Baker, Morgan was the largest single stockholder in Baker's bank; three Morgan partners sat on its board, and in enterprise after enterprise the Morgan and Baker banks joined forces. Both concerns had been interested in the Bankers Trust Company, founded in 1903 on the initiative of Henry P. Davison, who was then a vice-president in Baker's bank and later became a Morgan partner; the Bankers Trust grew rapidly, and in 1911 and 1912 absorbed the Mercantile and Manhattan trust companies. Both Morgan and Baker likewise stood back of the Guaranty Trust Company, into which, in 1910, were merged two other concerns, the Morton and the Fifth Avenue; the Guaranty's directors were named by a voting trust of three men—Baker, Davison (a Baker lieutenant turned Morgan lieutenant), and Porter (a Morgan partner). Similarly the influence of the two men, singly or jointly, reached in one way or another to the Chase National Bank (a majority of whose stock was owned by Baker), the Astor Trust Company, the Liberty National Bank, the Chemical Bank, and the National Bank of Commerce.

Nor was this all. For after 1907 the cool and silent James Stillman, who as head of the great National City Bank had previously been regarded principally as an ally of the Rockefeller family and the Standard Oil group generally, drew closer to Morgan. Morgan became a stockholder in the National City Bank, and his son became a director of it. And Stillman or his representatives came to have a say in the management of one of the institutions mentioned above—The National Bank of Commerce—as well as in the Farmers Loan & Trust Company.

Studying these developments, one could reasonably say that the Morgan-Baker-Stillman influence was strongly felt in most of the important banks of New York.

From banking it spread into insurance. For a time George W. Perkins had been both a Morgan partner and a vice-president of the New York Life Insurance Company; and in 1909 something else happened. Since 1905, when a series of scandals had rocked the insurance business, the ownership of another big company, the Equitable, had been in the hands of Thomas Fortune Ryan, who had set up, to supervise the concern, a board of three trustees which included Grover Cleveland and was calculated to put the management above suspicion. Later, Ryan had sold part of his stock interest in the Equitable to E. H. Harriman. At the end of 1909 Morgan bought Ryan's remaining interest; he also acquired the part which had gone to Harriman. (The doughty railroad emperor had died in the summer of 1909; a fortnight before the end, in a reconciliatory mood, he had invited Morgan to come to Arden and sit by his bed for a friendly talk.) Now in sure control of the Equitable, Morgan offered a quarter interest in his investment to Baker, and another to Stillman, if at any time they should care to buy these fractions; this they did after his death, but for the time being they were content that he should hold their shares. This was satisfactory to him; he wanted to put the Equitable, which was a huge purchaser of securities, into "safe hands"; and what safer than his own?

During the Pujo Committee's investigation in 1912, Samuel Untermyer, the committee counsel, questioned Morgan relentlessly about the purchase from Ryan. He had been struck by the fact that Morgan had paid a price which, at the usual dividend rate, would yield him only a small fraction of one per cent on his investment. Why had he been willing to pay so much, Untermyer wanted to know; and why had he wanted to buy control of the Equitable company anyhow?

"Because I thought it was a desirable thing for the situation to do that," said Morgan.

"But that is very general, Mr. Morgan, when you speak of 'the situation.' Was not the stock safe enough in Mr. Ryan's hands?"

"I suppose it was," answered Morgan, unwilling to suggest that Ryan might otherwise have disposed of the shares to people whom he distrusted. "I thought it was greatly improved by being in the hands of myself and these two gentlemen [Baker and Stillman], provided I asked them to do so."

Untermyer persisted with his questions, and in due course Morgan remarked that he had thought the purchase was "good business." The colloquy went on:

UNTERMYER. Where is the good business, then, in buying a security that only pays one-ninth of one per cent?

MORGAN. Because I thought it was better there than it was where it was. That is all.

UNTERMYER. Was anything the matter with it in the hands of Mr. Ryan?

MORGAN. Nothing.

UNTERMYER. In what respect would it be better where it is than with him?

MORGAN. That is the way it struck me.

And a little later:

UNTERMYER. Did Mr. Ryan offer this stock to you?

MORGAN. I asked him to sell it to me. . . .

UNTERMYER. What did he say when you told him you would like to have it, and you thought you ought to have it?

MORGAN. He hesitated about it, and finally sold it.

At last, under persistent hammering, Morgan was a little more specific. He explained that Ryan had not been in good health, and that when a man died and his stock went into his estate, it might get divided up into small lots and you could not tell what would become of it. But he insisted that "the only reason I did it, on which I am willing to stand up before the community, is that I thought it was the thing to do."

"This is a little nebulous, is it not?" asked Untermyer.

"You may call it so," replied Morgan, "but I do not look at it in that light."

3

So widely had the threads of the Morgan influence—and of the Morgan-Baker-Stillman influence—reached, that when the Pujo Committee made its report, at the conclusion of its hearings in 1912-13, and proclaimed its discovery of the existence of the "money trust" which it had decided in the first place to discover, it was able to produce some staggering statistics. It found that if you lumped together the Morgan partners and the directors of the First National and National City banks and the Bankers Trust Company and the Guaranty Trust Company, you had a group of men who between them held—

118 directorships in 34 banks and trust companies;
30 directorships in 10 insurance companies;
105 directorships in 32 transportation companies;
63 directorships in 24 producing and trading corporations;
25 directorships in 12 public utility corporations;

making, in all, 341 directorships in 112 corporations with aggregate resources or capitalization of over 22 billion dollars. And of these 341 directorships, the members of the firm of J. P. Morgan & Co. held no less than 72.

Said the Pujo Committee, toward the close of its report: "The acts of this inner group . . . have . . . been more destructive of competition than anything accomplished by the trusts, for they strike at the very vitals of potential competition in every industry that is under their protection, a condition which if permitted to continue will render impossible all attempts to restore normal competitive conditions in the industrial world."

That the Morgan firm actually exercised any controlling authority by means of these directorships, Morgan himself stoutly denied when he was called before the committee. He even went so far as to deny that voting trusts exercised such authority. When, for example, Untermyer asked him whether he, as a member of the voting trust which year after year chose the directors of the Southern Railway, was not in effect dealing with himself when the firm of J. P. Morgan agreed with the officials of the Southern Railway on the prices at which its securities should be issued to the public, he would not yield an inch. "I do not think so," said he. "We do not deal with ourselves."

"Let us see if you do not," persisted Untermyer. ". . . The voting trustees name the board, do they not?"

MORGAN. But when you have elected the board, then the board is independent of the voting trustees.

UNTERMYER. That is only until the next election?

MORGAN. It is during that time they act independently.

UNTERMYER. You think, therefore, that where you name a board of directors who remain in existence only a year and you have the power to name another board next year, that this board so named is in an independent position to deal with your banking house, as would a board named by the stockholders themselves?

MORGAN. I think it would be better.

UNTERMYER. You think it is a great deal better?

MORGAN. Yes, sir.

UNTERMYER. More independent?

MORGAN. Better.

UNTERMYER. Will you tell us why?

MORGAN. Simply because we select the best people we can find for the positions.

Questioned as to his alleged control of banks, he insisted likewise that the presence of Morgan partners on the boards of other banking institutions did not mean control. They were usually in a minority, and in a few banks; "there is no question of control," said he, "unless you have got a majority of the directors . . . in all banks." Often he shifted his ground in the debate with Untermyer as the zest of verbal battle seized hold of him, but the trend of his argument was plain: that the degree of influence which men exercised depended, in the long run, not upon charts and diagrams of "control," but upon their personal stature, and that in banking this was preeminently true.

He was, of course, heavily overstating a valid point. The House of Morgan exercised a strong and in some matters a determining influence, not only in the councils of many banks, but as we have already seen, in the affairs of many railroads and industrial corporations. This does not mean that the statistical compilations of the Pujo Committee bore much more resemblance to the living actuality than the "red network" diagrams subsequently drawn up by determined radical-baiters. Corporations often welcomed leading bankers on their directorates for the prestige value of their names, or for their astute advice, or for possible future assistance in financing; and the bankers in turn often used such directorships chiefly as listening posts. Where the relationship was more definitely supervisory than this, the supervision was usually very limited, as I have already noted. Yet that there was a reality behind the Pujo diagrams was scarcely deniable. A handful of strongly placed men with many plums at their disposal, and with similar points of view on many things, enjoyed working together, enjoyed putting friends into positions of authority (directorships and committee memberships in reorganized companies, for instance), and gradually began to regard most of the banks and a large number of important corporations as the natural instruments of their group. The high repute of these men in the financial community, their ability, their mutual trust, and their extending acquaintance with one another produced an association of interest that was much too informal to be labeled a "money trust," but that nevertheless was a nucleus of indefinable yet substantial power over a considerable sector of the national economy.

From this association of interest Pierpont Morgan himself, who had done so much to create it—and also to raise its ethical standards—was in his last years by degrees withdrawing. But at least part of his overpowering position in it was becoming institutionalized as his partners took over, though none of them would ever wield such commanding personal force as he had possessed.

4

To Morgan himself the last years brought many discouragements. The concept of social justice which had been making steady headway since the turn of the century had brought with it a popular distrust of great wealth and great economic power which dismayed him. The muckraking journalists and novelists, from Ida M. Tarbell with her history of the Standard Oil Company, and Lincoln Steffens with his *Shame of the Cities,* to Upton Sinclair with his portrayal of the horrors of the packing houses in *The Jungle,* had dramatized the sins of big business and the egregious influence of money on political life. Politicians of a new sort, from reform mayors like "Golden Rule" Jones of Toledo and Tom Johnson of

Cleveland to reform governors and senators like Robert La Follette of Wisconsin and Hiram Johnson of California, had learned to turn to practical administrative and legislative use the public indignation which Theodore Roosevelt had whipped up; and every one of these men had his group of eager young disciples, determined to scotch the "interests." Such varied events as the anthracite coal strike of 1902, the insurance scandals of 1905, the Ballinger disclosures of 1910, and the Triangle fire of 1911 had each in its own way documented to the public satisfaction the irresponsibility of greed. More and more laws to regulate business were being written into the statute books. So marked was the steady change in the political climate in which big business had to operate that after the very conservative Taft succeeded the belligerent Roosevelt in the White House in 1909, the number of prosecutions of large companies for restraint of trade not only did not diminish, but increased sharply. By 1912 Roosevelt's Bull Moose Progressives and the disciples of Woodrow Wilson's New Freedom were vying for the chance to take over the country from the Taft Republicans, with Wilson winning; and the Pujo investigation, shortly after Wilson's election, was but one of many signs that the era of untrammeled authority for the men who ran big business was over, because the public at large no longer trusted them.

Morgan could not understand the change. When, in 1911, the federal government brought suit against his own child, the Steel Corporation, under the anti-trust laws (a suit which the corporation later won), the news was a body blow. "Well, it has come to this!" he exclaimed sadly to Satterlee, and sat long brooding over this public affront. He was distressed, too, over the failure of the officials of New York City to appropriate money for a new building in which the Metropolitan Museum might house his vast collections, which he proposed to give or leave to it. Had he not saved the city's credit in 1907? Had he not always been a loyal citizen? It made matters no easier to reflect that such apparent official ingratitude was due to the fact that it was now politically safer to rebuff him than to co-operate with him. In April 1912, when the ship *Titanic,* pride of his International Mercantile Marine, sank with great loss of life, he was appalled to hear that some people were charging that a Morgan-directed policy of economy was responsible for the disaster. When he was called down to Washington in the fall of 1912 to testify before the Clapp Committee on his campaign contributions of earlier years, and then to face the Pujo Committee with its money-trust allegations, his depression deepened. He had done what he thought was right; had things indeed come to this?

Shortly after his sessions with the Pujo Committee he was off once more abroad, to Europe and then to Egypt, very tired and nervous. Just before his departure Colonel George Harvey of *Harper's Weekly,* who had for a time been a vehement backer of Woodrow Wilson, came to see Morgan in the Library, and in the course of their talk quoted the lines, "Who never to himself hath said, 'This is my own, my native land.' " Morgan sat still for a full half-minute, his eyes far away, and then said slowly to Harvey, "When you see Mr. Wilson, tell him from me that if there should ever come a time when he thinks any influence or resources that I have can be used for my country, they are wholly at his disposal." He was thinking, perhaps, of his gold purchase for Grover Cleveland in 1895, and wondering whether ever again his government would call upon him for anything except to answer implied charges of interference with the public interest.

In Egypt, where his daughter Louisa Satterlee accompanied him, he was in miserable health, a weak old man indeed. He decided to return to more familiar scenes, and got as far on his way home as Rome. There his condition took a turn for the worse. He summoned up enough strength to go to church on Easter Day; thereafter his appetite, his nerves, his strength rapidly deteriorated.

On the evening of March 30, 1913, his mind wandered. Louisa and her husband Herbert Satterlee—who had hurried abroad in response to an urgent cable—gathered from fragments of his talk that he was back in the old days at Hartford and Vevey. At last they heard him say, "I've got to go up the hill!" He did not speak again; and at four minutes after noon the next day—Monday, March 31, 1913—he died, at the age of not quite seventy-six years.

5

His body was brought back to New York, where on April 14 there was a great funeral at St. George's; he was buried at Hartford.

By his will—which disposed of an estate estimated at 68 million dollars (aside from his art collections)—his widow received for life the income of a trust fund of one million dollars, and by another provision was assured at least $100,000 a year; No. 219 and Cragston also went to her for life. His son Jack received an outright legacy of three millions. His married daughters, Louisa Satterlee and Juliet Hamilton, each received a life income from a trust fund of a million, and each of the two sons-in-law was granted a million outright. There were many other smaller personal bequests, to relatives, friends, and members of his household; and everybody in the employ of J. P. Morgan & Co. received the equivalent of a year's salary. There were institutional bequests, too, among them being the income from $500,000 for St. George's, $100,-000 for the local Episcopal diocese, and $100,000 for the House of Rest for Consumptives. The remainder of the estate—everything—went to his son, as residuary legatee, *including his art collection,* valued at anywhere up to an additional fifty millions.

This last-mentioned provision caused consternation at the Metropolitan Museum, whose officials had confidently expected to receive the treasures. It had certainly been Morgan's intention thus to bequeath them, and during his last year he had spent much time and energy arranging to have them packed up and shipped to the United States. But the failure of the city to provide space for them had so disturbed him that he had decided to hand the problem on to his son. The greater part of the collection did later go to the Metropolitan, but many things were sold or went to other institutions; thus what was probably the most remarkable single collection assembled in our century was in the end widely dispersed.

6

After Morgan's death, there were many who said that it was the Pujo investigation which had killed him; not merely his two-day ordeal before the committee, but his feeling that he was distrusted by hostile representatives of the American public. Certainly he was weaker after those sessions in Washington. Something had gone out of him. Yet it is possible that he had not had long to live in any case. And truly there was drama in his being thus called to account at the very conclusion of his life.

Many of those present on that December day of 1912, listening as Morgan sat in the witness chair at the end of the long committee table and submitted hour after hour to interrogation, must have felt that, regardless of his denials, he actually had come to exercise a dangerously extensive authority, and that if any such authority should ever become wholly institutionalized and further developed, so that one man or group of men could direct it at will, democracy might one day become a lost cause. Yet even as they felt this, I wonder if some of these listeners did not sense the man's moral weight, and ask themselves to what extent his own rise to power may have illustrated the point he was so vehemently making: that what mattered in any business was the caliber of the men who had the funds or the properties in their charge.

Over and over he stated this conviction, but never more effectively than in the passage which I have already quoted at the beginning of this book and now quote once more at its end, as Pierpont Morgan's final apologia.

"Is not commercial credit based primarily upon money or property?" asked Untermyer.

"No, sir," said Morgan; "the first thing is character."

"Before money or property?"

"Before anything else. Money cannot buy it. . . . Because a man I do not trust could not get money from me on all the bonds in Christendom."

What degree of truth there was in that contention, as applied to his own career, is something about which men will long differ. But in his last appearance before the bar of public opinion he had at least made his own powerful plea. And with that we may leave him, proceeding, each of us, to our own individual judgments upon the career of Pierpont Morgan.

SOURCES AND OBLIGATIONS

I have drawn very frequently upon the big biography by Herbert L. Satterlee of his father-in-law: *J. Pierpont Morgan, An Intimate Portrait* (Macmillan, 1939). Satterlee combed over a quantity of letters, diaries, and private family records, and interviewed many of Morgan's then surviving friends, and his work is especially useful as a source because of its wealth of specific detail—including such things as the dates of every trip abroad, the exact itinerary, etc.—and because of its severely chronological arrangement. (There is even more detail on Morgan's earlier years in Satterlee's earlier, privately printed volume covering Morgan's life only up to 1866: *The Life of J. Pierpont Morgan.*) My point of view is quite different from Satterlee's, but I acknowledge my heavy dependence upon his previous spadework.

The other two biographies of Morgan—*The Life Story of J. Pierpont Morgan,* by Carl Hovey (Sturgis & Walton, 1911), sometimes erroneously described as an "official" life, and the lively *Morgan the Magnificent,* by John K. Winkler (Garden City Publishing Co., 1930)—I have used only sparingly; and *The House of Morgan,* by Lewis Corey (G. Howard Watt, 1930), a sharply adverse book, has been useful chiefly as a guide to possible source material.

As will be clear from the detailed citation of sources, which will follow shortly, I have made much use of (1) various hearings before government commissions and committees, especially the Stanley Committee and the Pujo Committee, at which people who participated in great episodes of Morgan's career gave their own versions of what had happened and submitted to severe interrogation; (2) certain over-all studies of the period, including especially *Forty Years of American Finance,* by Alexander Dana Noyes, and Mark Sullivan's *Our Times*; (3) books of memoirs, or detailed biographies of other men, which introduce Morgan incidentally but sometimes enlighteningly—such as, for example, Burton J. Hendrick's *Life of Andrew Carnegie,* Ida M. Tarbell's *Life of Elbert H. Gary,* and the autobiographies of W. S. Rainsford and Lincoln Steffens, to mention only a few of many; (4) the files of the *Commercial & Financial Chronicle* and of the *New York Times* and *Tribune*; and (5) certain original documents to which the Morgan firm kindly gave me access, such as the original syndicate books for the gold operation of 1895, for the launching of the Steel Corporation, and for the launching of the International Mercantile Marine; the cable books for the periods of the 1895 operation and the Northern Pacific Panic; a private memorandum on the history of the London and New York firms written by J. P. Morgan (Jr.) in his last years, which Junius S. Morgan thoughtfully lent me; and various diaries, account books, and other documents of J. Pierpont Morgan's.

Few people who had known Morgan really well were living by the time I went to work. But I spent many hours questioning the late Thomas W. Lamont a few months before his death; and among others I should like especially to mention Leonhard A. Keyes of the House of Morgan, who provided me with many details of Morgan's office life, and also Belle da Costa Greene, librarian of the Morgan Library, who was helpful with first-hand information and impressions as well as with Morgan data in the Library files.

Some of the ground traversed in this book I had previously been over when I wrote *The Lords of Creation* in 1934-35; here and there I have relied upon the earlier book to save myself the labor of going back to certain original sources, and at one point, in the description of the Panic of 1907, I have lifted two paragraphs almost bodily from the previous work.

I should like especially to thank R. Gordon Wasson of J. P. Morgan & Co. for helping to make available to me the original material at 23 Wall Street, for patiently running down the answers to various questions of mine, and for reading the manuscript in rough draft and, with the aid of Mr. Keyes and others, catching errors and providing me with useful comments—always with complete respect for my independence of view.

I shall now proceed, chapter by chapter, to list my sources of material on matters which might be open to question or inquiry by other writers or scholars; and to save space I shall begin by listing here several sources to which reference will most frequently be made. The symbol which precedes each of the names is the one which will identify it in the pages which follow:

CFC—*Commercial & Financial Chronicle.*

H—*The Life of Andrew Carnegie,* by Burton J. Hendrick (Doubleday, Doran & Co., 1932).

L of C—*The Lords of Creation,* by Frederick Lewis Allen (Harper & Brothers, 1935).

N—*Forty Years of American Finance,* by Alexander Dana Noyes (G. P. Putnam's Sons, 1909).

P—Pujo Committee Hearings. (U. S. Banking & Currency Committee. House. 62nd Congress, 2nd and 3rd sessions. Money Trust Investigation. Investigation of the financial and monetary conditions in the United States, under House Res. 429 and 504.)

R—*The Story of a Varied Life,* by W. S. Rainsford (Doubleday, Page & Co., 1922).

S—*J. Pierpont Morgan, An Intimate Biography,* by Herbert L. Satterlee (Macmillan, 1939).

Stanley—Stanley Committee Hearings. (House Committee on Investigation of the U. S. Steel Corporation, under House Res. 148, 62nd Congress, 1st and 2nd sessions.)

Steffens—*The Autobiography of Lincoln Steffens* (Harcourt, Brace & Co., 1931).

Sullivan—*Our Times,* by Mark Sullivan (Charles Scribner's Sons), especially Vol. II (1929).

T—*The Life of Elbert H. Gary,* by Ida M. Tarbell (D. Appleton-Century Co., 1933).

Chapter I—Judgment Day

The details of Morgan's travels during 1912 follow Satterlee; the quotation beginning, "His feeling . . ." is from S 556. The account of Morgan's examination is from the Pujo Hearings, with quotations from P 1003, 1004, 1006, 1019, 1056, and (the final one, which appears again in Chapter XIII) 1084. The figures for deposits with J. P. Morgan & Co. are given not as stated at the outset of the hearing but as later corrected as it proceeded.

Chapter II—The Materials of a Career

The data on Joseph Morgan are from Satterlee; on Junius Spencer Morgan, from Satterlee, checked against the account of the Beebe firm in *Levi Parsons Morton,* by Robert McElroy (G. P. Putnam's Sons, 1930). Satterlee's earlier volume, the privately printed *Life of J. Pierpont Morgan,* contains a photograph of 26 Asylum Street before the building was destroyed; I visited the site in 1948. I have inspected some of Morgan's boyhood diaries at the Morgan Library but the items and quotations on the Diorama, his letters to Jim Goodwin, and his letters from Horta, are all from Satterlee. The 1871 account book from which I have quoted is in the Morgan Library. For the Rainsford "precious heirloom" quotation, see R 284. The first paragraph of the Morgan will is from Winkler, p. 12. My account of his western trip, his school and university days, and his early days in New York (including the New Orleans episode and his first marriage) is based on Satterlee; but the 1857 account-book items are from the original book, now at J. P. Morgan & Co. Incidentally, in a wallet of his at the Morgan Library I found a calling card on which in 1871 he recorded the full statistics of a voyage to England.

Chapter III—Groping for Direction

The draft figures of 1863 are from Morison and Commager's *Growth of the American Republic,* Vol. I, p. 602.

If the Hall Carbine Affair had been a major episode in Morgan's life I should have felt compelled to make my own lengthy investigation of the original documents. As it seemed to me of minor importance, I have relied upon R. Gordon Wasson's *The Hall Carbine Affair* (second revised edition, Pandick Press, 22 Thomas St., New York, 1948), which, though written by an officer of J. P. Morgan & Co. with the obvious intent of clearing Morgan's name, is so scrupulously detailed and reproduces or cites so many original documents that for the purposes of this book I have accepted its factual data. The figures I have quoted may be found in Wasson's summary on pp. 77-81, except for the amount of Morgan's commission, for which see pp. 22-23; the quotation from the War Department Commission is from p. 46.

For the gold speculation of 1863, see Winkler, pp. 58-59; *New York Times,* October 12 and 14, 1863; New York *Daily Tribune,* October 11, 1863. (These newspaper accounts, however, name no names.) For Morgan's personal income for 1864, see Corey, p. 64.

On the Susquehanna affair, I have followed in the main the careful and detailed account, virtually contemporary, by Charles Francis Adams in the *North American Review* for April 1871, as reprinted in *High Finance in the Sixties,* edited by Frederick C. Hicks (Yale University Press, 1929). Certain details are from the *New York Times* of August 7 and September 8, 1869. The Supreme Court quotation is from *Supreme Court of the State of New York, 1869,* I, 339. On the Pacific trip I follow S 130-133, but on the Susquehanna affair I have found the Satterlee version unsatisfactory and probably erroneous at more than one point.

The letter from Morgan's father about Drexel is from the recollection of a former Morgan partner. The amount added to reserves, 1871-75, I found listed on a sheet of paper in a wallet preserved at the Morgan Library. For Morgan's houses, travels, and recreation, my main source has been Satterlee. The quotation from William H. Vanderbilt about "public sentiment" is from CFC, November 29, 1879, quoting the New York *Tribune.*

Chapter IV—Morgan the Peacemaker

The Carnegie-Vanderbilt conversation is from H, II, 26. The *Corsair* conference has been picturesquely chronicled many times; for the route followed and the direct quotations I have followed S 225-226. For the remark to Judge Ashbel Green, S 226-227. The CFC comment on the *Corsair* compact comes from CFC, July 25, 1885. The passenger fares between New York and Chicago, from CFC, April 3, 1886. The quotation from the *Commercial & Financial Chronicle* on the anthracite coal combination, from CFC, March 27, 1886. The *New York Times's* comment on the anthracite combination, much shortened by me, is from an editorial on "The Proposed Coal Monopoly," February 16, 1886. For the data on Supreme Court action, the source is *The United States Since 1865,* by Louis M. Hacker and Benjamin B. Kendrick, p. 276. For the railroad conference of 1888-89, I have relied chiefly upon the daily press of the time, especially the New York *Daily Tribune,* January 11, 1889, which contains Morgan's reply to Roberts and a reference to the Windsor Hotel meeting; Morgan's reply may also be found in CFC, January 12, 1889; the ironical *Times* story appeared on January 11, 1889.

Chapter V—No. 219

Most of the material in this chapter is based upon facts set forth in Satterlee, about Morgan's daily and weekly routine, the developments at Cragston, *Corsair II,* the Corsair Club, Morgan's voting, and especially the account of electric wiring of No. 219 and the resulting troubles, which is based upon S 207-216. The ruins of Cragston are described as I saw them in September 1948. The long quotation on Morgan's confrontation of Everitt H. Johnson is from S 213. But the account of the interior of the Morgan house, especially the library, is from *Era of Elegance,* by Andrew Tully (Funk & Wagnalls, 1947); the details of the William H. Vanderbilt house are from *Mr. Vanderbilt's House and Collection,* described by Edward Strahan, published by George Barrie, in 2 volumes; the account of Rainsford's acceptance of the call to St. George's is from R 201; the Satterlee quotation on the prosperity of 1881 is from S 199; the William Graham Sumner quotation is from *What Social Classes Owe to Each Other* (1883), as quoted on p. 724 of Vol. II of *The Shaping of the American Tradition,* by Louis M. Hacker (Columbia University Press, 1947); and the account of the turning on of the electric lights in downtown New York is from *Edison: His Life, His Work, His Genius,* by William Adams Simonds (Bobbs Merrill, 1934).

Chapter VI—Railroad Reorganizer—And Emperor?

My most generally useful source for this chapter has been *The Reorganization of the American Railroad System, 1893-1900,* by E. G. Campbell (Columbia University Press, 1938). The Noyes figures on the bankrupt condition of the American railroads are from N 218 and N 276. The data on the Richmond Terminal legal agreements are from Campbell, p. 154, and also appear in Satterlee. For the testimony of William Z. Ripley before the Industrial Commission on reorganization stock and bond issues, see U. S. House Documents, Vol. 72, 57th Congress, 1st session, p. 291. The London *Economist*'s comments on the Erie reorganization charges appeared August 31, 1895, and are quoted in Campbell, pp. 169-170; its comments on the Baltimore & Ohio accounting scandals appeared December 26, 1896, and are quoted on p. 141 by Campbell, whose account of the adventures of the B & O at this time is useful.

As to the passage on the contest over the Reading Railroad, my data on the status of the New Haven road in 1892 are from CFC, *Investors' Supplement* for July 1892; the alleged "peanut stand" statement by McLeod is hesitantly quoted by Campbell but has been accepted by some other writers and sounds to me genuine; Morgan's part in the onslaught on Reading was tentatively suggested by Thomas F. Woodlock before the Industrial Commission (see U. S. House Documents, Vol. 72, 57th Congress, 1st session, p. 456) and was more definitely charged by McLeod as quoted in the *Railway World,* April 29, 1893, whence come the remarks by him which I have quoted. On the Richmond Terminal operation, my quotation of Clyde is from the recollection of a former Morgan partner.

Chapter VII—Gold for the Government

On the general condition of the gold reserve, my chief source has been Noyes; but see also Grover Cleveland's article on "The Cleveland Bond Issues," *Saturday Evening Post,* May 7, 1904, and the "endless chain" passage in Cleveland's Annual Message, December 3, 1894. The figures for withdrawals from the gold reserve in the last week of January 1895 are from CFC, February 2, 1895, p. 192. The Sullivan quotation on the general mood of unrest is from Sullivan, I, p. 137. The Drexel-Morgan partners' dinner at the Metropolitan Club comes from material in the files of J. P. Morgan & Co. The data on Bacon's college prowess are from *Robert Bacon: Life and Letters,* by James Brown Scott (Doubleday, Page & Co., 1923) as is the "lieutenants" quotation.

On the daily events beginning on Thursday, January 31, and continuing through the following week, I have had the advantage of being able to inspect and quote from the original cable books of J. P. Morgan & Co., in which copies of the cables, uncoded, were preserved in longhand—both those sent and those received from London. I have quoted many of them, and drawn from them at other points, as where I mention Morgan's private expectation of being able to compromise on 3⅝ per cent. And they proved especially useful in clearing up an awkward confusion as to the date of the crucial meeting at which Morgan persuaded Cleveland. According to Satterlee, this meeting took place Monday morning; according to Grover Cleveland's *Post* article, Thursday evening; according to Allan Nevins' *Grover Cleveland, A Study in Courage* (Dodd, Mead, 1932) there were apparently two sessions, one on Tuesday morning and a more important one on Thursday. After studying the testimony in the hearing held not long afterward by the Senate Committee on Finance (U. S. Senate, Committee on Finance, Investigation of the Sale of Bonds, 54th Congress, 2nd session, Senate Document 187, Vol. 5), I had pretty well made up my mind that the chief session was held Tuesday morning, with perhaps a supplementary one on Thursday (and of course a session at the Treasury on Friday morning, at which Cleveland was not present); and the fact that the daily papers recorded Cleveland as having had a state dinner at the White House on Thursday evening fortified me; the cables seem to me to clinch my case, especially the "we have carried our point" cable sent on Tuesday.

Morgan's hiding out at Mrs. Warren's is from S 286, as are most of my other statements about Morgan in Washington (checked, however, against other sources); the Cleveland-Morgan quotation on the guarantee is from S 292; the Cleveland quotation on his "watchfulness" of Morgan and the later quotation of his question to Morgan and Morgan's answer are both from *Recollections of Grover Cleveland*, by George F. Parker (Century Co., 1909), p. 325.

Morgan's subsequent testimony on the episode is from the hearings before the Senate Committee on Finance, as cited above. The specific figures on the actual profits are drawn from the original Syndicate Book, which still exists at J. P. Morgan & Co.

CHAPTER VIII—TRIANGULATION

Obviously there are four principal sources of the material in this chapter. The first is Steffens, I, 188-190. The second is Rainsford, the successive quotations being from R 277, 265, 278, 278, 285, and (the long series of quotations on the vestry meeting and its sequel) 278-284. The third is Satterlee, the passage on Morgan's start at collecting being from S 247-248, the one on the Spanish painting from S 443-444. The fourth is *Roger Fry*, by Virginia Woolf (Harcourt, Brace & Co., 1940), pp. 129-131 and 141; my comments upon Fry, Morgan, and the museum were based partly upon having had access to the (incomplete) file, at the Metropolitan Museum, of correspondence between Fry and the museum officials.

Various minor points: The quotation from the admiring writer on the Vanderbilt house is from the Introduction to *Mr. Vanderbilt's House and Collection* (cited above under Chapter V). The comparison between Morgan and Mrs. Gardner draws upon material in *Isabella Stewart Gardner and Fenway Court*, by Morris Carter (Houghton Mifflin, 1925). The Mitchell quotation on Morgan as a collector is from *Memoirs of an Editor*, by Edward P. Mitchell (Charles Scribner's Sons, 1924); the *Burlington* editorial comment on Morgan appeared in May 1913. As for the data on rich men's estates, I took my Carnegie figure from the *Dictionary of American Biography* and the others from *America's Sixty Families*, by Ferdinand Lundberg (Vanguard Press, 1937). The anecdote about Morgan's gift to the Harvard Medical School comes from an article by Joseph B. Gilder in the *Century Magazine*, Vol. 86, p. 461.

Chapter IX—Billion-Dollar Adventure

The Noyes quotation is from N 257. The size of the Carnegie income is conservatively stated; in 1900 it was about $25,000,000; see H, II, 53. The Hunter figures from *Poverty* may be found in *The Shaping of the American Tradition*, by Louis M. Hacker (Columbia University Press, 1947), II, 931-932. For Steffens on Dill, see Steffens, I, 192-196. The data on Morgan's travels and recreations in 1897 are from S 320-325, except that certain details, and the Newport quotation, are from contemporary issues of *Harper's Weekly*.

The story of the various steel promotions, culminating in the launching of U. S. Steel, has been frequently told (I have told it once before myself, in the first chapter of *The Lords of Creation*). For my quotations of dialogue, I have drawn chiefly upon Miss Tarbell's life of Gary, written while he was still living, and Hendrick's very careful life of Carnegie; and those books have been most useful in checking other points. To be more specific: the "You must be president" talk between Morgan and Gary is from T 94; the "I would not think of it" remark of Morgan's, from T 111; the account of Gates and Gary and Morgan's ultimatum, from T 122-123; the Morgan-Gary conversations about buying the Rockefeller ore mines, from T 118-120. My chief source on the plans of Frick and Phipps is H 77-86. On Morgan's being approached in this connection (before the "I would not think of it" approach), see H 84, quoting Robert Bacon's testimony in the suit against the Steel Corporation in 1913, pp. 5473-5474. On the struggle in 1900 between Carnegie and the other steel combinations, H 114-128; Carnegie's letter and cable to his associates, H 117-118; the Carnegie-Schwab talk about making tubes, H 123. On the University Club dinner, H 128-132. On the negotiations which followed, H 132-143. The Morgan call on Carnegie and the shipboard conversation are from H 139 and 142. The account of the call made by John D. Rockefeller, Jr., and Rogers on Morgan is from *John D. Rockefeller,* by Allan Nevins (Charles Scribner's Sons, 1940), Vol. II, pp. 419-420.

The data on total capitalization of U. S. Steel and the underlying values are from *Report on the United States Steel Corporation,* by the Bureau of Corporations, as quoted in *The Shaping of the American Tradition,* by Louis M. Hacker (Columbia University Press, 1947), II, 947; on the Pittsburgh Steel millionaires, from *The Romance of Steel,* by Herbert N. Casson (A. S. Barnes & Co., 1907); the quotations on the public reaction to the news of the launching of U. S. Steel are all taken from Sullivan, II, 351-355, including the subsequent quotation of John Brisben Walker.

The actual Syndicate profits are all from the original Syndicate Book at J. P. Morgan & Co. and the books of the firm for 1902. I might add that I have not set down the exact total profits because they could be computed in more than one way, since they would depend partly upon the value of the stock distributed and the participations in the new syndicate.

Incidentally, it may interest some readers to know that the syndicate which launched the Steel Corporation consisted of approximately three hundred participants, who were down in the Book for varying amounts totaling two hundred million dollars; that each participant was called upon to pay 12½ per cent of the amount of his participation, but no more; and that the participants who were down for amounts of $1,200,000 or more were as follows:

William H. Moore	$24,800,000
William B. Leeds	18,750,000
D. G. Reid	18,750,000
James Hobart Moore	12,500,000
J. P. Morgan & Co.	6,475,000
John W. Gates	6,000,000
R. H. Porter	5,000,000
E. H. Gary	4,500,000
William Eidenborn	3,275,000
First National Bank	3,125,000
William Rockefeller	3,125,000
James Stillman	3,125,000
Henry H. Rogers No. 1	3,125,000
N. Y. Security & Trust Co.	3,000,000
P. A. B. Widener	2,875,000
Kidder, Peabody & Co.	2,500,000
Wm. Nelson Cromwell	2,000,000
Marshall Field	2,000,000
John Lambert	1,900,000
Henry H. Rogers No. 2	1,875,000
Thomas F. Ryan	1,875,000
Thomas Dolan	1,650,000
E. C. Converse	1,300,000
N. Thayer	1,250,000
W. K. Vanderbilt	1,250,000
Samuel Mather	1,200,000

Chapter X—Pomp and Circumstance

My largest factual source of material in this chapter is Satterlee, but aside from the other sources mentioned below, I have used at many points facts and impressions which came from people who had known Morgan or the circumstances of his life at firsthand. The Gambetta quotation is from *The Edwardian Era,* by André Maurois (D. Appleton-Century Co., 1933), pp. 72-73. For the Satterlee quotation on fruit from Dover House, see S 387; for his climbing up the liner's side, S 336-337; for the Zodiac menu, S 406. The steel-mill-purchase anecdote is from Sullivan, II, 356. The "What's the use of bothering" quotation is from Edward Robinson's introduction to the *Guide to the Loan Exhibition of the J. Pierpont Morgan Collection* at the Metropolitan Museum,

1914. The Rigby anecdotes are from *Lock, Stock and Barrel: The Story of Collecting,* by Douglas and Elizabeth Rigby (Lippincott, 1944), pp. 13 and 34; the Rigbys did not use Duveen's name, but the Garland Collection anecdote appears also in *Art Treasures and Intrigue,* by James Henry Duveen (Doubleday, Doran & Co., 1935), p. 133, as a Duveen story. Mitchell's description of Morgan in his Library is from *Memoirs of an Editor* (cited above under Chapter VIII), p. 367. The episode of Morgan's making a baby a life fellow is from an address by Robert W. De Forest, quoted in *Bulletin of the Metropolitan Museum of Art,* April 1913. For his loan of a million dollars to a friend without security, see S 267-268. The story of the saving of the two uptown banks is told in detail in *Henry P. Davison,* by Thomas W. Lamont (Harper & Brothers, 1933). The story of the loss taken on the Cincinnati, Hamilton & Dayton deal is told in intricate detail in a pamphlet on file at J. P. Morgan & Co., briskly entitled *Before the Interstate Commerce Committee, in the Matter of the Cincinnati, Hamilton & Dayton Railway Co.; Its History since June, 1904; J. P. Morgan & Co.'s Connection with Its Affairs; Statement by Frederick W. Stevens, Compiled for Presentation to the Interstate Commerce Commission in Advance of Examination by Its Counsel.*

Chapter XI—The Limits of Triumph

There is some variation in the figures for holdings of Northern Pacific stock by the Harriman forces; I have used the same ones that I used previously in L of C, 52-53. Bacon's cable to Morgan about the big Harriman purchases of Northern Pacific stock is not in the cable book at J. P. Morgan & Co.; apparently it was sent (after coding) from Bacon's house, as an extra precaution for secrecy; there was a credit of some thirty or forty dollars to Bacon on the books of J. P. Morgan & Co. a little later for the expense of cabling. That Bacon knew that some purchasing was being done is shown by a cable of April 30 by Bacon, but in that message he says this was apparently being done "with intention at least asking for representation." The quotation from Morgan about his protective motive is taken as quoted on p. 31 of the Morgan brief in the Northern Securities case. The total of Morgan purchases on May 6 is taken from the actual books at J. P. Morgan & Co.

For Morgan's travels in 1901, my source is Satterlee. For Morgan's reaction to McKinley's death, see S 363; for Morgan's prior acquaintance with Hanna, S 316-317; for Roosevelt's dinner for Morgan and comment thereon, see *Theodore Roosevelt,* by Henry F. Pringle (Harcourt, Brace & Co., 1931), p. 227; for the Steel Corporation resolution on union labor, see L of C, 35; for the Mr. Dooley quotation, see Sullivan, II, 411; for the account of Morgan getting the news of the government's action while at dinner, Sullivan, II, 412-414; for the conversation between Morgan and Roosevelt about the Northern Securities action, see *Theodore Roosevelt and His Time,* by Joseph Bucklin Bishop, I, pp. 184-185.

On the formation of International Mercantile Marine and the British reaction thereto, see *Viscount Pirrie of Belfast,* by Herbert Jefferson (William Mullan & Son, Ltd.), pp. 272-277, and also S 381. The George F. Baer letter is reproduced in Sullivan, II, p. 425. The gift by Morgan toward the maintenance of a coal depot in New York comes from S 389. There is a good account of the *Corsair* conference between Root and Morgan in *Elihu Root,* by Philip C. Jessup (Dodd, Mead, 1938); for the rest of the anthracite strike arbitration, I have leaned heavily on the careful account in Sullivan; but John Mitchell's comment on Morgan and the strike is quoted from S 394.

The data on campaign contributions, and the quotation from Roosevelt, are from the Hearings before the Clapp Committee (Committee on Privileges and Elections, U. S. Senate, 1912, Hearing on Campaign Contributions). The Morgan contribution was there stated to have come from the firm, but I understand that it does not appear on the books of the firm, and therefore assume that it was charged to the partners separately. The Gridiron dinner is described in Sullivan, II, 220-221, quoting the Washington *Post*; and also in S 437-438. For the Morgan testimony on the troubles of U. S. Steel about 1903, see P 1027. On the International Mercantile Marine syndicate operation, I have quoted from the "Navigation Syndicate" notice of February 28, 1906, as it appears in the original Syndicate Book at J. P. Morgan & Co.

As to the New Haven Railroad, I have made considerable use of *The Fall of a Railroad Empire,* by Henry Lee Staples and

Alpheus Thomas Mason (Syracuse University Press, 1947), which tells the story in detail. The increase in capitalization is from the *Report of the Interstate Commerce Commission on the Financial Transactions of the New York, New Haven & Hartford Railroad Co.*, July 15, 1914, 63rd Congress, 2nd session, Senate Document No. 544; as are the figures on the cost of the New York, Westchester & Boston project. For Mellon's testimony, as quoted, see Staples 182-183; for his comment to Barron ("I took orders . . ."), see *More They Told Barron*: notes of the late Clarence W. Barron, edited and arranged by Arthur Pound and Samuel Taylor Moore (Harper & Brothers, 1931), p. 168; for his observations on the New York, Westchester & Boston, see Staples 168-169.

Chapter XII—Rock of Defense

On the Episcopal Convention at Richmond, I have consulted contemporary reports in *The Churchman.* The two passages quoted from Bishop Lawrence come from *Memories of a Happy Life,* pp. 251-252. The troubles of Heinze and his friends are recounted in more detail in L of C, 115-122.

In following Morgan's personal activity during the panic, I have made much use of Satterlee, who was with him much of the time; but for the financial operations he was carrying on, I have relied heavily upon the testimony brought out in the Stanley and Pujo investigations, trying always to bear in mind, when reading this testimony, what I thought the interrogator was trying to establish and what I thought the witnesses might be trying to establish or to hide. One can prove almost anything about the panic by approaching the evidence either as a prosecuting attorney or as a defense attorney; I have twice (in 1934-35 and in 1947-48) gone through volumes of testimony as judicially as I could, and have arrived both times at about the same conclusion. For the "sore point" statement and Thorne's testimony generally, see Stanley III, and note the letter from Melville E. Stone in Stanley III, 1687; also see Perkins' testimony in Stanley III, especially at 1472-1473 and 1504. The Satterlee quotation about waking up Morgan on Wednesday morning is from S 467. For the decision to save the Trust Company of America and the "This, then, is the place . . ." quotation, I have used Strong's account as it appears in Lamont's life of Henry P. Davison, p. 76. For the Wednesday evening meeting I have followed chiefly

S 471-473. The account of Morgan's drive downtown on Thursday morning is from S 473. For Thomas' own version of the attempt to prevent the Stock Exchange from closing on Thursday, see P. I, 355-358; for Satterlee's version, S 474-475. For Perkins' visit to Cortelyou on Friday morning, etc., and the "touch and go" quotation from him, see Stanley II, 1474-1476. The Satterlee description of Morgan barging down Nassau Street is from S 479. My Library scene description follows closely a preceding one in L of C, 134-135.

My account of the complex troubles of Moore & Schley and the purchase of Tennessee Coal & Iron is pieced together from testimony given before the Stanley Committee, especially by Schley, Ledyard, Perkins, and Gary; the scene in which the trust-company heads signed up is from Lamont's life of Davison, pp. 82-83; the purchase of New York City bonds is from the same book, pp. 85-87 (there is a reproduction of the longhand contract opposite p. 86). Morgan's reply to the banker who said he was below his legal reserve is from Perkins' testimony, Stanley III, 1612.

Chapter XIII—Envoi

The Cortesi item about driving about Rome is from *My Thirty Years of Friendships*, by Salvatore Cortesi (Harper & Brothers, 1927), p. 96, and the episode of the call on Cardinal Merry del Val from pp. 96-97. "How much for the stack?" is actual: it appears in Duveen's *Art Treasures and Intrigue* (cited above under Chapter X).

The data on the Morgan-Baker-Stillman influence in the New York banks are adapted from the Pujo Committee report, as quoted in *The Shaping of the American Tradition*, by Louis M. Hacker (Columbia University Press, 1947), II, 951-955, which is also the source of the quotation about "the acts of this inner group"; Morgan's testimony on his purchase of Equitable stock from Ryan is from P 1068-1070; his testimony on the Southern Railway voting trust, from P 1019; his reaction to the suit against the Steel Corporation is from S 531-532; the account of his last months and death is all from Satterlee. His will is taken from contemporary newspaper reports. As for the final quotation of the book, that, as already noted under Chapter I, where it previously appeared, is from P 1084.

INDEX

Set in Linotype Baskerville
Format by A. W. Rushmore
Manufactured by The Haddon Craftsmen
Published by HARPER & BROTHERS, *New York*